U0800191

“十四五”高等职业教育轨道交通类专业英语系列教材

城市轨道交通桥隧维修与养护

罗立娜　方恩权　李冕梧◎主　编
郭咏辉　李岳涛◎副主编

中国铁道出版社有限公司
CHINA RAILWAY PUBLISHING HOUSE CO., LTD.

内 容 简 介

本书是“十四五”高等职业教育轨道交通类专业英语系列教材之一，立足城市轨道交通行业发展现状，根据技术领域和岗位群的岗位要求，以培养职业能力为中心，结合桥隧养护相关规程编写而成。本书共3章，包括桥隧基础知识、桥梁作业和隧道作业。本书不仅具有科学性、系统性、实用性特点，而且具有较强的指导性、可操作性，使学生的专业技能与企业岗位无缝对接。

本书采用双语编写，适合作为高等职业教育铁道工程技术、地下与隧道工程技术、城市轨道交通工程技术、市政工程技术等专业教材，也可作为相关领域工程技术人员培训教材或参考书。

图书在版编目(CIP)数据

城市轨道交通桥隧维修与养护/罗立娜，方恩权，李冕梧主编.—北京：中国铁道出版社有限公司，2024.9
“十四五”高等职业教育轨道交通类专业英语系列教材
ISBN 978-7-113-30539-0

Ⅰ.①城… Ⅱ.①罗…②方…③李… Ⅲ.①城市铁路-轨道交通-铁路桥-维修-高等职业教育-教材②城市铁路-轨道交通-铁路隧道-维修-高等职业教育-教材 Ⅳ.①U448.135.7②U459.1

中国国家版本馆CIP数据核字(2023)第170470号

书　　名：城市轨道交通桥隧维修与养护
作　　者：罗立娜　方恩权　李冕梧

策　　划：韩从付　　　**编辑部电话：**(010)83527746
责任编辑：李中宝　李学敏
封面设计：曾　程
责任制作：刘　颖
责任校对：苗　丹
责任印制：樊启鹏

出版发行：中国铁道出版社有限公司(100054，北京市西城区右安门西街8号)
网　　址：https://www.tdpress.com/51eds/
印　　刷：天津嘉恒印务有限公司
版　　次：2024年9月第1版　2024年9月第1次印刷
开　　本：787 mm×1 092 mm 1/16　**印张：**14.25　**字数：**346千
书　　号：ISBN 978-7-113-30539-0
定　　价：53.00元

前 言

城市轨道交通行驶路线不受其他交通系统的干扰，可以大幅缩短城市时空距离，缓解地面交通拥堵，具有大运量、便捷、准时的优点，在城市交通体系发展中起到举足轻重的作用。中国城市轨道交通协会信息显示，截至2023年底，我国共有59个城市投运城市轨道交通线路11 224.54 km。

为确保城市轨道交通运输安全，桥梁隧道等基础设施养护维修已成为运营管理的重要工作之一。本书根据高等职业教育城市轨道交通工程技术、铁道工程技术等专业培养目标与教学要求，确定桥隧工典型工作任务，明确高职人才培养的素质、知识和能力要求，以培养职业能力为中心，梳理教学内容，划分项目和任务，内在逻辑合理，内容精练。第1章主要介绍桥隧基础知识；第2章详细阐述桥梁设施的常见病害与桥面、桥跨、墩台等养护维修作业；第3章详细阐述隧道设施的常见病害与防水、堵漏、加固等养护维修作业。本书不仅具有科学性、系统性、实用性的特点，而且具有较强的指导性和可操作性，有助于学生全面系统地掌握桥隧养护的相关知识和技能，使学生的专业技术与企业岗位无缝对接，能尽快适应桥隧养护维修工作。

党的二十大报告指出："教育、科技、人才是全面建设社会主义现代化国家的基础性、战略性支撑。必须坚持科技是第一生产力、人才是第一资源、创新是第一动力，深入实施科教兴国战略、人才强国战略、创新驱动发展战略，开辟发展新领域新赛道，不断塑造发展新动能新优势。"本书采用双语编写，适合作为高等职业教育铁道工程技术、地下与隧道工程技术、城市轨道交通工程技术、市政工程技术等教材，也可作为相关领域工程技术人员培训教材或参考书，让学生既掌握城市轨道交通桥隧维修技术，又加强专业英语训练，从容应对国际化的机遇和挑战。与此同时，本书也是响应我国开展相关海外国际培训需求，助力轨道交通国际化人才培养，践行"一带一路"倡议，推进区域协同发展的一项成果。

本书由广州铁路职业技术学院罗立娜、广州地铁集团有限公司方恩权和深圳地铁运营集团有限公司李冕梧任主编，广州铁路职业技术学院郭咏辉、深圳地铁运营集团有限公司李岳涛任副主编。具体编写分工如下：李冕梧负责编写第1章中1.1节的中文部分；广州铁路职业技术学院江晓芳负责编写第1章中1.1节的英文部分；罗立娜负责编写第1章中1.2、1.3节和第2章的英文部分，以及第3章的中英文部分；方恩权负责编写第1章中1.3节的中文部分；郭咏辉负责编写第1章中1.2节和第2章中2.1～2.4节的中文部分；李岳涛负责编写第2章中2.5节的中文部分。在编写过程中，北京城建设计发展集团股份有限公司雷刚和广东省交通规划设计研究院集团股份有限公司谢卓雄给予了大力支持和帮助，在此表示衷心的感谢。

由于编者水平有限，书中难免会出现疏漏与不当之处，恳请广大读者批评指正。

编　者

2023年5月

目 录

第 1 章　桥隧基础知识

Chapter 1　Basic Knowledge of Bridges and Tunnels

学习目标（Learning Objectives）

1. 能力目标

1. Capability objectives

(1)能够进行桥隧设施限界检查；

(1) Be able to conduct gauge inspection of bridge and tunnel facilities;

(2)能够识别不同类型的桥梁和隧道及其构造组成。

(2) Be able to identify different types of bridges and tunnels and their structural components.

2. 知识目标

2. Knowledge objectives

(1)熟悉车辆限界、设备限界和建筑限界的概念；

(1) Be familiar with the concepts of vehicle gauge, equipment gauge and construction gauge;

(2)熟悉桥梁、隧道的分类和荷载组成；

(2) Be familiar with the classification and load composition of bridges and tunnels;

(3)掌握桥梁、隧道的基本构造及各组成部分的作用。

(3) Master the basic structure of bridges and tunnels and the role of component.

3. 素质目标

3. Quality objectives

通过让学生了解桥隧工岗位的工作内容和重要性，培养学生爱岗敬业、勇于承担社会责任的职业观。

By introducing the work content and importance of workers in bridge and tunnel maintenance, cultivate students to love their jobs and assume social responsibility.

1.1　桥隧建筑限界

1.1　Structure gauge of bridge and tunnel

为了保证列车在线路上运行安全，列车的外轮廓线始终与周围的一切建(构)筑物和各种设备的轮廓线之间保持一个空间性的安全距离，以防止列车在运行中与沿线建(构)筑物和设备发生互相碰撞。限界就是为此而规定的轮廓尺寸线，即保障轨道交通安全运行、限制车辆断面尺寸、限制沿线设备安装尺寸及确定建筑结构有效净空尺寸的图形及坐标参数。隧道的大小和桥梁的宽窄,都是根据限界确定的。限界越大,行车安全度越高,工程量和工程投资也随之增加。限界的确定,既要考虑保证列车运行的安全,又要考虑系统建设成本。

In order to ensure the safe operation of trains on the line, a spatial safety distance is always maintained between the outer contour line of the train and the contour lines of all surrounding buildings (structures) and various equipment to prevent the train from colliding with buildings (structures) and equipment along the line during operation. The gauge is the contour dimension line specified for this purpose. It refers to the graphic and coordinate parameters that ensure the safe operation of rail transit, limit the cross-section size of vehicles and the installation size of equipment along the line, and determine the effective clearance size of building structures. The size of tunnel and the width of bridge is determined by the gauge. The larger the gauge, the higher the driving safety, the greater the amount of engineering and investment also increase. When the gauge is determined, the safety of train operation and the cost of system construction should be taken into consideration.

总体上看,限界是保证车辆运行安全的有效空间,是车辆与沿线固定建筑物及其设备安装空间关系总体协调后得到的净空尺寸图形坐标。

The gauge is an effective space to ensure the safe operation of vehicles. It is the graphical coordinate of the clearance size based on the overall installation space relationship between vehicles and fixed buildings and their equipment along the line.

1.1.1 限界的种类

1.1.1 Types of gauges

城市轨道交通车辆在隧道内或高架上运行,一方面,隧道或高架要有足够的空间,可供车辆通行并配置线路结构、通信、信号、供电、给排水等设备;另一方面,为了确保列车安全运行,凡接近城市轨道交通线路的各种建筑物及设备,必须与线路保持一定的距离。因此,城市轨道交通限界主要分为车辆限界、设备限界和建筑限界,如图 1-1 所示。

When urban rail transit vehicles run in tunnels or on elevated, on one hand, there should be enough space in the tunnel or elevated for vehicles to pass and configure equipment of line structure, communication, signals, power supply, water supply and drainage; on the other hand, in order to ensure train safe operation, all kinds of buildings and equipment close to the urban rail transit line must be kept at a certain distance from the line. Therefore, the gauge of urban rail transit are mainly divided into vehicle gauge, equipment gauge and construction gauge, as shown in Figure 1-1.

1. 车辆限界

1. Vehicle gauge

车辆限界是车辆在正常运行状态下形成的最大动态包络线。为了能确保城市轨道交通车辆的正常运行以及安全,车辆限界根据车辆的轮廓尺寸,考虑其弹簧挠度、各项间隙、磨耗、误差等技术参数的影响,对车辆在运行中可能出现的最大横向和竖向的偏移进行分析计算确定。直线地段车辆限界分为隧道内车辆限界和高架或地面线车辆限界,高架或地面线车辆限界应在隧道内车辆限界基础上，另加当地最大风荷载引起的横向和竖向偏移量。此外，受电弓限界或受流器限界也是车辆限界的组成部分。

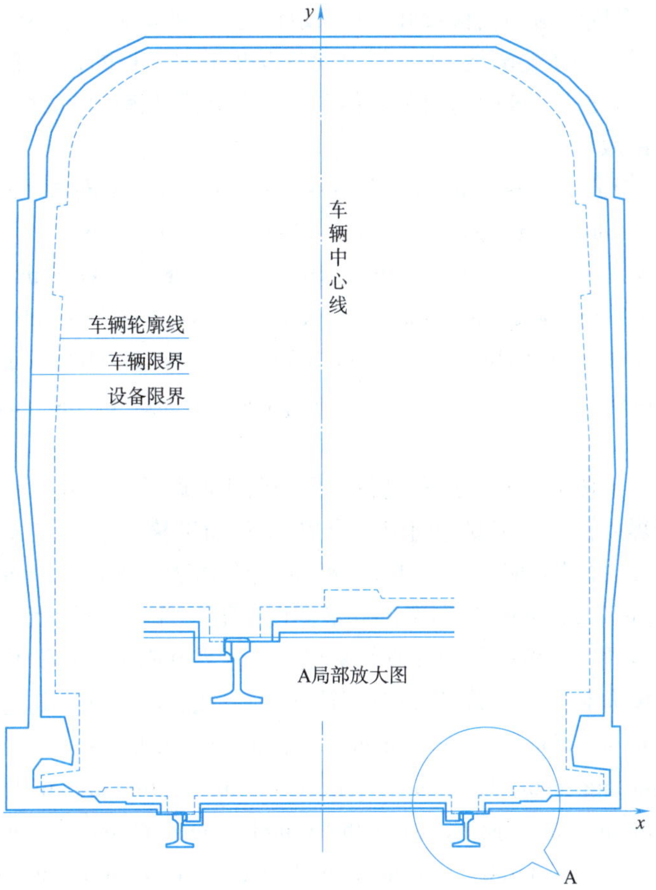

图 1-1　隧道内直线地段车辆轮廓线、车辆限界和设备限界示意图

Figure 1-1　Schematic diagram of vehicle contour, vehicle gauge, and equipment gauge in the tunnel on straight line

车辆轮廓线：vehicle contour line　　车辆限界：vehicle gauge

设备限界：equipment gauge　　A 局部放大图：partial enlarged view of A

Vehicle gauge is the maximum dynamic envelope formed by the vehicle in normal operation. In order to ensure the normal operation and safety of urban rail transit vehicles, the vehicle gauge is calculated based on the influence of the spring deflection, the gap, the wear, the error, and the maximum horizontal and vertical offset of the vehicle in operation. Vehicle gauge in the straight line section shall be divided into tunnel vehicle gauge and elevated or ground line vehicle gauge. Elevated or ground line vehicle gauge shall be based on vehicle gauge in the tunnel, plus the horizontal and vertical offset caused by the local maximum wind load. In addition, the pantograph gauge or the flow collector gauge is also an integral part of the vehicle gauge.

2. 设备限界

2. Equipment gauge

设备限界是在车辆限界的基础上，考虑轨道的轨距、水平、方向、高低等在某些地段上出现最大容许误差，引起车辆的附加偏移量，以及在设计、施工、列车运行中不可预计因素在内的安全预留量。设备限界是一条轮廓线，所有固定设备以及土木工程的任何部分都不得侵入此轮廓线内，保证城市轨道交通系统中的列车等移动设备在运营过程中的安全。其中，接触轨限界属于设备限界的辅助限界。

The equipment gauge is determined on the basis of the vehicle gauge, taking into account the maximum allowable error of rail gauge, level, direction, height, etc. in some sections, the additional offset of vehicles, and the safety reserve including unpredictable factors in design, construction and vehicle in operation. Equipment gauge is a contour line, all fixed equipment and any part of the civil works is not allowed to invade it for the safety of mobile equipment such as trains in the urban rail transit system. The contact rail gauge belongs to the auxiliary gauge of the equipment gauge.

设备限界按所处地段分为直线地段设备限界和曲线地段设备限界。直线地段设备限界是在直线地段车辆限界外扩大一定安全间隙后形成：车体肩部横向向外扩大 100 mm，边梁下端横向向外扩大 30 mm，接触轨横向向外扩大 185 mm，车体竖向加高 60 mm，受电弓竖向加高 50 mm，车下悬挂物下降 50 mm。转向架部件最低设备限界离轨顶面净距：A 型车为 25 mm，B 型车为 15 mm。曲线地段设备限界应在直线地段设备限界基础上，按平面曲线不同半径、过超高或欠超高引起的横向和竖向偏移量，以及车辆、轨道参数等因素计算确定。

Equipment gauge is divided into equipment gauge in straight line section and equipment gauge in curve section according to the location. Equipment gauge of the straight line section is formed after expanding a certain safety gap outside the vehicle gauge of the straight line section. The shoulder of vehicle body is laterally expanded by 100 mm, the lower end of boundary beam is laterally expanded by 30 mm, the conductor rail is laterally expanded by 185 mm, the vehicle body is vertically increased by 60 mm, the pantograph is vertically increased by 50 mm, and the suspension under the vehicle is lowered by 50 mm. The clear distance from the minimum equipment gauge of bogie components to the specified top of track: 25 mm for model A vehicle and 15 mm for model B vehicle. The equipment gauge in curve zone shall be determined on the basis of equipment gauge in straight line section according to the different radius of plane curve, horizontal and vertical offset caused by over-high or under ultra-high, as well as the factors of vehicle and parameters.

3. 建筑限界

3. Structure gauge

建筑限界是在设备限界基础上，考虑了设备和管线安装尺寸后的最小断面积。它规定了桥隧结构的形状、尺寸、位置，地下车站及站台的位置，地面建筑物（包括接触网支柱、声屏障和站台门等）的位置。建筑限界和设备限界之间的空间，应能安排各种电缆线、消防水管及消防栓、动力照明箱、信号箱及信号灯、照明灯、扩音器、通风管、架空接触网及其固定设备或接触轨及其固定设备等。在宽度方向上设备和设备限界之间应留出 20 ~ 50 mm 安全间隙。当建筑限界侧面和顶面没有设备或管线时，建筑限界和设备限界之间的间隙不宜小于200 mm，困难条件下不得小于 100 mm。相邻的双线，当两线间无墙、柱及其他设备时，两设备限界之间的安全间隙不得小于 100 mm。

Structure gauge is the minimum cross-sectional area which considers the dimensions of equipment and pipeline installation based on the equipment gauge. It specifies the shape, size, location of the bridge and tunnel structure, the location of underground stations and platforms, the location of ground buildings (including OCS mast, sound barrier and platform screen door, etc.). The space between building gauges and equipment gauges shall be arranged for various cables, fire pipes and fire hydrants, power lighting boxes, signal boxes and signal lights, lighting lamps, loudspeakers, ventilation pipes, overhead contact line and their fixed equipment or contact rails and their fixed equipment, etc. There should be a safety gap of 20 - 50 mm between the equipment and the equipment gauge in width. When there is no equipment or pipeline on the side and top of structure gauge, the gap between the structure gauge and the equipment gauge shall not be less than 200 mm and should not be less than 100 mm under difficult conditions. Adjacent double lines, between which there are no walls, columns and other equipment, the safety gap between two equipment gauges shall not be less than 100 mm.

1.1.2　建筑限界设计原则

1.1.2　Design principles for structure gauges

建筑限界规定了城市轨道交通构造物的形状、尺寸、位置、车站及站台位置以及其他建筑物（包括接触网支柱、声屏障和站台屏蔽门等）的位置，涉及施工误差、测量误差及结构永久变形在内，任何永久性建筑物均不得向内侵入此限界。

The structure gauge specifies the shape, size, and position of urban rail transit structures, the positions of stations and platforms, as well as the positions of other buildings (including overhead contact system pillars, sound barriers, and platform screen doors). The design of structure gauge should take construction errors, measurement errors, and permanent structural deformation into consideration, and make sure that permanent structures shall not intrude into the gauge.

城市轨道交通建筑限界设计的原则主要有以下五个方面：

The principles of urban rail transit structure gauge design mainly include the following five aspects:

①建筑限界是确定行车轨道周围构筑物净空大小的依据，是管线和设备安装位置的依据，是专业间共同遵守的技术规定，应经济、合理、安全可靠。

①The structure gauge is the basis for determining the clearance size of structures around the running track, the basis for the installation position of pipelines and equipment, and the technical regulations that are commonly followed among professions. It should be economical, reasonable, safe, and reliable.

②建筑限界应依据车辆的轮廓尺寸和技术参数、轨道特性、受电方式、施工方法、设备安装等综合因素进行分析、计算确定。

②The structure gauge should be analyzed and calculated based on the overall dimensions and technical parameters of the vehicle, track characteristics, power supply methods, construction methods, equipment installation, and other comprehensive factors.

③建筑限界一般按平直线路的条件进行制定。

③The structure gauge is generally formulated based on the conditions of a straight line.

④在制定建筑限界时,对结构变形误差、设备制造和安装误差,以及设计、施工、运营过程中难于预计的其他因素在内的安全留量等,都应分别进行研究确定。

④ When designing structure gauges, safety allowances, including structural deformation errors, equipment manufacturing and installation errors, as well as other factors that are difficult to predict during design, construction, and operation, should be studied and determined separately.

⑤车辆在曲线上运行时,转向架中心点可以随曲线的弯度转动,但转向架上的车体是一个刚性整体。车体两端突出于曲线外侧,中间部分向曲线内侧偏移,因此,曲线内外侧都需要进行加宽,如图 1-2 所示。

⑤When the vehicle is running on a curve, the center point of the bogie can rotate with the curvature of curve, but the body on the bogie is a rigid whole. The two ends of vehicle protrude from the outside of the curve, and the middle part shifts towards the inside of the curve. Therefore, both the inside and outside of the curve need to be widened, as shown in Figure 1-2.

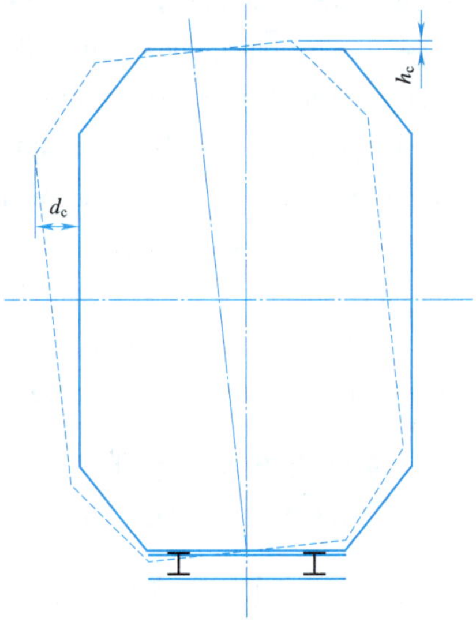

图 1-2 超高使车厢倾斜而引起的加宽和加高示意图

Figure 1-2 Schematic diagram of widening and heightening caused by the carriage tilting due to superelevation

1.1.3 桥隧建筑限界

1.1.3 Structure gauge of bridge and tunnel

桥隧建筑限界是桥梁、隧道建筑物不得侵入的规定轮廓线,以确保机车车辆和超限装载货物安全顺利地通过桥隧建筑物。

The structure gauge of bridge and tunnel is the prescribed contour line that the bridge and tunnel buildings shall not invade, which ensures that locomotives and overloaded goods can pass through the bridge and tunnel buildings safely and smoothly.

隧道建筑限界按结构形式分为矩形隧道建筑限界(明挖法)、圆形隧道建筑限界(盾构法)和马蹄形隧道建筑限界(矿山法),如图 1-3 所示。

The structure gauges of tunnels are divided into rectangular tunnel structure gauge (open cut method), circular tunnel structure gauge (shield method) and horseshoe tunnel structure gauge (mining method) according to the structural form, as shown in Figure 1-3.

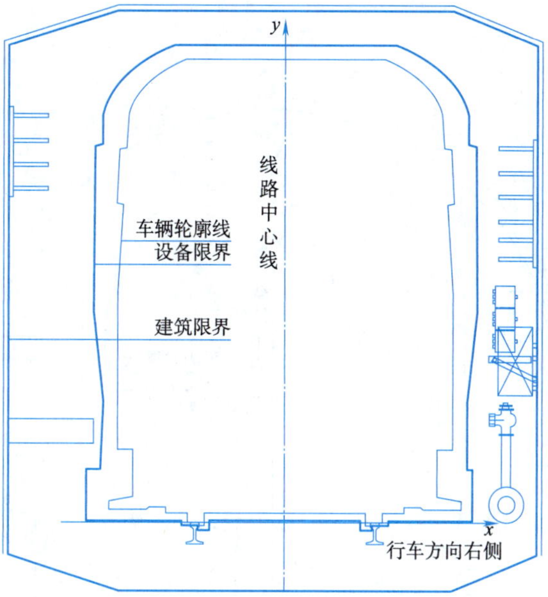

（a）矩形隧道建筑限界（明挖法）
Rectangular tunnel structure gauge (open cut method)

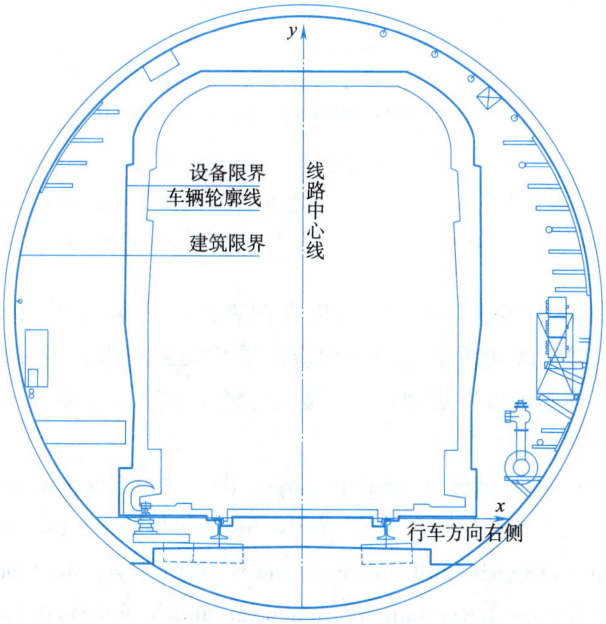

（b）圆形隧道建筑限界（盾构法）
Circular tunnel structure gauge (shield method)

图 1-3　隧道建筑限界示意图
Figure 1-3　Schematic diagram of tunnel structure gauge

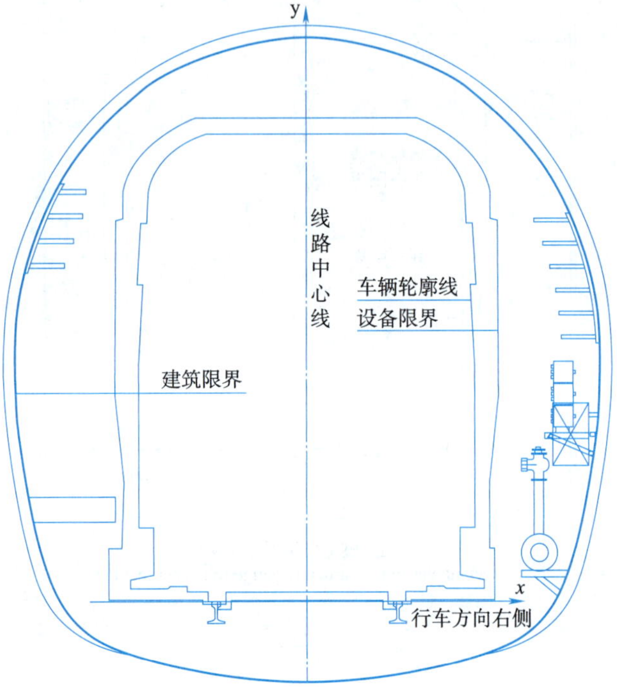

（c）马蹄形隧道建筑限界（矿山法）
Horseshoe tunnel structure gauge (mining method)

图 1-3 隧道建筑限界示意图（续）
Figure 1-3 Schematic diagram of tunnel structure gauge (continued)
线路中心线：central line of track 建筑限界：structure gauge

桥梁建筑限界较基本建筑限界稍大，可以在两者之间安装照明、通信以及信号设备，如图 1-4 所示。新建及修复、改建桥梁的净空均应满足桥梁建筑限界的要求。位于曲线上的下承桁梁及半穿式梁，其横断面净空需要加宽的数值，除与前述曲线半径、外轨超高和车辆长度有关外，尚与梁长有关。

The structure gauge of bridge is slightly larger than the fundamental structure gauge, so lighting, communication and signal equipment can be installed between the two gauges, as shown in Figure 1-4. The clearance of newly built, repaired and rebuilt bridges shall meet the requirements of bridge structure gauge. For the lower support truss beam and half through beam on the curve, the value of the cross-section clearance should be widened according to the aforementioned curve radius, superelevation, vehicle length and beam length.

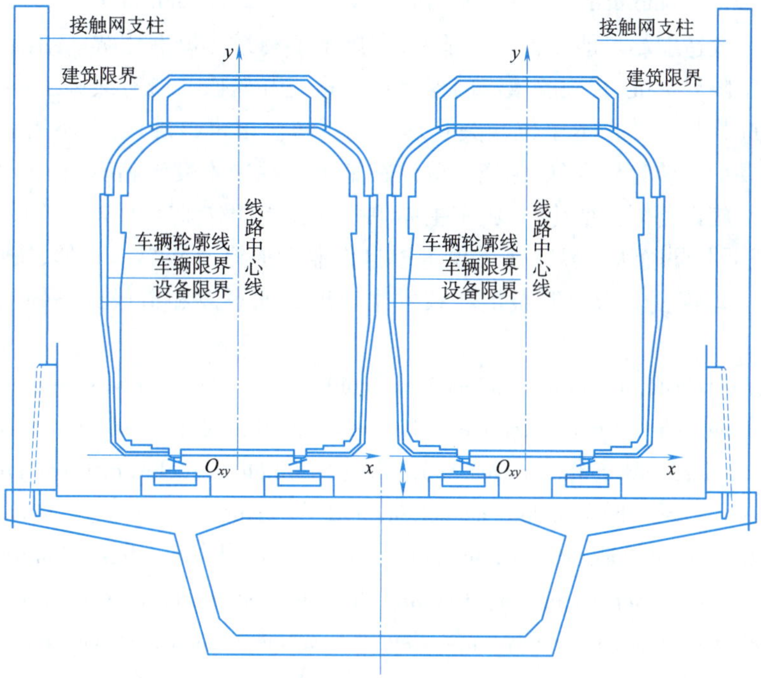

图 1-4　桥梁建筑限界示意图

Figure 1-4　Schematic diagram of bridge structure gauge

接触网支柱:OCS mast

1.1.4　限界的检查和管理

1.1.4　Inspection and management of gauges

限界检查是指对既有设施设备在距轨面不同高度处最接近线路中心线的点共同构成的横断面轮廓的检查和测量。一切设施设备均不得侵入轨道交通桥隧建筑限界,与机车车辆有直接相互作用的设备除外,但在使用中不得超过规定的侵入范围。

Gauge inspection refers to the inspection and measurement of the cross-sectional contour formed by the points closest to the central line of track at different heights from the track surface of existing facilities and equipment. All facilities and equipment shall not invade the structure gauge of rail transit bridge and tunnel, except for the equipment that directly interacts with the vehicles, but shall not exceed the specified scope in use.

各设备管理单位要健全限界管理机构,明确管理职责,掌握限界变化情况,确保资料完整、准确。为规范桥隧建筑限界的管理,确保轨道交通运输安全,结合各单位工作特点,应制定相应的限界检查和管理办法。

All equipment management units should improve the management organization of the gauges, clarify the management responsibilities, grasp the changes of the gauges, and ensure the integrity and accuracy of the data. In order to standardize the management of gauge of bridge and tunuel, and ensure safe running of rail transit, the corresponding gauge inspection and management measures should be formulated combined with the working characteristics of each unit.

既有线技术改造应尽可能改善限界条件,原则上不得缩小既有限界。沿线新建设施设备应符合相关规定限界标准,相关验收部门据此进行审查和验收。既有线施工需要临时缩小限界时,应制定临时限界,并报本单位相关管理部门审核。未审核确认前,不得临时缩小限界。安全监察部门要加强监督检查,确保施工单位在施工过程中不突破临时限界。施工维修作业可能造成其他设施设备限界变化时,施工主体单位须在组织作业前通知相关设备管理中心到现场,作业完成后共同确认限界。违反规定擅自作业造成既有限界缩小的,按照“谁改变,谁整治”的原则,立即恢复。未及时整治导致发生轨道交通事故和造成经济损失的,严肃追究责任。

The technical transformation of existing line should improve the gauges as far as possible, and in principle, the gauges should not be reduced. The newly built facilities and equipment along the line shall meet the standards about the gauges, according to which the relevant acceptance departments shall make a review and check before acceptance. If the gauges need to be temporarily reduced during the construction of existing lines, temporary gauges should be established and exterminated by the relevant management departments of the unit. The gauges shall not be temporarily reduced before examination and confirmation. Safety supervision department should strengthen supervision and inspection to ensure that the construction unit does not break through the confirmed gauges in the construction. When the maintenance operation may cause gauge changes in other facilities and equipment, the main construction unit shall notify the relevant equipment management unit to the site before operation and jointly confirm the gauge after work. If the existing gauge is reduced due to unauthorized operation in violation of regulations, the responsible party shall renovate it immediately. Those who fail to rectify in a timely manner and cause rail transit accidents and economic losses shall be held accountable.

各设备管理单位在新建、改建线路提前介入时,要对设施设备限界进行监督检查,发现问题及时通知建设管理单位、施工单位整改。新建、改建工程竣工验收前,建设管理单位须按规定向设备管理单位移交限界资料。新建、改建工程竣工验收时,各设备管理单位应现场测量和复核设施设备限界,并做好记录。不满足要求时,严禁开通使用。

When the equipment management unit get involved in the new or reconstruction lines, it shall supervise and inspect the gauges of facilities and equipment, and timely notify the construction management unit and the construction unit for rectification if problems are found. Before the acceptance of a new or reconstruction project, the construction management unit shall hand over the materials about gauges to the equipment management unit according to the provisions. During the completion acceptance of new and reconstruction projects, each equipment management unit shall measure and recheck the gauges of facilities and equipment on site, and make records. If the requirements are not met, it is forbidden to open and put into use.

设备管理单位应加强对沿线设施设备的巡视检查,掌握限界变化情况。当限界发生变化时,行车设施设备中心应立即采用相应安全措施,保障行车安全。设备管理单位应建立完整、准确、可靠的设施设备限界资料台账,并由专人负责管理。每年对线路技术设备进行定期检查时，各设备管理单位须认真检测核查其限界变化情况。原始限界测量记录及后期变化须永久保存。测量工具应满足限界测量准确度要求，定期进行计量检定或校准。严禁使用非标测量工具。

The equipment management unit should strengthen the inspection of the facilities and equipment along the line, and grasp the gauge changes. When the gauge changes, the facilities and equipment center shall immediately adopt corresponding safety measures to ensure the safe movement of the vehicle. The equipment management unit shall establish a complete, accurate and reliable ledger for facilities and equipment gauge which is managed by special personnel. During the regular inspection of equipment on the line every year, each equipment management unit shall carefully detect and check the gauge changes. The original gauge measurement records and later changes must be kept all the time. Measurement tools shall meet the accuracy requirements of gauge measurement and conduct regular measurement verification or calibration. Non-standard measuring tools are strictly prohibited.

受不可抗力或客观条件限制影响，设施设备侵限或已侵限设施设备限界进一步缩小时，各设备管理单位须填写"限界缩小报告单"。经审核确认后，将具体情况（形成原因、目前状况、运输限制条件等）及安全保障措施以书面形式报相关部门。各设备管理单位须建立侵限设施设备台账，实行销号管理，并于每年年底汇总侵限的设施设备。各设备管理单位应积极组织开展侵限设施设备整治工作，应制定整治方案并纳入年度工作计划，所需费用纳入财务预算。整治完成后，各设备管理单位及时将限界数据上报相关管理部门。对设施设备违规侵限的单位和个人，应责令其限期整改，造成行车事故的，按有关条款追责。

Affected by force majeure or objective conditions, when the gauges of facilities and equipment are violated or the gauges of facilities and equipment that have been violated are further reduced, each equipment management unit must fill in the gauge reduction report. After review and confirmation, the specific conditions (formation reasons, current conditions, transportation restrictions, etc.) and safety measures shall be reported to relevant departments in written form. Each equipment management unit shall establish the accounts for the facilities and equipment intruding into gauges, implement the cancellation management, and summarize the information of the facilities and equipment violating the limit. All equipment management units shall actively rectify the facilities and equipment that invades the gauge, formulate rectification plans, incorporate them into the annual work plan, and put the required expenses into the financial budget. After the rectification, each equipment management unit shall timely report the gauge data to the relevant management departments. Units and individuals that invade facilities and equipment gauge shall be ordered to rectify within a time limit. If any driving accident is caused, the responsibility shall be pursued according to the relevant provisions.

限界数据包括基础数据、文档资料、应用数据内容及格式等，是加强限界管理，确保轨道交通运输安全的重要保障。相关设备管理单位应严格审核限界数据，确保数据完整、准确、更新及时。

Gauge data, which includes basic data, document data, content and format of application data, etc., is an important guarantee to strengthen gauge management and ensure the safe driving. Relevant equipment management units shall strictly review the gauge data to ensure that the data is complete, accurate and timely updated.

限界数据被全覆盖动态管理,设施设备限界数据临时发生变化时,各设备管理单位应及时上报,并及时更新限界数据。遇下列情况各设备管理单位须立即按程序更新限界数据:

The gauge data is fully covered and dynamically managed. In case of temporary changes, each equipment management unit shall timely report and update the gauge data. In case of the following situations, each equipment management unit shall update the gauge data immediately according to the procedure:

①年度整理中发现需更新限界数据时。

①When gauge data needs to be updated in the annual sorting.

②日常使用过程中发现限界数据不完整、不准确时。

②When gauge data is incomplete and inaccurate during daily use.

各设备管理单位对录入的限界数据完整性、准确性负责,并确保及时更新;设备限界发生变化,未及时按规定报告和更新的,由相关设备管理单位负责;施工时,缩小限界未按规定办理有关手续或提供的限界数据不准确的,由建设管理单位负责。限界数据表空白处,视为在规定的检测范围内无任何设施设备。

Each equipment management unit shall be responsible for the completeness and accuracy of the input gauge data, and ensure timely updating. If the equipment gauge changes and can't be timely reported and updated, relevant equipment management units shall be responsible; if the gauge is reduced failing to go through relevant procedures as required or the gauge data provided is inaccurate, the construction management unit shall be responsible. The blank space in the data sheet shall be deemed to have no facilities and equipment within the specified range.

有关部门应切实掌握管辖范围内桥隧、立交桥、天桥、渡槽及其他建筑物的精确实测断面和各部分距离线路中心线的尺寸。一般地,重要线路的桥隧限界每 5 年,其他线路的桥隧限界每 10 年检查一次。

The relevant departments should obtain the accurate cross sections of the bridges, tunnels, overpasses, flyovers, aqueducts and other buildings and the dimensions of each part from the track central lines within their jurisdiction. Generally, the gauges of bridges and tunnels for important lines shall be inspected every 5 years, and the gauges of bridges and tunnels for other lines shall be inspected every 10 years.

1.2 桥梁设施基础知识
1.2 General knowledge of bridge infrastructure

1.2.1 桥梁的组成与分类
1.2.1 Components and classification of bridge

桥梁是主要承载公路和铁路交通或任何其他移动载荷而建造的结构。它使移动载荷跨越洼地、间隙、障碍物，例如河流、渠道、峡谷、山谷、交通繁忙的道路等。

Bridges are the structures built for carrying mostly road and railway traffic or any other moving loads over a depression or gap or obstruction such as a river, channel, canyon, valley, heavy traffic road, etc.

桥梁是城轨线路的重要组成部分。它构造复杂，技术性强，造价高，加固和修复都比较困难。桥梁必须保持完好状态，以保证列车按规定的速度，安全、平稳和不间断地运行。

Bridges are an important part of urban rail transit lines. They are complex in structure, exquisite in technology, high in cost, and difficult to reinforce and repair. Therefore, bridges must be kept in good condition to ensure safe, stable and uninterrupted operation of trains at specified speeds.

1. 桥梁的组成

1. Components of bridge

桥梁由四个基本部分组成，即上部结构、下部结构、支座和附属设施，如图 1-5 所示。

The main components of a bridge are the superstructure, substructure, bearing, and the ancillary facility, as shown in Figure 1-5.

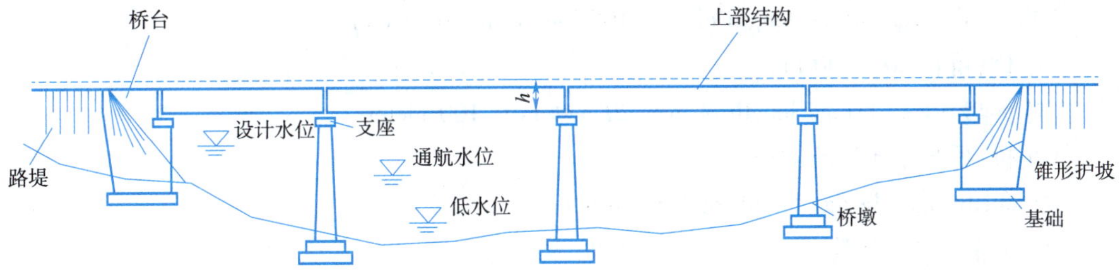

图 1-5　桥梁的组成

Figure 1-5　Components of bridge

路堤：embankment　桥台：abutment　设计水位：design water level
通航水位：navigable water level　低水位：low water level　上部结构：superstructure
桥墩：pier　锥形护坡：conical slope　基础：foundation
支座：bearing

上部结构是在线路中断时跨越障碍的主要承重结构，是桥梁支座以上（无铰拱起拱线或刚架主梁底线以上）跨越桥孔的总称；当跨越幅度越大时，上部结构的构造也就越复杂，施工难度也相应增加。

Superstructure is the main load-bearing structure for crossing obstacles when the line is interrupted. It is the general name of crossing bridge holes above the bridge support (above the springing line of non hinged arch or above the bottom line of rigid frame main beam); When the span is greater, the structure of the superstructure is more complex, and the difficulty of construction increases accordingly.

下部结构包括桥墩、桥台和基础。

The substructure consists of piers, abutments, and foundations.

支座是设在墩(台)顶,用于支承上部结构的传力装置,它不仅要传递很大的荷载,并且要保证上部结构按设计要求能产生一定的变位。

Bearing: it is a force transmission device located at the top of the pier (abutment) for supporting the superstructure, which not only transmits a large load, but also ensures that the superstructure can produce a certain displacement according to the design requirements.

附属设施包括桥面系、伸缩缝、桥梁与路堤衔接处的桥头搭板和锥形护坡等。

The ancillary facilities: including bridge decking, expansion joint, transition slab at bridge head at the junction of bridge and embankment, conical slope, etc.

2. 桥梁的分类

2. Classification of bridge

(1)按桥梁长度分类

(1) in relation to length of bridge

①特大桥:桥长 500 m 以上。

①Long-span bridge: bridge length of over 500 meters.

②大桥:桥长 100 ~ 500 m。

②Major Bridge: bridge length of over 100 meters to 500 meters.

③中桥:桥长 20 ~ 100 m。

③Minor bridge: bridge length of over 20 meters to 100 meters.

④小桥:桥长小于等于 20 m。

④Small bridge: bridge length of 20 meters or less.

(2)按桥跨材质分类

(2) in relation to material of bridge span

① 钢桥:梁拱材料为钢。

① Steel bridges: made of steel.

② 圬工桥:梁拱材料为石、砖、混凝土、钢筋混凝土、预应力钢筋混凝土。

② Masonary bridges: made of stone, brick, concrete, reinforced concrete, pre-stressed concrete.

③ 混合桥:一座桥上有两种以上不同的材质。一般指同时使用钢材与钢筋混凝土。

③ Composite bridge: made of more than two different materials, generally steel and reinforced concrete at the same time.

④ 木桥:梁拱材料为木。

④ Timber bridges: made of wood.

(3)按桥面位置分类

(3) According to the position of bridge deck relative to superstructures

① 上承式桥:桥面位于桥跨的顶部。

① Deck bridge: The bridge deck is located at the top of the bridge span.

② 下承式桥:桥面位于两主梁(桁梁或板梁)或两拱肋之间。

② Through bridge: The bridge deck is located between two main beams(truss or slab) or two arch ribs.

③ 中承式桥:桥面设置在桥跨主要承重结构(桁梁、拱肋、主梁等)中部。

③ Half through bridge: The bridge deck is located in the middle of the main bearing structures (truss, arch rib, main beam) of the bridge span.

(4)按桥梁受力体系分类

(4) based on the structural system

① 梁桥。梁桥的主要结构部件是在两端支撑的水平梁。当梁只跨越单个跨度时,它们被两点支撑;当梁跨越两个或多个跨度时,它们多点连续支撑。按照主梁的静力体系,梁桥分为简支梁桥、连续梁桥和悬臂梁桥,如图 1-6 所示。悬臂梁和连续梁都是利用支座上的卸载弯矩去减少跨中弯矩,使梁跨内力分配更合理,以同等抗弯能力的构件断面就可建成更大跨径的桥梁。

① Beam bridge. The main structural element of a beam bridge is a horizontal beam that is supported at each end. They can be simply supported when the beams only connect across a single span, or continuous when the beams are connected across two or more spans. According to the static system of the main beam, it is divided into simply supported bridge, continuous bridge and cantilever bridge, as shown in Figure 1-6. Both the cantilever beam and the continuous beam can reduce the bending moment in the middle of the span by utilizing the unloading bending moment on the support, so that the internal force distribution of the beam span is more reasonable and the component section with the same bending ability can be used to build a bridge with a larger span.

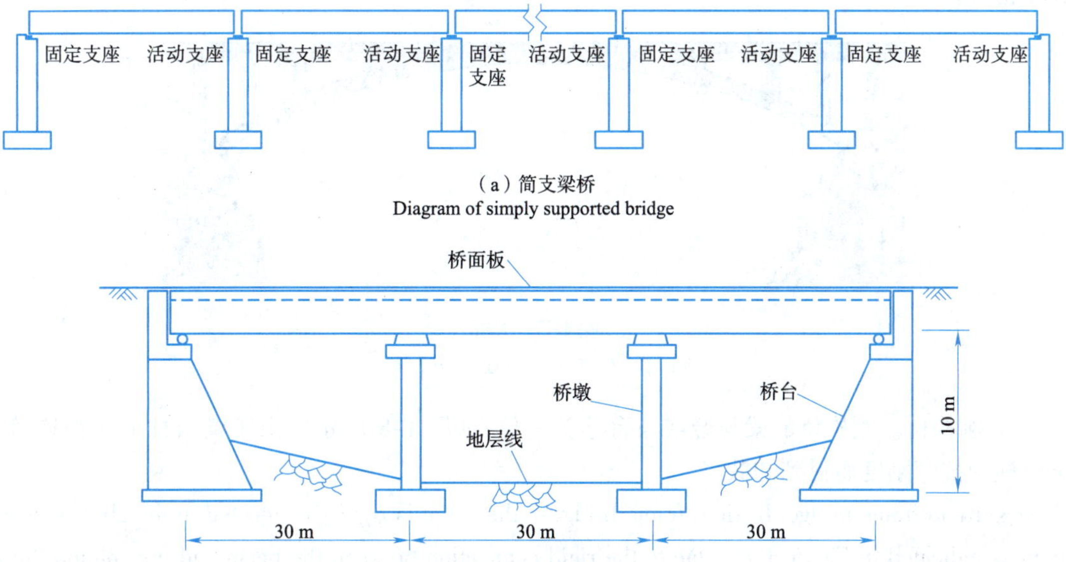

(b) 连续梁桥
Diagram of continuous bridge

图 1-6 梁桥

Figure1-6 Diagrams of beam bridges

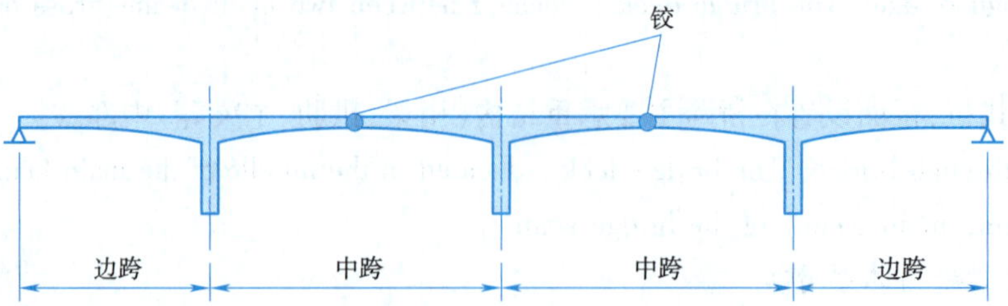

（c）悬臂梁桥
Diagram of cantilever bridge

图 1-6　梁桥（续）

Figure 1-6　Diagrams of beam bridges (continued)

固定支座：fixed　活动支座：movable　桥面板：deck　边跨：side span
地层线：rock line　铰：articulations　中跨：mid span

② 拱桥。拱式体系的主要承重结构是拱肋（或拱箱），以承压为主，采用抗压能力强的圬工材料（石、混凝土与钢筋混凝土）来修建，如图 1-7 所示。拱承受的荷载传递到基础上，对地基产生较大的水平推力，因此，拱桥对地基要求较高，一般常建于地基良好的地区。

② Arch bridge. The main load-bearing structure of the arch system is the arch rib (or arch box), which is mainly under pressure and built of strong compressive materials (stone, concrete and reinforced concrete), as shown in Figure 1-7. Arches are stable and capable of larger spans and supporting considerable loads than horizontal beams. The downward load of an arch must be transmitted to its foundations, generating a significant horizontal thrust on the foundation. Therefore, arch bridges have high requirements for the foundation and are usually built in areas with good foundations.

图 1-7　拱桥

Figure 1-7　Diagram of arch bridge

③ 刚构桥。刚构桥的梁与墩或与台连为一体，如图 1-8 所示。由于梁与柱的刚性连接，梁因柱的抗弯刚度而得到卸载。

③ Rigid frame bridge. In rigid frame bridges, the beam is rigidly connected to the abutments or piers as indicated in Figure 1-8. Due to the rigid connection between the beam and the column, less moments in deck being partly transferred to the supporting members.

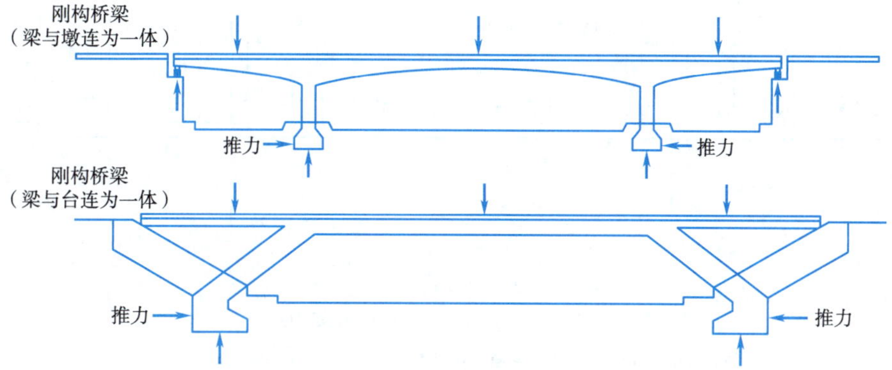

图1-8 刚构桥

Figure 1-8 Diagram of rigid frame bridge

刚构桥：rigid frame bridge　　推力：thrust

梁与墩连为一体：the beam and pier are connected as a whole

梁与台连为一体：the beam and abutment are connected as a whole

④ 悬索桥。悬索桥指以悬索为主要承重结构的桥，由悬索、索塔、锚碇、吊杆、桥面系等部分组成，如图1-9所示。主缆悬挂在塔架之间，最终连接到桥梁两端的锚碇上，垂直吊杆承受桥面系的自重和上面的交通荷载。主要承载构件是主缆，主缆是由高强度钢制成的受拉构件。主缆有良好的承载能力，且不存在屈曲问题。因此，桥梁结构的自重大大减轻，可以实现更大的跨径。此外，与其他类型的桥梁相比，悬索桥的美学外观是另一个优势。

④ Suspension bridge. A suspension bridge is a type of bridge in which the deck is hung below suspension cables on vertical suspenders, as shown in Figure 1-9. The basic structural components of a suspension bridge system include suspension cables, main towers, suspenders, bridge deck system, and anchorages for the cables at each end of the bridge. The main cables are suspended between towers and are finally connected to the anchorages at the bridge ends, and vertical suspenders carry the weight of the deck and the traffic load on it. The main load carrying member is the main cables, which are tension members made of high-strength steel. The whole cross-section of the main cable is highly efficient in carrying the loads and buckling is not problem. Therefore, the deadweight of the bridge structure can be greatly reduced and longer span becomes possible. In addition, the esthetic appearance of suspension bridges is another advantage in comparison with other types of bridges.

⑤ 组合体系。

⑤ Combination system.

a. 梁、拱组合体系：这类体系中有系杆拱、桁架拱、多跨拱梁结构等，如图1-10所示。它们利用梁的受弯与拱的承压特点组成联合结构。

a. Beam-arch combination system: this kind of system includes tied arch, truss arch, multi-span arch beam structure, etc, as shown in Figure 1-10. They use the bending characteristics of the beam and the compression characteristics of the arch to form a combined structure.

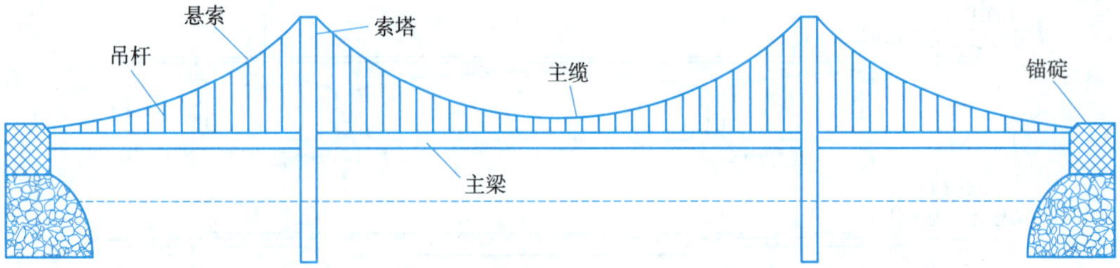

图 1-9 悬索桥

Figure 1-9 Diagram of suspension bridge

吊杆:suspender 索塔:tower 主缆:main cable

主梁:main girder 锚碇:anchorage 悬索:suspension cables

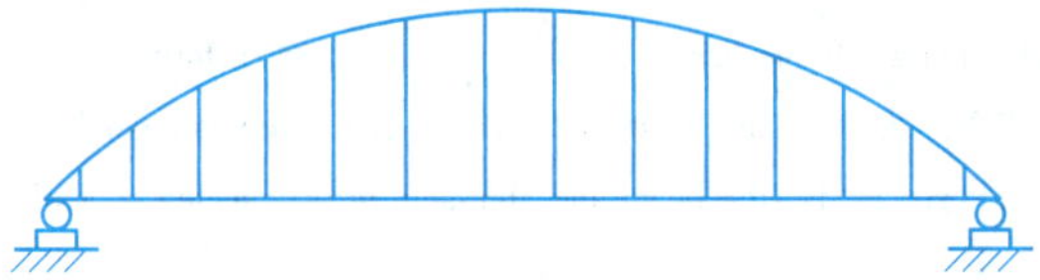

(a) 系杆拱

Tied arch

(b) 桁架拱

Truss arch

(c) 多跨拱梁结构

Multi-span arch beam structure

图 1-10 梁、拱组合体系

Figure 1-10 Diagram of beam-arch combination system

b. 斜拉桥:在塔之间的每个跨度中有几个点用斜拉索向上支撑的结构,由索塔、拉索和主梁组成,如图 1-11 所示。桥面重量由多条张力接近直线的斜拉索支撑,斜拉索直接延伸至一个或多个索塔,塔架通过垂直压缩将索力传递至基础,缆绳中的张力也使桥面受到水平压缩。斜拉桥外形优美,跨越能力强。

b. Cable-stayed bridge: a structure with several points in each span between the towers supported upward in a slanting direction with inclined cables and consists of main towers, cables, and main girders, as shown in Figure 1-11. The weight of the deck is supported by a number of nearly straight diagonal cables in tension running directly to one or more towers. The towers transfer the cable forces to the foundations through vertical compression. The tensile forces in the cables also put the deck into horizontal compression. Cable-stayed bridge has aesthetic appearance and strong spanning ability.

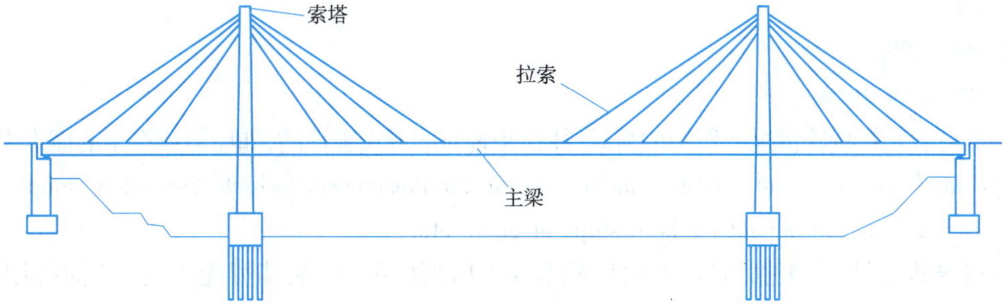

图 1-11 斜拉桥

Figure 1-11 Diagram of cable-stayed bridge

拉索:cable

1.2.2 桥梁的荷载

1.2.2 Loads on bridges

桥梁荷载是指桥梁结构设计所应考虑的各种可能出现的荷载统称。按照《地铁设计规范》(GB 50157—2013)的规定:桥梁荷载可以分为主力、附加力和特殊荷载。

Loads on bridges covers all kinds of possible loads that should be considered in the design of bridge structure. According to *Code for Design of Metro* (GB 50157—2013), the load of bridge can be divided into main force, additional force and special load.

1. 主力

1. main force

主力是正常的、经常发生的或时常重复出现的,又可分为恒载和活载。

The main force is normal, frequent or repeated, and can be divided into dead load and live load.

恒载一般指结构自重、土压力、静水压力及浮力、预加应力等,其大小和作用点一般是固定不变的,故称恒载。

Dead loads, known as permanent or static loads, are those that remain relatively constant over time, such as structure weight, earth pressure, hydrostatic pressure and buoyancy, prestress, etc.

活载主要指列车重量以及列车运动引起的荷载,一般指列车竖向静活载、列车离心力、无缝线路纵向水平力、人群荷载等。

Live loads on bridges refer to the train weight and the loads caused by train movement, including vertical static live load of train, centrifugal force of train, longitudinal force due to continuous welded rail, pedestrain load, etc.

2. 附加力

2. additional force

附加力是偶然作用的荷载,其最大值并不经常出现,而各种附加力同时出现最大值的机会就更少。

Additional forces belong to accidental loads, which result from low probability events, such as vehicle or ship impact, explosion, acts of terrorism or earthquake. Their maximum values do not often appear, and there are fewer opportunities for the maximum values of various additional forces at the same time.

3. 特殊荷载

3. special loads

特殊荷载是在特殊情况下作用的荷载,往往是暂时的或灾害性的,如船只或汽车的撞击力等。

Special loads are loads acting under special circumstances, which are often temporary or disastrous, such as the impact loads of ships or cars, etc.

桥梁结构设计,应根据结构的特性,按表 1-1 所列的荷载,就其可能出现的最不利组合情况进行计算。

Based on its structural characteristics, the bridge should be designed in the case of the most disadvantageous combination of loads listed in Table 1-1.

表 1-1 桥梁结构荷载分类表

<table>
<tr><th colspan="2">荷载分类</th><th>荷载名称</th></tr>
<tr><td rowspan="3">主力</td><td>恒载</td><td>结构自重
附属设备和附属建筑自重
预加应力
混凝土收缩及徐变影响
基础变位的影响
土压力
静水压力及浮力</td></tr>
<tr><td>活载</td><td>列车竖向静活载
列车竖向动力作用
列车离心力
列车横向摇摆力
列车活载产生的土压力
人群荷载</td></tr>
<tr><td>无缝线路
纵向水平力</td><td>伸缩力
挠曲力</td></tr>
<tr><td colspan="2">附加力</td><td>列车制动力或牵引力
风力
温度影响力
流水压力</td></tr>
<tr><td colspan="2">特殊荷载</td><td>无缝线路断轨力
船只或汽车的撞击力
地震力
施工临时荷载
列车脱轨荷载</td></tr>
</table>

注:① 如杆件的主要用途为承受某种附加力,则在计算此杆件时,该附加力应按主力计。
② 无缝线路纵向水平力不与本线制动力或牵引力组合。
③ 无缝线路断轨力及船只或汽车撞击力,只计算其中一种荷载与主力相组合,不与其他附加力组合。
④ 流水压力不与制动力或牵引力组合。
⑤ 计算中要求考虑的其他荷载,可根据其性质,分别列入上述三类荷载中。

Table 1-1 Classification of loads for bridge structures

Load classification		Load name
Main force	Dead load	Structure weight Self-weight of ancillary equipment and ancillary buildings Prestress Influence of concrete shrinkage and creep Influence of foundation displacement Earth pressure Hydrostatic pressure and buoyancy
	Live load	Vertical static live load of train Vertical dynamic action of train Centrifugal force of train Longitudinal force due to continuous welded rails lateral swaying force of train Earth pressure generated by vertical static live load of train Pedestrian load
	Longitudinal force due to continuous welded rail	Expansion-constriction force Discrete force
Additional force		Train braking force or tractive force Wind load Thermal stresses Effect of water current
Special loads		Breaking force of continuous welded rail Impact load of ships or cars Seismic load Construction temporary load Derailment load

Note: ① If the main purpose of the member is to bear some additional force, the additional force should be calculated as the main force when calculating this member.

② The longitudinal force due to continuous welded rail shall not be combined with the braking force or tractive force of the line.

③ For the breaking force of continuous welded rail and the impact force of ships or cars, only one of the loads is combined with the main force, not with other additional forces.

④ The flowing water pressure is not combined with the braking force or tractive force.

⑤ When other loads are required to be considered in the design, they can be included in the above three types of loads according to their properties.

1.2.3 桥梁上部结构

1.2.3 Superstructure of bridge

1. 桥跨结构

1. Bridge span structure

桥跨结构按材质主要分为钢结构和圬工结构。从桥梁养护角度出发，对钢结构梁最重要的要求是防止钢材锈蚀、防治构件裂纹及保持钉栓连接的紧密完好；对圬工梁拱的主要要求是圬工质量密实，排水设备有效完好、防止钢筋锈蚀、防治裂纹病害。

The bridge span structure refers to the part of the bridge that bears the load across the space. Based on material, it is mainly divided into steel structure and masonry structure. From the perspective of bridge maintenance, the most important problem for steel beam is to prevent steel corrosion, prevent component cracks and keep the nail bolt connection tight and intact; the beam or arch made of masonary requires dense construction quality, effective drainage equipment, the prevension and treatment of reinforcement corrosion and crack disease.

挠度是检验桥跨结构综合技术状态的一个重要指标,检修部门应切实掌握和了解管辖范围内桥梁梁跨挠度的现状及变化。

Deflection is an important index to check the comprehensive technical status of bridge span structure. The maintenance department should effectively grasp the status and trends of bridge span deflection within its jurisdiction.

《地铁设计规范》规定在列车竖向静活载作用下,桥跨结构梁体竖向挠度不应大于表 1-2 的规定值。

According to *Code for Design of Metro*, the elastic deflection of beam under vertical live load of train shall not exceed the specified value in Table 1-2.

表 1-2 梁体竖向挠度的限值

跨度 L	竖向挠度容许值
$L \leqslant 30$ m	$L/2\ 000$ m
$30 < L \leqslant 60$ m	$L/1\ 500$ m
$60 < L \leqslant 80$ m	$L/1\ 200$ m
$L > 80$ m	$L/1\ 000$ m

Table 1-2 Limitation of vertical deflection of beam

Span L	Allowable value of vertical deflection
$L \leqslant 30$ m	$L/2\ 000$ m
$30 < L \leqslant 60$ m	$L/1\ 500$ m
$60 < L \leqslant 80$ m	$L/1\ 200$ m
$L > 80$ m	$L/1\ 000$ m

2. 轨道梁的截面形式

2. Section type of track beam

目前,轨道梁主要采用的截面主要有 T 形截面、箱形截面和 U 形截面。

At present, T section, box section and U section are mainly used in track beam.

(1) T 形截面

(1) T section

T 形梁是我国最广泛采用的梁式。T 形梁材料几何分布与结构受力配合得最好。混凝土面积集中在受压区,受拉区仅仅是为设置预应力束的马蹄块,跨中剪力小、腹板很薄,到支座附近随着剪力增加而加厚,如图 1-12 所示。T 形梁一般在工厂预制,用架桥机吊装就位,施工快捷方便。

T section beam is the most widely used in China. The geometric distribution of T section beam material matches the structural stress best. The concrete area is concentrated in the compression area, and the tension area is only the horseshoe block with prestressed tendons. The shear force in the middle of the span is small, so the web is very thin. It thickens with the increase of shear force near the support, as shown in Figure 1-12. T section beams are generally prefabricated in the factory and hoisted in place by bridge erecting crane, so the construction is fast and convenient.

它的缺点是横向刚度和抗扭刚度比较差,必须加强横隔板以及梁间现浇湿接头以期改善;对平面线形的适应性差,在曲线上一般采用折线平分中矢布置。

However, T section beams have disadvantages of the poor lateral integrity, lateral stiffness and torsional stiffness, so it is necessary to strengthen the diaphragms and the cast-in-place wet joints between beams. Be directed against the poor adaptability to the plane line, the bisector midsagittal layout of broken line is generally adopted on the curve.

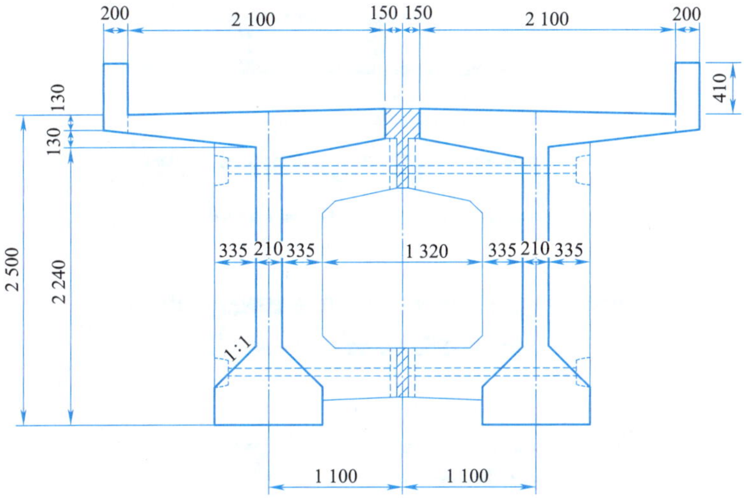

图 1-12　T 形截面(单位:mm)

Figure 1-12　T section(Unit: mm)

(2)箱形截面

(2) Box section

箱梁是目前国内轨道交通高架采用最多的梁式之一。它的特点是建筑高度适中,力学性能好(竖向刚度、横向刚度和抗扭刚度都好),整体性好,特别适用于曲线梁桥。它既可用于标准区段,也可用于变宽、道岔区段,平面上适应性比较强;既适宜做简支梁,也可做连续梁。箱梁外观线形比较流畅、美观,设计和施工经验比较成熟。它的缺点是建筑高度较大,断面空间利用不佳。

At present, box girder is one of the most used girder types for elevated rail transit in China. It is characterized by moderate building height, good mechanical properties (vertical stiffness, lateral stiffness and torsional stiffness) and good integrity, and suitable for both simply supported beam and continuous beam. It can be used not only in standard sections, but also in widened and turnout sections, which ensures that the cantilevers are of constant length, so it has strong adaptability in plane. The clean lines of box girders bridges, usually with no visible external stiffening, is generally considered to give a excellent appearance and durability, since there are no traps for dirt and moisture. However, all the features of box girder mentioned above lead to more complex and more costly fabrication.

在箱形截面中,把由顶板、底板和边腹板围成的每一个闭环,称作一个“箱”;每一个“箱”内再由中腹板分成若干“室”,如图 1-13 所示。

In the box section, each closed loop surrounded by top plate, bottom plate and side web is called a “box”; Each “box” is divided into several “cells” by the middle web, as shown in Figure 1-13.

(a) 单箱单室
Single cell section

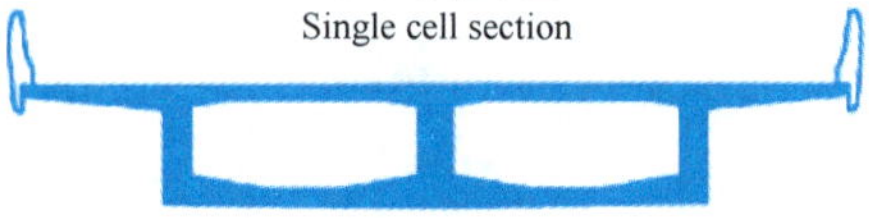

(b) 单箱双室
Single box double cells section

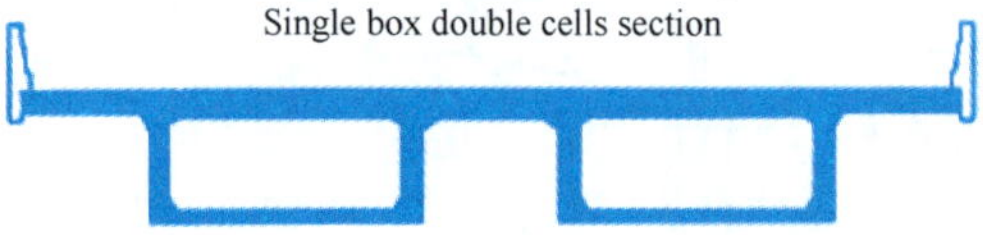

(c) 双箱单室
Two boxes single cell section

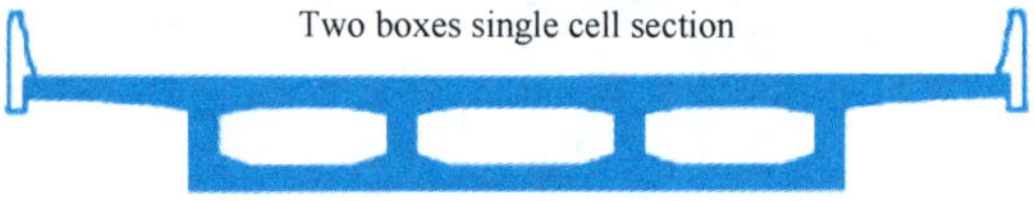

(d) 单箱三室
Single box triple cells section

(e) 双箱双室
Two boxes double cells section

(f) 三箱单室
Triple boxes single cell section

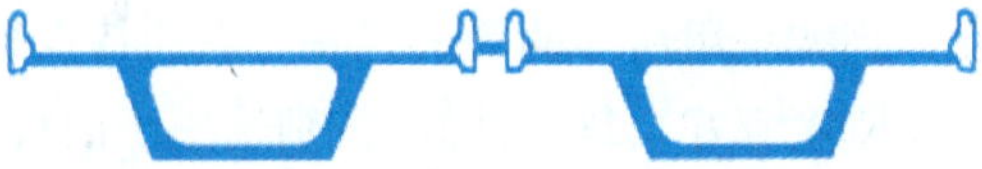

(g) 分离式箱形截面(由两个单箱单室组成的截面)
Separated box section (composed of two single cell section)

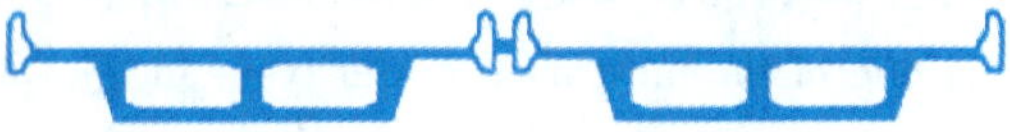

(h) 分离式箱形截面(由两个单箱双室组成的截面)
Separated box section (composed of two double cells section)

图 1-13 箱梁的箱与室

Figure 1-13 Box and cell of box girder

（i）组合箱梁截面
Composite box girder section

图 1-13 箱梁的箱与室(续)
Figure1-13 Box and cell of box girder(continued)

(3)U 形截面

(3) U section

U 形梁属于一种下承式的开口薄壁结构,梁体由底板,两侧的腹板和腹板顶部的翼缘板连成 U 形横截面的通道,多应用于城市轨道交通高架线路中,如图 1-14 所示。车辆荷载作用在桥面板上,荷载通过桥面板传给横梁,再由横梁传给主梁。主梁实际承受下端受拉荷载,对混凝土结构而言,这是不利的受力状态。荷载除引起主梁的弯曲外,还会引起主梁的扭转,存在弯扭效应。

U section beam is a through type open thin-walled structure, which is composed of the bottom plate, webs on both sides and flange plates on the top of web to form a U section cross section channel, as shown in Figure 1-14. It is mostly used in urban rail transit elevated lines. The vehicle load acts on the bridge deck, and the load is transmitted to the beam through the bridge deck, and then from the beam to the main beam. The main beam actually bears the tensile load at the lower end, which is an unfavorable stress state for the concrete structure. In addition to the bending of the main beam, the load will also cause the torsion of the main beam, which has the bending torsion effect.

随着环保要求的提高、人性化设计的提倡,在 U 形梁的主梁翼缘下可以安装管线;轨道交通车辆行驶于 U 形梁两腹板中间,轮轨走行系统的噪声受到两侧主梁上翼缘及腹板阻隔,在一定程度上减少了车辆噪声对周围环境的影响;两侧主梁能防止出轨列车倾覆下落,给行车安全提供了可靠的保证;顶板还可以作为紧急逃生通道,使乘客的生命安全更有保障。

With the improvement of environmental protection requirements and the promotion of humanized design, pipelines can be installed under the flange of the main beam of the U section beam. Rail transit vehicles run between the two webs of the U section beam, and the noise of the wheel rail running system is blocked by the upper flanges and webs of the main beams on both sides, which reduces the impact of vehicle noise on the surrounding environment to a certain extent. The main beams on both sides can prevent the derailed train from overturning and falling, which provides a reliable guarantee for driving safety. The roof can also be used as an emergency escape passage to ensure the life safety of passengers.

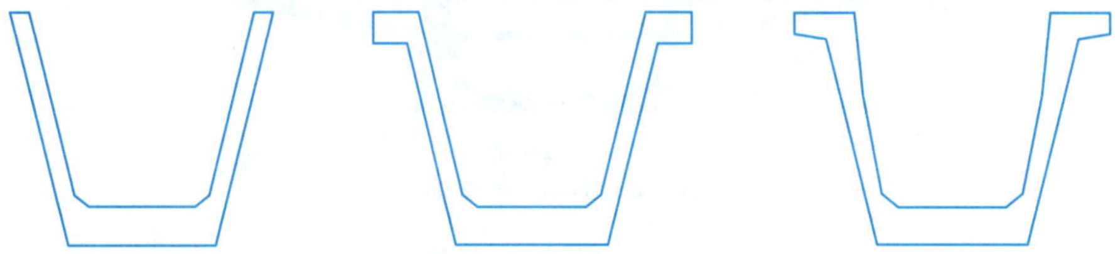

图 1-14 U 形截面

Figure 1-14 U section

1.2.4 桥梁下部结构

1.2.4 Substructure of bridge

桥梁下部结构是指支承桥跨结构并将其荷载传递至地基的构造物,由桥墩、桥台和基础等组成。

The structure of the bridge below the level of bearings is known as the substructure, which consists of abutments, piers, foundation, etc. Substructure supports the bridge span structure and transmits its load to the foundation.

桥墩是一种延伸到地下或水中的结构,用于支撑桥梁上部结构并将荷载传递至基础,如图 1-15 所示。桥墩应具有足够的强度,以承受垂直和水平荷载。如果桥梁跨越水面,桥墩不应阻碍水流或潮汐。桥墩根据其结构分为重力式桥墩和轻型桥墩。

A bridge pier is a type of structure that extend to the ground below or into the water, as shown in Figure 1-15. It is used to support bridge superstructure and transfer the loads to the foundation. The bridge piers can be constructed to be substantially strong in order to withstand both vertical and horizontal loads. It also does not hinder water flow or tide if the bridge spans the water. Piers are categorized into two major types based on its structure which include solid piers and open piers.

桥台常设置在全桥两端,除了支承边跨上部结构之外,还与路堤相衔接,以抵御路堤土压力,防止填土滑坡和坍落。对于跨河桥,桥台还保护路堤免受水流冲刷。桥台通常包括道砟墙、台身、翼墙和基础,如图 1-16 所示。桥台具有多种形式,主要分为重力式桥台、U 形重力式桥台、悬臂式桥台、扶壁式桥台、柱式桥台等。桥台的形式取决于路堤填土高度、上部结构、水文、地质、地形地貌等因素。

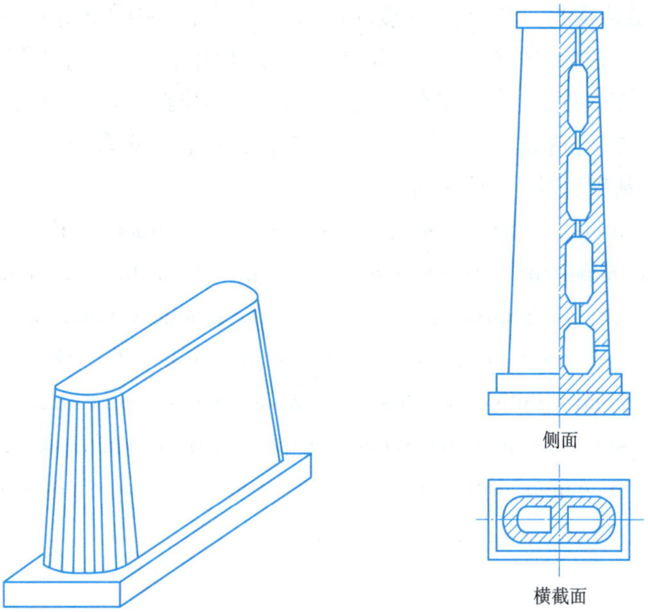

（a）重力式桥墩
Solid pier

（b）轻型桥墩
Open pier

图 1-15 桥墩类型

Figure 1-15 Types of piers

侧面：side view 横截面：cross section

As a component of a bridge, the abutment provides the vertical support to the bridge superstructure at the bridge ends, connects the bridge with the approach roadway, and retains the roadway base materials from the bridge spans. For a river bridge, the abutment also protects the embankment from scour of the stream. An abutment typically include ballast wall, abutment wall, wing wall and foundation, as shown in Figure 1-16. There are different abutment types including gravity abutments, U-shaped gravity abutments, cantilever wall abutments, counterfort abutments, spill-through abutments, etc. The selection of abutment types depends on the filling height of embankment, superstructure, hydrology, geology, landform and other factors.

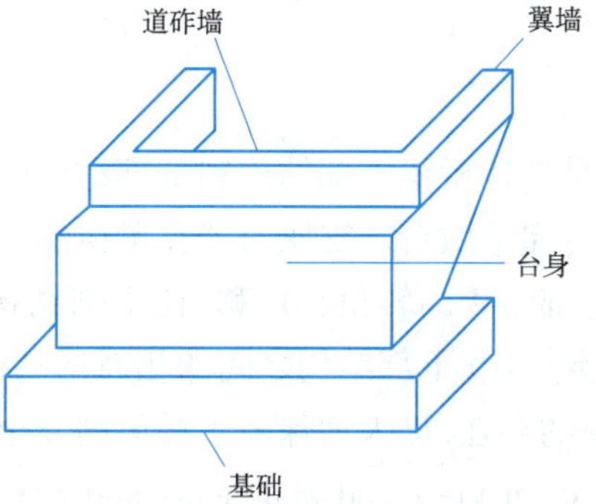

图 1-16 桥台的组成

Figure 1-16 Components of the pier

道砟墙：ballast wall 台身：abutment wall 翼墙：wing wall

桥梁基础是桥梁结构物直接与地基接触的最下部分，是桥梁下部结构的重要组成部分。它将荷载从下部结构（桥台、桥墩、挡土墙等）传递到地层中，而不会发生任何破坏或受到冲刷的影响。为了保证桥梁的正常使用和安全，地基和基础必须具有足够的强度和稳定性，变形也应在容许范围之内。按构造和施工方法不同，桥梁基础类型可分为：明挖基础、桩基础、沉井基础、沉箱基础和管柱基础，如图 1-17 所示。

The bridge foundation is the lowest part of the bridge structure that directly contacts the foundation, and is an important component of the bridge substructure. It transfers loads from the substructure (abutment, pier, retaining wall, etc.) to the ground without any damage or impact of erosion. In order to ensure the normal use and safety of the bridge, the ground and foundation must have sufficient strength and stability, and the deformation should also be within the allowable range. According to different structures and construction methods, bridge foundations can be classified into open foundation, pile foundation, well foundation, caisson foundation and pipe-column foundation, as shown in Figure 1-17.

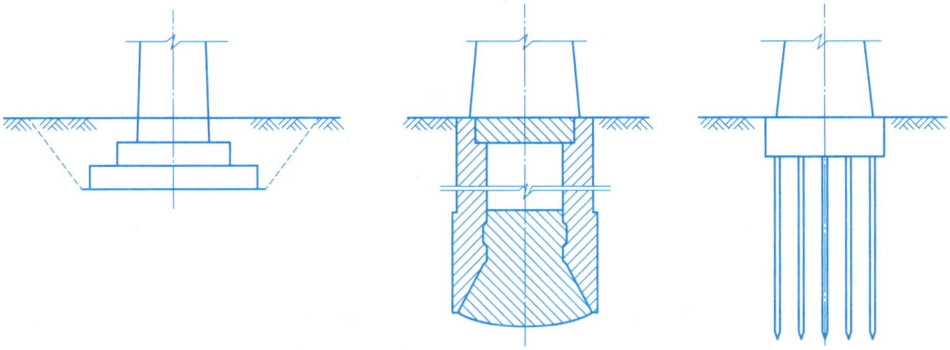

（a）明挖基础 Open foundation　（b）沉井基础 Well foundation　（c）桩基础 Pile foundation

图 1-17 桥梁基础

Figure1-17 Foundation of bridge

1.2.5 支座

1.2.5 Bearing

桥梁支座架设于墩台上，是连接桥梁上部结构和下部结构的重要结构部件，支撑着整个梁体及上部载荷，并将这些载荷传递给墩台。支座布置在梁体的两端，在荷载、温度、混凝土收缩和徐变、地震作用下，能适应上部结构的转角和位移，使上部结构可自由变形而不产生额外的附加内力。桥梁支座还为上部结构和下部结构之间的相对运动留出了空间，例如，水平和横向的旋转运动和平移运动。支座的存在，极大地保障了桥梁的安全。

Bridge bearings are installed on piers and abutments and are important structural components that connect the upper and lower structures of the bridge. They support the entire beam and upper loads, and transmit these loads to the piers and abutments. The bearings, which are arranged at both ends of the beam body, can adapt to the rotation angle and displacement of the upper structure under load, temperature, concrete shrinkage and creep, and earthquake, and allow the upper structure to deform freely without generating additional internal forces. Bridge bearings also makes rooms for relative movements between superstructure and substructure, such as rotation movements and translational movements in horizontal and transverse direction. Therefore, bearings greatly ensure the safety of bridge.

桥梁支座按其变形性能分为固定支座、单向活动支座和多向活动支座；按其材料分为简易支座、钢支座、橡胶支座、钢筋混凝土支座和特种支座等；按支座的结构形式可分为弧形支座、摇轴支座、辊轴支座、板式橡胶支座、四氟滑板橡胶支座、盆式支座、球面与柱面支座等；按支座所能实现的功能分为常规支座和减隔震支座。常规支座一般用于七度及以下地震区，支座本体不具备减、隔震功能，减隔震支座则可以在一定程度上消减地震能量对桥梁的作用。

Bridge bearings are divided into fixed bearings, unidirectional movable bearings and multi-directional movable bearings according to their deformation properties. According to its materials, it is divided into simple bearings, steel bearings, rubber bearings, reinforced concrete bearings and special bearings. According to the structures, bearings can usually be divided into arc bearings, rocking shaft bearings, roller bearings, plate rubber bearings, PTFE rubber bearings, basin bearings, spherical and cylindrical bearings, etc. According to the functions, bridge bearings can be divided into conventional bearings and isolation bearings. The conventional bearings can't reduce and isolate earthquakes, so they are generally used in earthquake areas of 7 degree and below. The isolation bearings can reduce the effect of seismic energy on the bridge to a certain extent.

1. 钢支座

1. Steel bearing

钢支座通过钢部件的滚动、摇动和滑动实现支座的位移和转动功能。它承载能力强，能适应桥梁的位移和转动，广泛应用于城市轨道交通桥梁。

The three basic configurations in steel bearings are sliding, rockers, and rollers, which realize the displacement and rotation of the steel bearing. With strong load-bearing capacity, steel bearings are widely used in urban rail transit to adapt to the displacement and rotation of bridges.

钢支座分为铸钢支座和新型钢支座：

Steel bearings are divided into cast steel bearings and new steel bearings:

（1）铸钢支座使用碳素钢或优质钢经过制模、翻砂、铸造、热处理、机械加工和表面处理制成，是一种传统型式的支座。铸钢支座承载能力较大，但其构造尺寸大、耗钢量多、刚度过大、传力急剧，容易造成下部结构损坏。铸钢支座易锈蚀，养护费用高，维修较困难。目前，铁路桥梁开始使用盆式橡胶支座。视跨度与荷载大小，钢支座常见种类有平板支座、摇轴支座和辊轴支座等。

(1) Cast steel bearing is a kind of traditional bearings made of carbon steel or high-quality steel through molding, sand casting, casting, heat treatment, mechanical processing and surface treatment. Cast steel bearings have a large load-bearing capacity, but their large structural

dimensions, high steel consumption, strong stiffness and rapid force transmission can easily cause damage to the substructure. Moreover, cast steel bearings have the disadvantages of easy corrosion, high maintenance costs and difficult maintain. At present, pot rubber bearings are being used in railway bridges instead of cast steel support. Depending on the span and load, common types of steel bearings include flat plate bearings, rocker bearings, roller bearings etc.

(2)新型钢支座根据材料可划分为不锈钢支座、合金钢支座、滑板钢支座和球型钢支座。它们的特点包括:①采用不锈钢或高级合金钢材料制造,可封闭在油箱内,以防生锈并减少维护或免维护;②对承受接触应力的部分进行表面硬化处理,以提高其容许承载力;③支座的转动部分采用钢制或黄铜制成的球冠形,在球冠的上、下分别设置聚四氟乙烯板以减少摩擦阻力。

(2) The new steel bearings are divided into stainless steel bearing, alloy steel bearing, sliding plate steel bearing and spherical steel bearing. Their characteristics include: ① they are made of stainless steel or high-grade alloy steel materials, and can be enclosed in the oil tank to prevent rust and reduce maintenance or avoid maintenance; ② The allowable bearing capacity is improved by surface hardening of the part that bears contact stress; ③ The rotating part of bearing adopts a spherical crown shape made of steel or brass, and PTFE plates are installed above and below the spherical crown to reduce frictional resistance.

2. 球型钢支座

2. Spherical steel bearing

球型钢支座由球冠衬板与球面滑板之间的滑动实现竖向转角。根据上部结构与支座转动中心的相对位置,球面转动方向可以与平面滑动方向一致或相反,如图 1-18 所示。球型钢支座按结构类型可分为普通球型支座、球型减隔震支座、垫板式调高支座和填充式调高支座。

The spherical steel bearing rotates vertically by sliding between the spherical crown liner and the spherical sliding plate. Depending on the relative position of the superstructure to the center of rotation of the support, the rotation direction of the spherical surface can be consistent with or opposite to the direction of plane sliding, as shown in Figure 1-18. According to the structures, spherical steel bearings can be divided into ordinary spherical bearings, spherical vibration bearings, plate height-adjusting bearings and filled height-adjusting bearings.

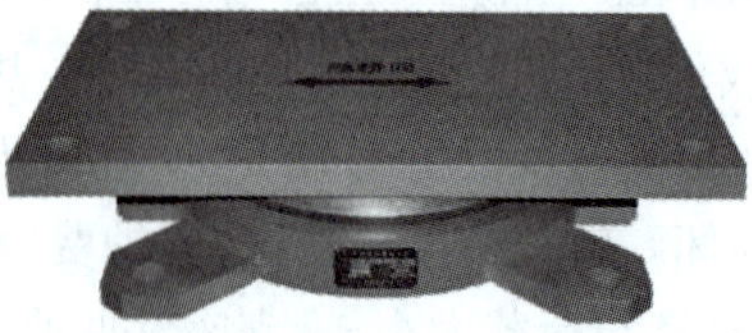

图 1-18 球型钢支座实物图

Figure 1-18 Physical drawing of spherical steel bearing

球型钢支座是钢构件做成的球形支座，传力可靠，各向转动性能一致，不仅具备盆式橡胶支座承载能力大、水平位移大的特点，而且能适应大转角的需要，适用于大跨宽桥、曲线桥。由于承压部件不使用橡胶件，不存在橡胶低温脆性等影响，因此特别适用于低温地区。

The spherical steel bearing is a spherical bearing made of steel components, with reliable force transmission and consistent rotation performance in all directions. It doesn't only have the characteristics of large bearing capacity and large horizontal displacement of basin rubber bearing, but can also adapt large angles. It is suitable for large-span wide bridges and curve bridges. Since there are no rubber parts used for the pressure bearing, there is no influence such as low-temperature brittleness of rubber, so it is especially suitable for low-temperature areas.

3. 板式橡胶支座

3. Plate rubber bearing

板式橡胶支座由多层橡胶片与薄钢板硫化、黏合而成，如图 1-19 所示。它有足够的竖向刚度，能将上部构造的反力可靠的传递给墩台；有良好的弹性，以适应梁端的转动；又有较大的剪切变形能力，以满足上部构造的水平位移。支座的橡胶材料以氯丁橡胶为主，也可采用天然橡胶或者是由天然橡胶配方的耐高温橡胶支座。氯丁橡胶一般用于最低气温不超过 -25 ℃的地区。

The plate rubber bearing is made of multiple layers of rubber sheets vulcanized and bonded with thin steel plates, as shown in Figure 1-19. It has enough vertical rigidity and can reliably transmit the reaction force of superstructure to the pier platform. It also has good elasticity to adapt to the rotation of the beam end and large shear deformation capacity to meet the horizontal displacement of superstructure. The rubber material of bearing is mainly neoprene, and natural rubber or high-temperature resistant rubber bearing formulated by natural rubber can also be used. Neoprene is generally used in areas where the minimum temperature is not less than -25 ℃.

(a) 实物图
Physical drawing

(b) 截面图
Sectional drawing

图 1-19　板式橡胶支座

Figure 1-19　Plate rubber bearing

板式橡胶支座在竖直荷载作用下，嵌入橡胶片之间的钢板将约束橡胶的侧向膨胀，使垂直变形相应减小从而提高了支座的竖向刚度。支座的水平位移仅与支座橡胶的净厚有关。为防止薄钢板的锈蚀，在板式橡胶支座的上、下面及四周均有橡胶保护层。

Under vertical loads, the steel plate embedded between rubber sheets restrains the lateral expansion of the rubber, which reduces the vertical deformation accordingly and improves the vertical stiffness of the bearing. While the horizontal displacement of bearing is only related to the net thickness of bearing rubber. In order to prevent the corrosion of thin steel plate, there is a rubber protective layer on the top, bottom and around the plate rubber bearing.

板式橡胶支座具有构造简单、安全方便、节省钢材、价格低廉、养护简便、易于更换等特点。它的力学特性也很优异:板式橡胶支座有足够的竖向刚度以承受垂直荷载,且能将上部结构的压力可靠地传递给墩台;有良好的弹性以适应梁端的转动;有较大的剪切变形以满足上部构造的水平位移;有良好的防震作用,可减少动载对桥跨结构与墩台的冲击作用。根据形状,板式橡胶支座可分为矩形板式橡胶支座、圆形板式橡胶支座和球形板式橡胶支座,适用于中小型桥梁。

The plate rubber bearing has the characteristics of simple structure, safe and convenient, steel saving, low price, simple maintenance and easy replacement. It also has excellent mechanical properties: The plate rubber bearing has sufficient vertical stiffness to withstand the vertical load and can reliably transmit the pressure of superstructure to the pier abutment; It has good elasticity to adapt to the rotation of beam end; There is a large shear deformation to meet the horizontal displacement of superstructure; It has a good shockproof effect, which can reduce the impact effect of dynamic loads on the span and pier of bridge. According to the shapes, the plate rubber bearing can be divided into rectangular plate rubber bearing, circular plate rubber bearing and spherical plate rubber bearing, which are suitable for small and medium-sized bridges.

设计规范规定,跨度不大于 20 m 的梁可采用板式橡胶支座,并应设横向限位装置。

The design code stipulates that beams with a span of no more than 20 m can be supported by plate rubber bearings, and a transverse limiting device should be installed.

4. 盆式橡胶支座

4. Pot rubber bearing

盆式橡胶支座由钢构件与橡胶组合构成,是一种特殊类型的桥梁支座,具有承载能力大、水平位移量大、转动灵活等特点,广泛应用于支座反力大的大型桥梁,如图 1-20 所示。设计规范规定,跨度大于等于 20 m 的桥梁宜采用盆式橡胶支座。

Pot rubber bearing composed of steel components and rubber is a special type of bridge bearing with the characteristics of high bearing capacity, large horizontal displacement, and flexible rotation, as shown in Figure 1-20. They are widely used in large bridges with large bearing reactions. According to the design specification, pot rubber bearing should be adopted for beams with a span of more than or equal to 20 m.

盆式橡胶支座一般可分为固定支座、单向活动支座和双向(多向)活动支座,如图 1-21 所示。固定支座在所有方向上不得移动。带有钢导边的单向活动支座只能在一个方向上移动。不锈钢滑动件和高分子滑动件进一步降低了摩擦系数,当水平载荷相对较小(小于垂直载荷的 20%)时,最好使用单向活动支座。双向(多向)活动支座可以在所有方向上移动。

Generally, pot rubber bearing is classified into fixed pot bearing, guided pot bearing and free sliding pot, as shown in Figure 1-21. Fixed pot bearing is unmoved in all directions. Guided pot bearing with steel guide edge can be only moved in one direction. The stainless steel slide and PTFE

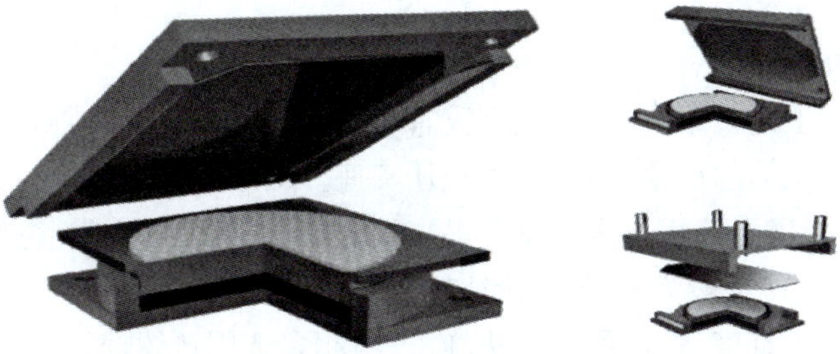

图 1-20　盆式橡胶支座

Figure 1-20　Pot rubber bearing

slide further reduce the friction coefficient and guided pot bearing is used best when horizontal loads are relatively small (less than 20% of vertical load). Free sliding pot bearing can be movable in all directions. The added PTFE and stainless steel sliding surface between the piston and the sole plate creates a bearing assembly that allows horizontal movement in any direction.

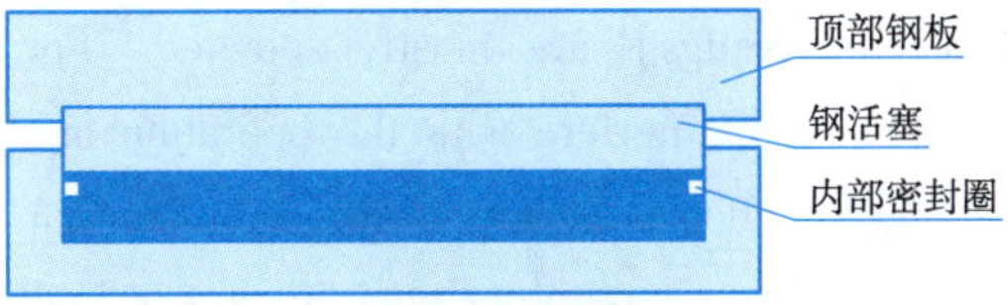

（a）固定支座结构
Fixed pot bearing structure

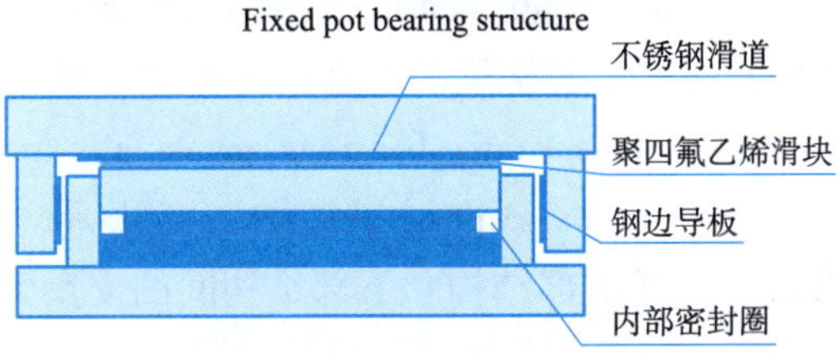

（b）单向活动支座结构
Guided pot bearing structure

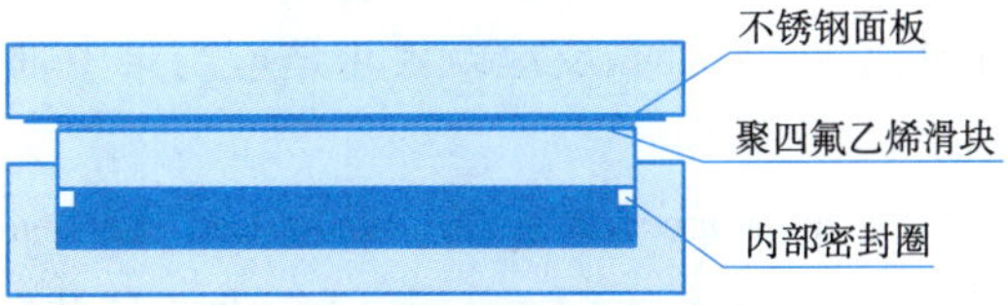

（c）双向（多向）活动支座结构
Free sliding pot bearing structure

图 1-21　盆式橡胶支座的种类

Figure 1-21　Types of pot rubber bearing

顶部钢板：top steel plate　　钢活塞：steel piston

内部密封圈：internal sealing ring　　聚四氟乙烯滑块：PTFE slide

不锈钢滑道：stainless steel slide　　不锈钢面板：stainless steel panel

钢边导板：steel edge guide

5. 特种支座
5. Special bearing

对于处于地震带上的桥梁，为减小地震灾害，现多选用抗震支座或减隔震支座产品。对于上部结构存在向上的反力的桥梁，一般选用拉压支座。对于悬索桥、斜拉桥等存在漂浮结构的桥梁，在梁体横向一般需要选用抗风支座产品。对于沿海及跨海桥梁，为保证支座使用寿命，则多选用耐蚀支座产品（一般为耐蚀球型钢支座）。对于跨铁路、高山、峡谷的桥梁，为了不干扰铁路运行和减小施工难度，多选用转体法施工，因此多选用转体球铰产品。对于在高纬度地区低温环境，为保证钢材应力，多选用低温用支座。

For bridges in the seismic zone, in order to reduce seismic disasters, seismic bearings or seismic isolation bearings are mostly selected. For bridges with upward reaction force in the superstructure, tension and compression bearings are generally selected. For suspension bridges, cable-stayed bridges and other bridges with floating structures, wind-resistant bearing products are generally required in the transverse direction of the beam body. For coastal and cross-sea bridges, in order to ensure the service life of the bearing, corrosion-resistant bearing products (generally corrosion-resistant spherical steel bearings) are mostly selected. For bridges across railways, mountains and canyons, in order not to interfere with the operation of the railway and reduce the difficulty of construction, the rotary method is mostly used for construction, so the rotating ball hinge products are mostly selected. For the low temperature environment in high latitude areas, in order to ensure the stress of the steel, low temperature bearings are mostly selected.

为了充分发挥支座的作用，通常结合桥梁的上部结构类型布置支座，基本原则如下：

In order to fully utilize the role of bearings, bearings are usually arranged in combination with the superstructure types of bridges. The basic principles are as follows:

(1)支座要求必须能够可靠传递上部结构和下部结构间的支反力。

(1) The support requirement must be able to reliably transmit the support reaction force between superstructure and substructure.

(2)当桥梁的上部结构是空间结构时，支座既要求适应与梁中轴线方向相同的力，也要适应与桥梁中轴线方向垂直的力。

(2) When the superstructure of bridge is a spatial structure, the bearings are required to adapt to the same force as the central axis of beam, and also to adapt to the force perpendicular to the central axis of bridge.

(3)桥梁支座能够承受因为梁体变形而产生的横向、竖向的转角和位移。

(3) The bridge bearing can withstand the transverse and vertical rotation and displacement caused by the beam deformation.

(4)在每联梁体上通常必须布置一个固定支座。

(4) A fixed bearing must usually be arranged on each beam.

(5)在有较大的支座反力的地方适合设置固定支座。

(5) It is suitable to set up a fixed bearing in the place where there is a large support reaction.

(6)位于同一桥墩上的几个支座应具有相同或者相近的转动刚度。

(6) Several bearings located on the same pier should have the same or similar rotational stiffness.

(7)在连续梁可能发生支座沉陷的位置,应考虑将支座高度设置成可调节的。固定支座的布置不仅需考虑上部结构传来的纵向和竖向荷载的作用,还需考虑桥梁发生挠曲变形时的支座转动。

(7) At the position where the bearing subsidence of continuous beam may occur, the bearing height should be adjustable. The arrangement of fixed bearings should take into account the longitudinal and vertical loads transmitted from the superstructure, as well as the rotation of bearings due to bridge deflection.

城市轨道交通运营过程中,由于受到环境荷载和车辆荷载等影响,支座性能一旦劣化,将会对桥梁的稳定性、安全性造成严重影响。因此,对桥梁支座进行正确的安装与定期的养护是保证其正常工作、延长其使用寿命的重要措施。

During the operation of urban rail transit, due to environmental loads and vehicle loads, once the performance of bearings deteriorates, it will have a serious impact on the stability and safety of bridge. Therefore, correct installation and regular maintenance of bridge bearings are important measures to ensure their normal operation and extend their service life.

1.2.6 桥梁基本附属设施

1.2.6 Basic auxiliary facilities of bridge

1. 桥面铺装

1. Bridge pavement

桥面设施包括:保护层和防水层、轨道结构、挡砟墙(采用有砟轨道时)、防护墙(采用无砟轨道时)、排水系统、人行道及栏杆、电缆槽、接触网立柱、声屏障、避车台等。铺设道砟的桥面为道砟桥面,不设桥面板的钢结构桥梁才会做成明桥面。桥梁上轨道结构与路基上的轨道结构基本相同,但还需要按规定铺设护轨、人行道、避车台等,如图 1-22 所示。

Bridge deck facilities include: protection layer and waterproof layer, track structure, ballast wall (when using ballasted track), protective wall (when using ballastless track), drainage system, pedestrian walkways and railings, cable trays, overhead contact system columns, sound barriers, refuge platforms, etc. The bridge deck paved with ballast is called the ballast bridge deck. The steel bridge without deck is not paved with ballast, thus sleepers are directly paved on the longitudinal beam to become the open bridge deck. Different from the track on the subgrade, the guardrail, sidewalk, refuge platform, etc. need also to be laid on the bridge deck structure according to the regulations, as shown in Figure 1-22.

(1)护轨

(1) Guard rail

护轨位于基本轨内侧,当机车车辆在桥头或桥上脱轨时,护轨可将脱轨车轮引导并限制于护轨与基本轨之间的轮缘槽内继续顺桥滚出,以免机车车辆向旁偏离撞击桥梁或自桥上坠下,造成严重事故。

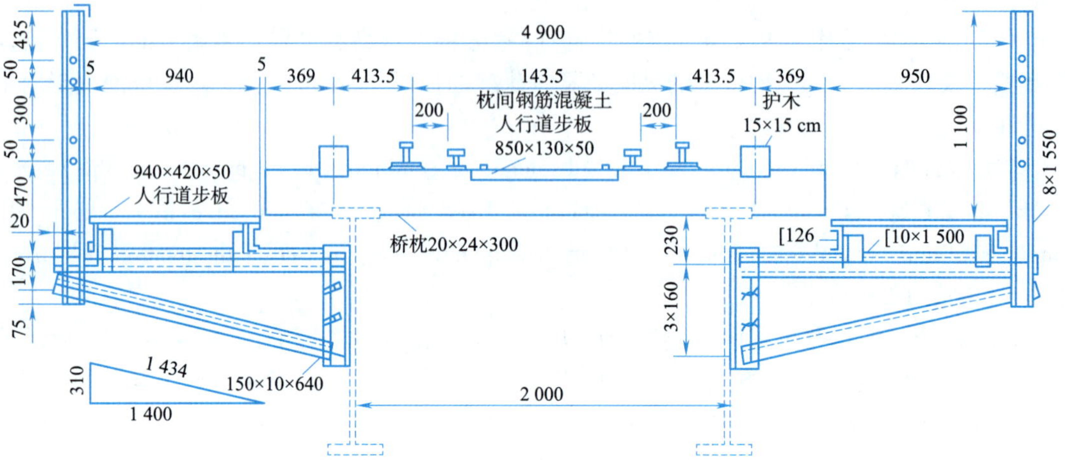

（a）明桥面
Open deck

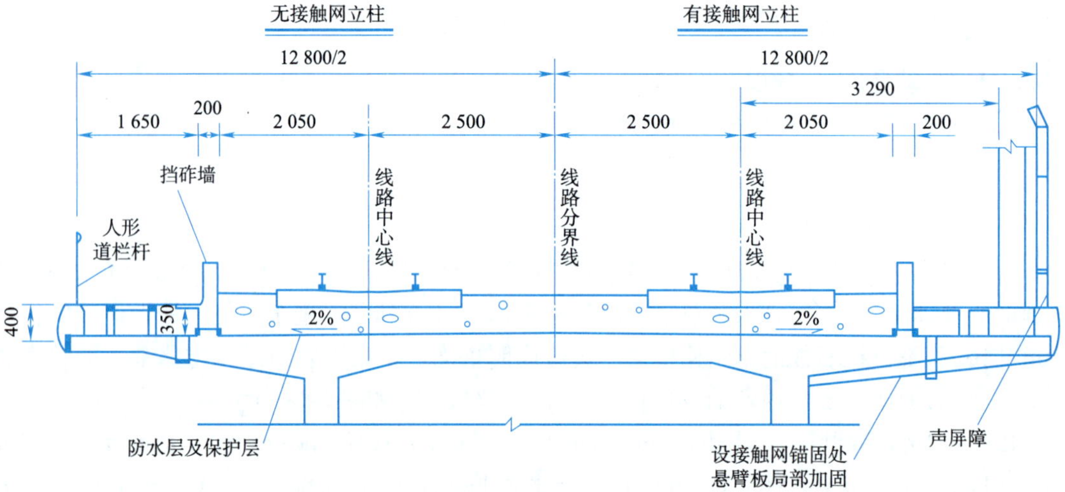

（b）道砟桥面
Ballasted deck

图 1-22　桥面一般构造图(单位:mm)

Figure 1-22　Structure of bridge deck (Unit: mm)

枕间钢筋混凝土人行道步板:reinforced concrete sidewalk slab between sleepers　　人行道步板:sidewalk slab

护木:fender　　桥枕:bridge sleepers

无接触网立柱:without OCS column　　有接触网立柱:with OCS column

挡砟墙:ballast retaining wall　　人行道栏杆:handrail of sidewalk

线路分界线:line boundary line　　防水层及保护层:waterproof layer and protective layer

设接触网锚固处悬臂板局部加固:locally strengthened with cantilever plate in the anchorage zone of OCS column

声屏障:sound barrier

The guard rails are located inside the stock rails. When the locomotive derails at the bridgehead or on the bridge, the guard rails can limit the derailed wheels to the flange clearance between the guard rail and the stock rail, and guide it to roll out along the bridge. It can prevent the locomotive and vehicle from deviating sideways, hitting the bridge or falling from the bridge, which results in serious accidents.

桥面护轨两端应伸出桥台挡砟墙以外,直轨部分长度应不少于5 m;在直线上桥长大于50 m,曲线上桥长大于30 m的桥梁则为10 m,然后弯曲交汇于线路中心,并将轨端切成斜面联结。弯轨部分的长度不应少于5 m,轨端超出台尾的长度不应少于2 m。自动闭塞区间在护轨交汇处应安装绝缘衬垫。

Both ends of the guard rails on the deck shall extend beyond the ballast retaining walls of abutments, and the length of straight part shall not be less than 5 m. For the bridge that has the straight line of above 50 m and the curve of above 30 m, the length of straight part shall be 10 m, hence, the guard rails on the deck shall be bent and connected at the center of the lines by cutting their ends into inclined planes. The length of curve part shall not be less than 5 m, and the rail length beyond abutment shall not be less than 2 m. Insulators shall be installed at the intersection of guard rails in automatic block sections.

铺设护轨时,护轨顶面不应高出线路钢轨顶面5 mm,也不应低于线路钢轨面25 mm。考虑到车轮轮缘宽最小为140 mm,脱轨时为使车轮能沿槽滚出桥梁,护轨与基本轨头部间净距为:明桥面钢梁桥定为220 mm;有砟桥面为500 mm;当桥上设有伸缩调节器时为320~350 mm。

When laying the guard rail, the top surface of guard rail should not be 5 mm higher than the top surface of line rail, nor should it be 25 mm lower than the top surface of line rail. Considering that the minimum width of wheel flange is 140 mm, in order to allow the wheel to roll out of the bridge along the groove during derailment, the clear distance between guard rail and basic rail head is: 220 mm for steel beam bridge on open deck; 500 mm for ballasted deck; 320 - 350 mm when the expansion rail joints are set on the bridge.

(2)钢轨伸缩调节器

(2) Expansion rail joints

在荷载与温度变化影响下,桥梁上的钢轨会随同桥梁一起伸长或缩短。桥梁上部结构的连续长度越长,伸缩量就越大。钢轨接头的间距越大,车轮经过该处时产生的冲击力就越大,甚至影响行车安全。因此,在轨道上安设钢轨伸缩调节器,利用尖轨或基本轨相对错动调节轨线的胀缩。钢轨伸缩调节器常用在大跨度钢梁桥上、桥头上和无缝线路需调节钢轨伸缩量地段,一般应根据线路、桥梁和轨道系统设计,如图1-23所示。

Under the influence of load and temperature changes, the rail on the bridge will elongate or shorten with the bridge. The longer the continuous superstructure of the bridge, the greater the expansion amount. The bigger the rail joint gap, the greater the impact force generated by wheels passing through, which even affects the running safety. Therefore, a expansion rail joints is installed on the track to adjust the expansion and contraction of track line using the relative displacement of the switch rail or stock rail. The expansion rail joints, which are commonly used on large-span steel bridges, bridge heads, and the sections where the continuous welded rail expansion needs to be adjusted, should be designed based on the line, bridge, and track system, as shown in the Figure 1-23.

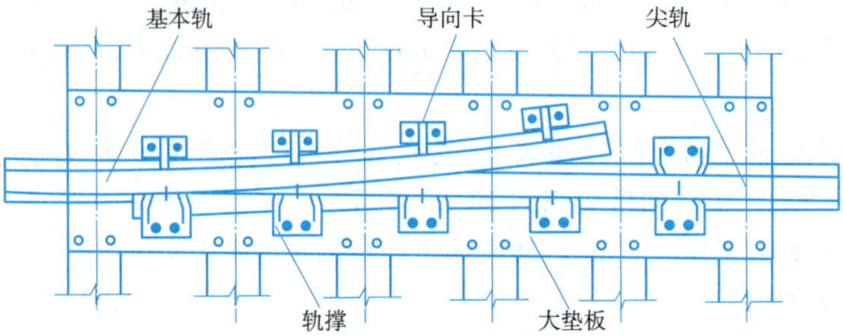

图 1-23 钢轨伸缩调节器

Figure 1-23 Expansion rail joints

基本轨:stock rail 导向卡:guide plate 尖轨:switch rail
轨撑:rail brace 大垫板:large pad

(3)人行道、避车台

(3) Sidewalk and refuge platform

桥梁人行道主要供桥梁维修养护人员工作通行,可根据桥梁结构采用不同结构形式。一般对于采用 T 形梁的桥梁结构可通过预埋 U 形螺栓将预制支架连接固定到桥面板上,预制步板则铺设在支架上,如图 1-24 所示。个别情况下,当桥上允许非养护人员通过时,线路中心至人行道栏杆内侧的净距应根据具体需要考虑,并在人行道和线路之间采取可靠的安全分隔措施。

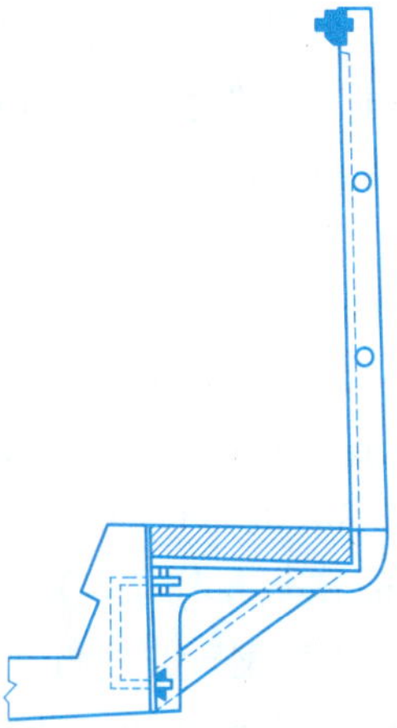

图 1-24 人行道

Figure 1-24 Sidewalk

The bridge sidewalk is mainly used for bridge maintenance personnel to work and pass, and different structures can be adopted according to the bridge structure. Generally, for T section beams, prefabricated brackets can be connected and fixed to the deck by embedding U-shaped bolt, and prefabricated step plates can be laid on the brackets, as shown in Figure 1-24. In particular cases, when non maintenance personnel are allowed to pass through the bridge, the clear distance from the center of the line to the inside of the sidewalk railing should be considered according to specific needs, and reliable safety separation measures should be taken between sidewalk and line.

避车台是供检修养护工作人员避车的场所,其支架构件与梁体的预埋螺栓栓接。在两桥台台尾之间,沿桥梁全长每隔 30 m 左右,在人行道栏杆外侧各设置避车台一座。单线桥在两侧人行道上按间隔 30 m 左右交错设置避车台;双线及多线桥在每一侧各相距 30 m 左右设置避车台。线路中心至避车台内侧的净距不小于 3. 75 m,避车台应尽量设在桥墩处。

The refuge platform is a place for maintenance personnel to avoid vehicles, and its support members are bolted to the embedded bolts of the beam. Between the two abutments, a refuge platform shall be set outside the sidewalk railing every 30 m along the bridge. For single-track line bridges, refuge platforms are staggered on both sides of sidewalks at an interval of about 30 m. For double-track bridges and multi-track bridges, refuge platforms are set up on each side of sidewalks at a distance of about 30 m. The clear distance from the line center to the inside of the refuge platform shall not be less than 3.75 m, and the refuge platform shall be set at the pier as far as possible.

(4)防排水系统

(4) Waterproof and drainage system

为了迅速排除桥面上的雨水,防止雨水渗入梁体引起锈蚀而影响桥梁的耐久性、稳固性,确保桥梁的正常运营,除了在桥面铺装内设置防水层外,还应设置排水设施。

In order to quickly drain the rainwater off the beck, prevent access of water to the parts of the structure and eliminate unfavorable aggressive actions, both waterproof layers and drainage facilities shall be set up in the bridge deck pavement.

桥面排水设施主要包括桥面纵横坡和一定数量的泄水管。根据不同的桥面轨道结构形式,桥面采用不同的排水方式。保护层施工时,轨台间桥面根据排水需要设置2%横向流水坡,当梁体设置于平坡时,可根据泄水孔位置沿纵向设置3‰左右的流水坡,让积水通过排水管引到桥下。实际使用时,排水方式根据桥面轨道类型和桥梁所处的环境确定。泄水管的孔径和数量应根据桥梁所处环境的暴雨强度确定,为防止长桥桥头、凹点线路桥梁位置桥面积水,在桥面保护层施工时,应在泄水孔纵向坡度下坡端位置设置横向挡水堰,实施分区排水,并根据汛期汇水量调整桥头、凹点线路处局部泄水孔的设置间距和孔径。采用集中排水时,应在施工时预埋连接固定排水管的滑行槽道,保证排水管的伸缩变形,避免漏水。为防止杂物堵塞排水管道,泄水管口均设置了管篦或管盖。

The drainage facilities on bridge deck mainly include the longitudinal and transverse slopes of bridge deck and a certain number of drainage pipes. According to different track structures, the bridge deck adopts different drainage measures. During the construction of protective layer, a 2% transverse flow slope can be set on the bridge deck between the rail and abutment according to the drainage needs. When the beam is set on a flat slope, a flowing slope of about 3‰ can be set longitudinally according to the position of outlet, and the ponding is led to the under bridge through a drainage pipe. In their applications, the drainage method is determined based on the type of bridge deck track and the environment around the bridge. The hole diameter and number of drain pipes shall be determined according to the rainstorm intensity of bridge's environment. In order to prevent ponding at the bridgehead and concave line of the long bridge, during the construction of protective layer, a transverse retaining weir shall be set at the downslope end of the longitudinal slope of the drain hole to implement drainage by zones, and the spacing and hole diameter of local drain holes at the bridgehead and concave line shall be adjusted according to the water catchment in flood season. For concentrated drainage, a sliding channel connecting and fixing the drainage pipe should be embedded during construction to ensure the expansion and deformation of the drainage pipe and avoid water leakage. A pipe grate or a pipe cover is set up at the scupper of the drain pipe to prevent trucks from blocking.

桥梁上常用的泄水管有竖向泄水管道、横向泄水管道和封闭式泄水管道等形式。桥上泄水管道一般采用 PVC 管。当桥长较短时,纵向排水管的出水口,可以设在桥梁两端的桥台处;对于长大桥,除了在桥台处设置出水口外,还需在某些桥墩处布置出水口,并利用竖向管道将水引到地面。纵向排水管道一般可设在箱梁中或梁肋内侧;竖向排水管可布置在墩台壁的预留槽中或布置在桥台内部预留孔道中,也可用管卡固定于墩身上。

Vertical drainage pipes, horizontal drainage pipes and closed drainage pipes are commonly used on bridges. When the bridge is short, the outlet of the longitudinal drainage pipe can be set at the abutments. For long bridges, in addition to setting water outlets at the abutments, it is also necessary to set water outlets at some piers and use vertical pipes to divert water to the ground. The longitudinal drainage pipe can generally be set in the box girder or inside the beam rib. Vertical drainage pipes can be arranged in reserved grooves on the pier and abutment walls or in reserved holes inside the abutment, or can be fixed to the pier body with pipe clamps

桥面排水系统可分为开放式排水和封闭式排水。

The bridge deck drainage system can be divided into open drainage and closed drainage.

桥面开放式排水系统通过护栏中的槽孔或路缘线桥面直接将水排出桥面,如图 1-25 所示。该系统可能会发生杂物堵塞,并导致混凝土劣化,如腐蚀和剥落,故需要长期维护。而垂直泄水管穿过并延伸至桥面以下。在不考虑对桥下径流造成的环境影响或潜在洪水的情况下,采用开放式排水系统。

The open system for deck drainage directly discharges water through the open slot in barrier or the bridge deck at curb line, as shown in the Figure 1-25. This system may experience clogging by debris and cause other deterioration mechanisms for concrete such corrosion and spalling, and thus needs continuous maintenance. Comparatively, the vertical drainage pipe passes through and extends below the bridge deck. Open drainage systems are adopted without considering the environmental impact or potential floods on the runoff under the bridge.

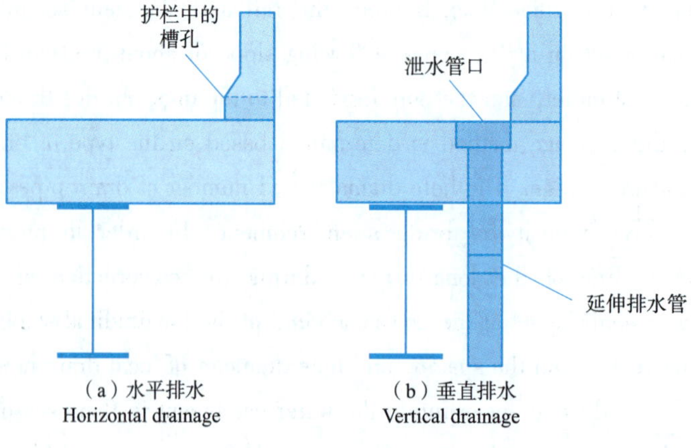

图 1-25 开放式排水系统

Figure 1-25 Open deck drainage system

护栏中的槽孔:open slot in barrier　泄水管口:scupper　延伸排水管:extension pipe

与开放式排水系统相比，封闭式排水系统通常由排水孔或进水口收集桥面汇水，再经封闭管道将排水口的径流向下传输至地面的排水入口点，如图 1-26 所示。封闭排水系统预留适当的位置用于后期维护。它适用于存在环境相关问题的地方，如侵蚀、洪水。

Compared to the open deck drainage systems, the closed one consists normally of scuppers/inlets made at the deck surface; however, with a closed piping which transmits the runoff from the scuppers down to a drainage inlet point at the ground level, as shown in the Figure 1-26. Closed systems are equipped with proper preset locations for maintenance works making them suitable for application where there are environmental-related issues, such as erosion or floods.

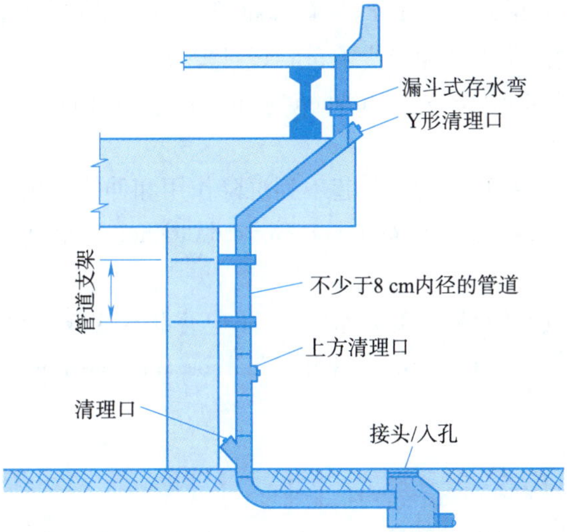

图 1-26　封闭式排水系统

Figure 1-26　Closed deck drainage system

漏斗式存水弯：funnel trap　Y 形清理口：Y cleanout　管道支架：pipe supports as required
清理口：cleanout　上方清理口：upward cleanout　不少于 8 cm 内径的管道：8″Min. pipe
接头/入孔：junction/manhole

2. 伸缩缝与沉降缝

2. Expansion joint and settlement joint

伸缩缝是为解决与圬工结构热胀冷缩而设置，可保证上部结构自由伸缩，并能承受车辆荷载作用。伸缩缝应具有经久耐用、良好的平整度、防水、防尘等功能，便于养护更换。

The expansion joint is designed to solve the expansion and cold contraction of the masonry structure, which can ensure the free expansion of the superstructure and bear the load action of the vehicle. The expansion joint should be durable, good flatness, watertight, dustproof and easy to maintain and replace.

沉降缝是解决圬工结构因基础不均匀沉降而发生的上下错动问题。因此，沉降缝自墙身至基础都是直通的，留缝的距离也与基础地质有密切关系，如土石分界处，必须设置沉降缝。

Settlement joint is used to prevent uneven settlement of the bridge due to the different bearing capacity of the foundation or the large difference in the load of each part. Therefore, the settlement joint is straight from the wall to the foundation. The distance of the gap is also closely related to the basic geology, such as the boundary between soil and rock, the settlement joint must be set.

伸缩缝和沉降缝的设置要求有：

The setting requirements of expansion joint and settlement joint are as follows:

① 伸缩缝和沉降缝的宽度,一般为 1 ~2 cm,中间填塞沥青浸制的麻筋、木板或其他具有弹性的材料。

① The width of expansion joint and settlement joint is generally 1 to 2 cm, and the middle is filled with hemp bar, wood board or other elastic materials soaked with asphalt.

② 沉降缝和伸缩缝的位置和构造必须符合设计要求。

② The location and structure of settlement joint and expansion joint must meet the design requirements.

③ 缝口要直,不能歪斜扭曲。否则,起不到沉降作用和伸缩作用。

③ The seam should be straight and not crooked. Otherwise, it will not play the role of settlement and expansion.

④ 沉降缝和伸缩缝应具有较好的防水作用,不应有漏水或漏土现象发生。

④ The settlement joint and expansion joint shall be waterproof without water leakage or soil leakage.

3. 锥体填土及护坡

3. Cone filling and Slope protection

锥体填土的作用是加强桥台与路基的连接并包裹桥台,增加桥台的稳定性。锥体填土宜用渗水土填筑。锥体护坡的作用是保护锥体填土和桥头路堤免被水流冲刷以保证线路的稳定。一般以全高防护,并根据水流流速、流冰、流木等情况决定防护标准。填土坡脚埋入深度应考虑一般冲刷的影响。

Cone filling is used to strengthen the connection between abutment and subgrade, wrap the abutment and increase its stability. Cone filling shall be filled with permeable soil. Cone slope protection can protect cone filling and bridge approach embankment from erosion by current, so as to ensure the line stability. Generally, protection over the entire height is adopted, and the protection standard is determined according to the flow velocity, drift ice, driftwood, etc. The influence of general scouring shall be considered for the buried depth of fill slope toe.

4. 台后填土

4. Filling behind abutment

为排除台后积水,减少列车通过时桥台与路堤之间的变位差,提高列车运行的平稳性、舒适度,需在台后的一定距离之内设置过渡段。台后基坑应以混凝土回填或以碎石分层填筑压实。

The transition section, which is set within a certain distance behind abutment, can eliminate the ponding behind the abutment, reduce the displacement difference between abutment and embankment when a train passes by, and improve the stability and comfort of the train running. The foundation pit behind abutment shall be backfilled and compacted with concrete or crushed stones in layers.

5. 检查设备

5. Facilities for inspection

为经常检查桥梁建筑物各部位的情况和保证桥梁养护维修人员的正常工作及操作安全，需要在桥梁的不同部位配备与其相应的检查设备。设计规范规定，桥下应设养护、维修便道，使自行走行升降式桥梁检修车能进行检修作业；高度超过 20 m、桥下无条件设置养护维修便道处，可设置专门检查设备以便日常维修。常见的检修设备有：

In order to frequently check the bridge condition and ensure maintenance personnel to work safely, corresponding inspection facilities need to be equipped at different parts of a bridge. The design specification stipulates that maintenance access shall be set under the bridge to enable the self-propelled lifting bridge maintenance vehicle to carry out maintenance operations. If the bridge height exceeds 20 m and the maintenance and repair road under the bridge is unconditionally set up, and special inspection facilities shall be set up for daily maintenance, as following:

① 围栏：一般为栅栏式，高 1 m，立柱用圆钢或角钢埋入墩台顶帽。

① Fence: generally fence type, with a height of 1 m. The banisters are embedded in the pier cap with round steel or angle steel.

② 吊篮：供进行检查或维修时，穿越梁部左右侧及梁端部进行工作之用。通常桥台设单侧吊篮，桥墩设双侧吊篮。一般采用预先焊好的角钢支架，通过预埋的 U 形螺栓固定在桥墩台的托盘或顶帽上，吊篮里的步行板可铺设钢筋混凝土板。

② Hanging basket: it is used for working through the left and right sides of beam and beam-ends during inspection or maintenance. Generally, hanging baskets are set on one side of the abutment and on both sides of the pier. The pre welded angle steel supports are fixed on abutment cap or pier cap with embedded U-shaped bolts. The walking plate in the hanging basket can be paved with reinforced concrete plate.

③ 检查梯：便于从桥面下到墩台顶和进行支座检查用的设备。

③ Ladder for inspection: convenient to go down from deck to the top of pier and abutment and inspect facilities.

④ 简易台阶：当桥头路堤高度大于 3 m 时，应根据需要在路堤边坡上设置简单台阶。

④ Simple steps: when the height of the embankment at the bridge end is greater than 3 m, simple steps shall be set on the embankment slope as required.

⑤ 长大与重要的桥梁应根据构造特点和需要，设置专门的检查设备。

⑤ Large-scale and important bridges shall be equipped with special inspection facilities according to structural characteristics and needs.

1.3 隧道设施基础知识
1.3 General knowledge of tunnel infrastructure

城市轨道交通区间隧道是连接两个地下车站之间的建筑物。区间隧道施工方法、衬砌结构与构造主要取决于隧道的用途、沿线地形、水文地质、工程地质条件、环境要求、维修管理、工期要求及投资额等因素。

Urban rail transit interval tunnel is a building connecting two underground stations. The construction method, lining structure and architecture of the interval tunnel mainly depends on the use of the tunnel, terrain, hydrogeology, geology, construction methods, environmental requirements, maintenance management, construction period requirements, investment amount and other factors.

1.3.1 地下结构的荷载
1.3.1 Loads on underground structures

按照《地铁设计规范》的规定:作用在地下结构上的荷载,可以分为永久荷载、可变荷载和偶然荷载,见表1-3。

According to *Code for Design of Metro*, the loads acting on underground structures can be divided into permanent loads, variable loads and accidental loads, see Table 1-3.

表1-3 隧道结构荷载分类

<table>
<tr><th colspan="2">荷载分类</th><th>荷载名称</th></tr>
<tr><td colspan="2" rowspan="8">永久荷载</td><td>结构自重</td></tr>
<tr><td>地层压力</td></tr>
<tr><td>结构上部和破坏棱体范围的设施及建筑物压力</td></tr>
<tr><td>水压力及浮力</td></tr>
<tr><td>混凝土收缩及徐变影响</td></tr>
<tr><td>预加应力</td></tr>
<tr><td>设备重量</td></tr>
<tr><td>地基下沉影响</td></tr>
<tr><td rowspan="6">可变荷载</td><td rowspan="4">基本可变荷载</td><td>地面车辆荷载及其动力作用</td></tr>
<tr><td>地面车辆荷载引起的侧向土压力</td></tr>
<tr><td>地铁车辆荷载及其动力作用</td></tr>
<tr><td>人群荷载</td></tr>
<tr><td rowspan="2">其他可变荷载</td><td>温度变化影响</td></tr>
<tr><td>施工荷载</td></tr>
<tr><td colspan="2" rowspan="3">偶然荷载</td><td>地震作用</td></tr>
<tr><td>沉船、抛锚或河道疏浚产生的撞击力等灾害性荷载</td></tr>
<tr><td>人防荷载</td></tr>
</table>

注:设计中要求考虑的其他荷载,可根据其性质分别列入上述三类荷载中。

Table 1-3　Classification of loads for tunnel structures

Load classification		Load name
Permanent Load		Self-weight of structural members
		Earth pressure
		Pressure from facilities and buildings in the upper part of structure and the range of damaged prism
		Hydrostatic pressure and buoyancy
		Influence of concrete shrinkage and creep
		Prestress
		Self-weight of ancillary equipment
		Influence of foundation settlement
Variable load	Basic variable load	Vehicle load on the ground and its dynamic action
		Lateral earth pressure caused by ground vehicle load
		Metro vehicle load and its dynamic action
		Pedestrian load
	Other variable load	Influence of temperature change
		Construction load
Accidental load		Influence of seismic
		Catastrophic loads such as impact force caused by ship sinking, anchoring or river dredging
		Load of civil defense

Note: Other loads, which are required to take into accout in the design, can be sorted in the above three types of loads according to their properties.

1.3.2　隧道施工方法
1.3.2　Methods of tunnel construction

隧道及地下工程的类型很多,工程特点各异,相应的施工方法和技术也各不相同。表 1-4 为我国目前地下工程中应用于城市轨道交通区间隧道的施工方法及其特点。

There are many types of tunnels and underground engineering with different engineering characteristics, and corresponding construction methods and technologies are also different. Table 1-4 shows the construction methods and their characteristics of urban rail transit interval tunnels currently used in underground engineering in China.

表 1-4　隧道施工方法及特点

序号	施工方法	场地要求	优　点	缺　点
1	明挖法	城市郊区场地开阔区域;软岩和土体	进度快、工作面大、造价低	破坏环境生态、影响交通、产生尘土和噪声污染
2	矿山法(新奥法)	岩石或坚硬土体	地面干扰小、造价低	进度慢、劳动强度高、风险大
3	浅埋暗挖法	埋深较浅,需对土体进行冻结、注浆、深层搅拌桩加固地基、管棚法加固	地面干扰小、造价低、施工灵活多变	机械化程度低、劳动强度高、环境恶劣、风险大

续表

序号	施工方法	场地要求	优　点	缺　点
4	盾构和顶管法	软弱地层、深埋	地面影响小、机械化程度高、安全、劳动强度低、进度快	机械设备复杂、价格昂贵、工艺烦琐、需要专业施工队伍
5	沉管法	跨越江河湖海、软地层	造价低、速度快、隧道断面大	封锁江河水面，需要专门的驳运、下沉、对接设备；属于水下作业，风险大
6	凿岩机法（TBM 法）	坚硬岩石地层	速度快、机械化程度高、安全、无地面干扰	造价高、使用技术复杂，刀具易磨损
7	沉井法	软弱地层、地域空旷	造价低、速度快	对环境影响大、泥浆污染、地面下沉

Table 1-4　Tunnel construction methods and their characteristics

No.	Construction method	Site requirements	Advantages	Disadvantages
1	Open cut method	Open areas in the suburbs; Soft rock or soil	Fast progress, large working surface, low cost	Destroy the environment and ecology, affect the traffic, and cause dust and noise pollution
2	Mining method (NATM)	Rock or hard soil	Small interference to the ground and low cost	Slow progress, high labor intensity and high risk
3	Shallow mining method	Shallow buried, the soil should be frozen, grouted, reinforced by deep mixing pile, and reinforced by pipe shed method	Small interference to the ground, low cost and flexible construction	Low mechanization, high labor intensity, bad environment and high risk
4	Shield method and pipe-jacking method	Weak stratum, deep buried	Small interference on the ground, high mechanization, safety, low labor intensity and fast progress	Complex machinery and equipment, high cost, complicated process, and professional construction teams are needed
5	Immersed tube method	Across rivers, lakes and seas, soft stratum	Low cost, fast speed and large tunnel section	The water surface shall be blocked, special lightering, sinking and docking equipment shall be used. It's underwater operation with high risk
6	TBM method	Hard rock stratum	High speed, high mechanization, safety and no interference to the ground	High cost, complex technology and easy wear of tools
7	Open caisson method	Weak stratum, open space	Low cost and fast progress	Environmental impact, mud pollution and ground subsidence

1.3.3　隧道结构形式

1.3.3　Types of tunnel structures

区间隧道一般有矩形、拱形、圆形、多圆形及椭圆等断面形式。矩形断面分单跨、双跨两种，其内轮廓与区间隧道建筑限界接近，便于顶板上敷设城市地下管网设施；圆形断面形式具有结构受力合理、断面形状不会因线路纵向坡度和平面曲线半径变化而改变、对内净空影响小等特点。双圆盾构的使用在有效利用地下空间、减少施工周期等方面取得一定优势。

Interval tunnels generally have rectangular, arched, circular, multi circular and elliptical sections. Rectangular section can be divided into single span and double span, and its inner contour is close to the structure gauge of tunnel, which is convenient for laying the facilities of urban underground pipe network on the roof. Circular section has the characteristics of reasonable mechanic property, consistent section shape and small impact on internal clearance. The use of double circle shield has some advantages in effectively using underground space and reducing construction time.

1. 明挖法隧道结构形式

1. Structure of open cut tunnel

明挖法施工的隧道结构通常采用矩形断面,一般为整体浇筑或装配式结构,由于其内轮廓与地下铁道建筑限界接近,内部净空可以得到充分利用,结构受力合理,顶板上便于敷设地下管网设施。

The tunnel structure constructed by open cut method usually adopts rectangular cross-section, which is generally cast-in-one or fabricated structure. For the inner contour is close to the subway structure gauge, the internal clearance can be fully utilized, the structure loading is reasonable, and the underground pipe network can be laid on the roof.

(1)整体式衬砌

(1) Integral lining

整体式衬砌结构断面分单跨、双跨等形式,如图1-27所示,由于其整体性好,防水性能容易得到保证,故可适用于各种工程地质和水文地质的条件,但施工工序较多,施工速度较慢。

The integral lining structural section is divided into single span, double span and other forms, as shown in Figure 1-27. Due to its good integrity and waterproof performance, it can be applied in various engineering geological and hydrogeological conditions, but there are many construction procedures and the construction speed is slow.

(a) 单跨
Single span

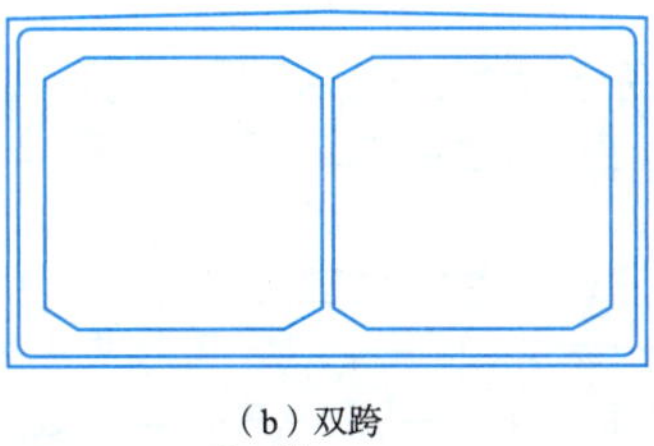

(b) 双跨
Double span

图1-27　明挖法整体式衬砌结构

Figure 1-27　Structure of open cut integral lining

(2)预制装配式衬砌

(2) Prefabricated lining

预制装配式衬砌的结构形式,应根据工业化生产水平、施工方法、起重运输条件,场地条件等因地制宜选择,目前以单跨和双跨较为通用,如图1-28所示。预制装配式衬砌整体性较差,对于有特殊要求(如防护、减震)的地段,要慎重选用。

The structure of prefabricated lining shall be selected according to the industrial production level, construction method, lifting and transportation conditions, site conditions and other local conditions. At present, single span and double span are common, as shown in Figure 1-28. The integrity of prefabricated lining is poor, so the sections with special requirements (such as protection and vibration reduction) should be carefully selected.

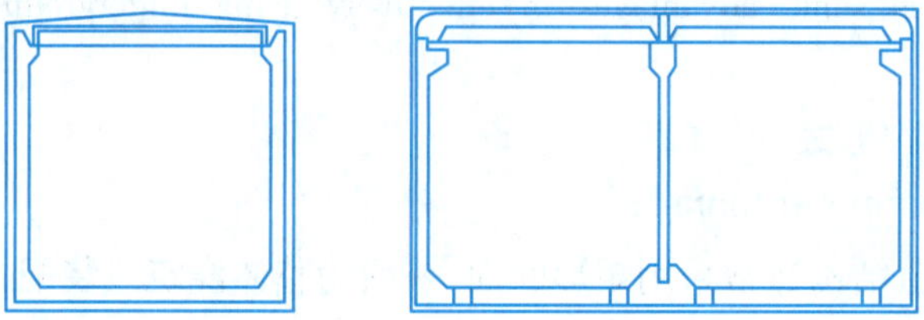
(a)

(b)

图 1-28 明挖法预制装配式衬砌结构

Figure 1-28 Structure of open cut prefabricated lining

(3)喇叭口衬砌

(3) bell mouth lining

喇叭口衬砌通常都采用整体式钢筋混凝土结构,图 1-29 表示非对称喇叭口衬砌结构。

The bell mouth lining is usually an integral reinforced concrete structure. Figure 1-29 shows the asymmetric bell mouth lining structure.

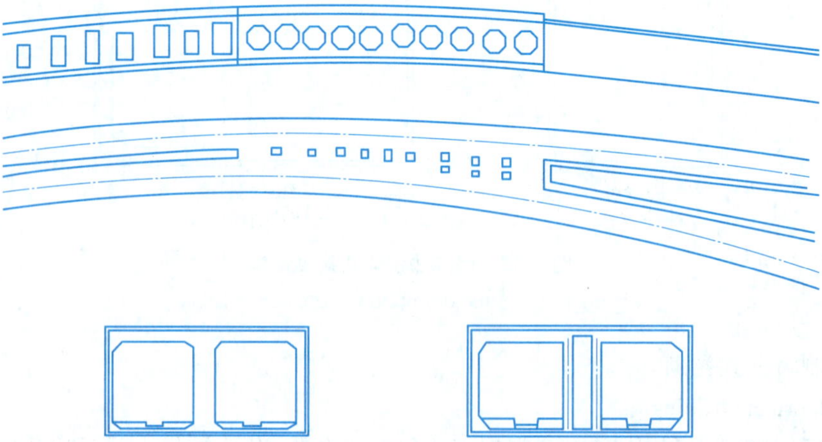

图 1-29 非对称喇叭口衬砌结构

Figure 1-29 Asymmetric bell mouth lining structure

2. 矿山法隧道结构形式

2. Tunnel structures by mining method

轨道交通区间隧道采用矿山法施工时，一般采用拱形结构，其基本断面形式为单拱、双拱和多跨连拱，如图 1-30 所示，前者多用于单线或双线的区间隧道或联络通道，后两者多用在停车线、折返线或喇叭口岔线上。

When the rail transit interval tunnel is constructed by mining method, the arch structure is generally adopted, and its basic sections are single arch, double arch and multi span multiple arch, as shown in Figure 1-30. The former is mostly used for the single line or double line section tunnel or connecting passage, while the latter is mostly used for the vehicle parking lines, round line or bell mouth branch line.

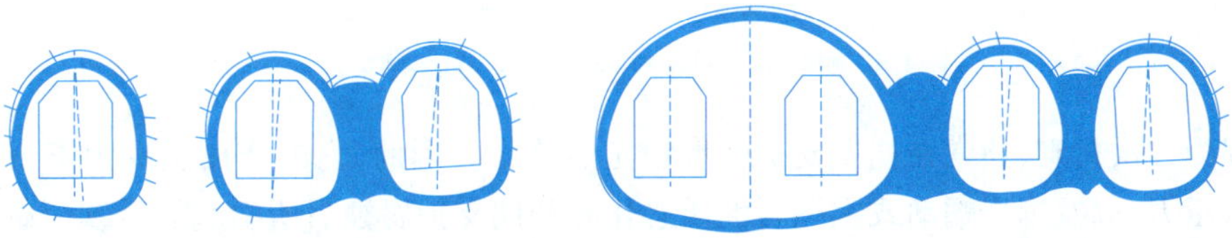

图 1-30　矿山法隧道衬砌结构形式

Figure 1-30　Structural form of tunnel lining by mining method

根据围岩条件、地下水状况、地表下沉的控制标准、断面大小和施工方法等，隧道可以采用复合式衬砌及其衍生方案。

According to surrounding rock conditions, groundwater conditions, control standards of surface subsidence, section size and construction methods, the tunnel can adopt composite lining and its derivative structures.

(1)复合式衬砌

(1) Composite lining

复合式衬砌由初期支护、防水隔离层和二次衬砌所组成，如图 1-31 所示。外层为初期支护，其作用为加固围岩，控制围岩变形，防止围岩松动失稳，是衬砌结构中的最重要承载单元。一般应在开挖后立即施作，并应与围岩密贴，所以最适宜采用喷锚支护，即根据具体情况，选用锚杆、喷混凝土、钢筋网和钢支撑等单一或并用而成。

Composite lining is composed of primary support, waterproof isolation layer and secondary lining, as shown in Figure 1-31. The outer layer is the primary support, which is the most important bearing unit in the lining structure. It can strengthen the surrounding rock, control the deformation of the surrounding rock, and prevent the surrounding rock from loosening and instability. Generally, it shall be constructed immediately after excavation and shall be closely attached to the surrounding rock. Therefore, shotcrete anchor support is most suitable, that is, anchor bolt, shotcrete, reinforcing mesh, steel support or combined ones are selected according to the specific situation.

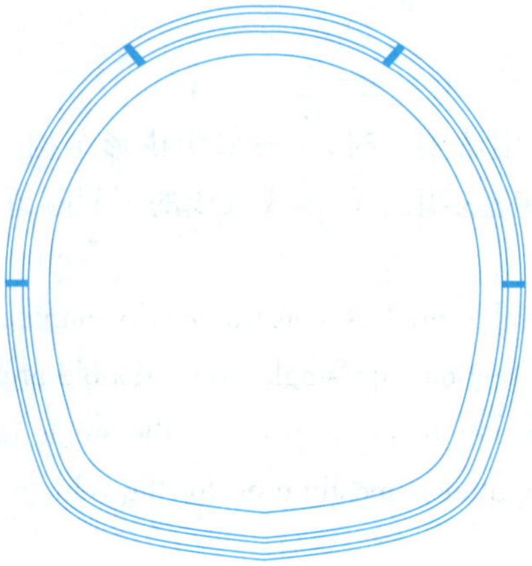

图 1-31　复合式衬砌结构

Figure 1-31　Composite lining structure

内层为二次衬砌，通常在初期支护变形稳定后施作。因此，它的作用主要为安全储备，并承受静水压力，以及围岩蠕动或因围岩性质恶化和初期支护腐蚀后所引起的后续荷载，并提供光滑的通风表面。

The inner layer is the secondary lining, which is usually constructed after the deformation of the primary support is stable. It can bear hydrostatic pressure and subsequent load caused by creep or deterioration of surrounding rock and corrosion of primary support. In addition to being a safety margin, the secondary lining also provides a smooth ventilation surface.

二次衬砌一般采用模筑混凝土。一般地，在初期支护和二次衬砌之间一般需要敷设不同类型的防水隔离层。

The secondary lining is generally made of cast-in-place concrete. Generally, different types of waterproof isolation layers need to be laid between the primary support and the secondary lining.

(2)衍生方案

(2) Derivative structures

在干燥无水的坚硬围岩中，区间隧道衬砌亦可采用单层的喷锚支护，不做防水隔离层和二次衬砌，但此时对喷混凝土的施工工艺和抗风化性能都应有较高的要求，衬砌表面要平整，不允许出现大量的开裂。

In the dry hard surrounding rock, the lining of interval tunnel can also be supported by single-layer shotcrete and anchor, without waterproof isolation layer and secondary lining. However, at this time, there should be higher requirements for the shotcrete construction process and weathering resistance. The lining surface should be flat without large cracks.

当岩层的整体性较好，基本无地下水，衬砌结构防水要求不高，从开挖到衬砌这段时间围岩能够自稳时，可采用单层整体现浇混凝土衬砌或装配式衬砌，不做初期支护和防水隔离层。根据不同的围岩条件，整体式衬砌可做成等截面直墙式和等截面或变截面曲墙式，前者适用于坚硬围岩，后者适用于软弱围岩。

When the rock stratum has good integrity without groundwater, the lining structure doesn't have high standards of waterproof, and the surrounding rock can be self stable from excavation to lining, a single-layer integral cast-in-situ concrete lining or fabricated lining can be used without initial support and waterproof isolation layer. Based on different surrounding rock conditions, the integral lining can be made into constant section straight wall and constant section or variable section curved wall. The former is applicable to hard surrounding rock, while the latter is applicable to soft surrounding rock.

一般要求在衬砌做好后向衬砌背后注浆,填充空隙,改善衬砌受力状态,减少围岩变形。同时,衬砌混凝土本身需有较高的自防水性能。

After the lining is completed, grouting is generally required to fill the gap behind the lining, which improves the stress state of lining and reduce the deformation of surrounding rock. At the same time, the lining concrete itself should to have high self waterproof performance.

3. 盾构法隧道结构形式

3. Structures of shield tunnel

盾构法修建的隧道衬砌有预制装配式衬砌(见图 1-32)、预制装配式衬砌和模筑钢筋混凝土整体式衬砌相结合的双层衬砌(见图 1-33)以及挤压混凝土整体式衬砌三大类。

Tunnel linings constructed by shield method are divided into three categories: prefabricated lining (see Figure 1-32), double-linings (see Figure 1-33) of prefabricated lining and molded reinforced concrete integral lining, and extruded concrete integral lining.

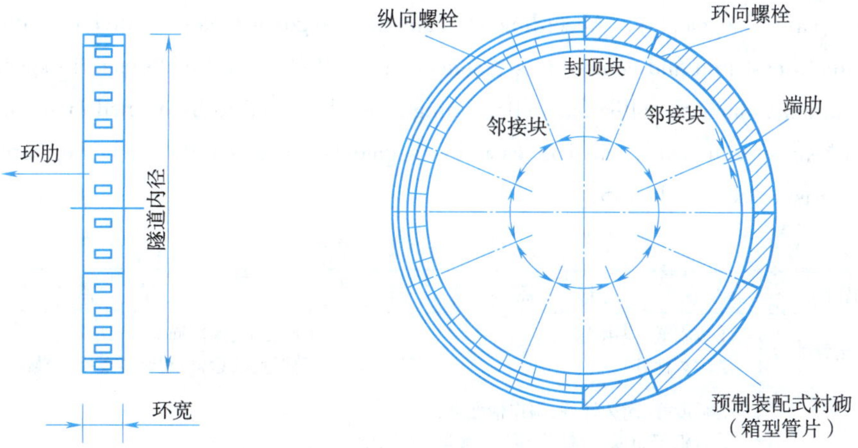

图 1-32　单层预制装配式衬砌圆环结构

Figure 1-32　Single layer prefabricated lining ring structure

环肋:ring rib　环宽:ring width　隧道内径:tunnel inner diameter
纵向螺栓:longitudinal bolt　环向螺栓:circumferential bolt
封顶块:capping block　邻接块:adjacency block　端肋:end rib
预制装配式衬砌(箱型管片):prefabricated lining (box segment)

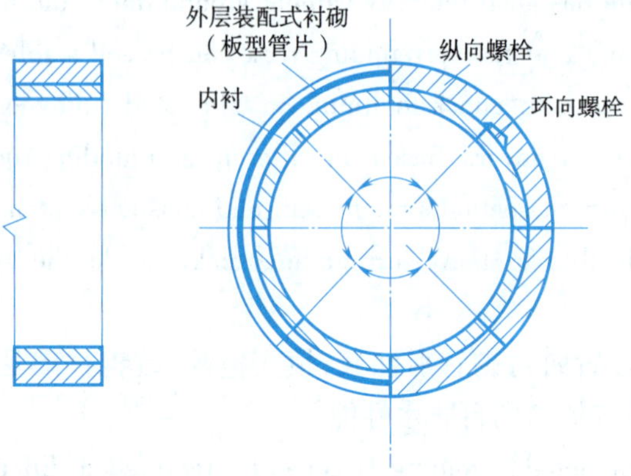

图 1-33 双层衬砌圆环结构

Figure 1-33 Double lining ring structure

外层装配式衬砌（板型管片）：outer fabricated lining (plate segment)　　内衬：lining

(1) 预制装配式衬砌

(1) Prefabricated lining

预制装配式衬砌采用工厂预制的构件（称为管片）在盾构尾部拼装而成。管片种类按材料可分为钢筋混凝土、钢、铸铁以及由几种材料组合而成的复合管片。在区间隧道的特殊地段，如集水井、需要开口的衬砌环或预计将承受特殊荷载的地段，一般采用钢或铸铁管片。管片类型比较见表 1-5。

The prefabricated lining is assembled at the tail of the shield with factory prefabricated components (called segments). According to materials, segments can be divided into reinforced concrete, steel, cast iron and composite segments composed of several materials. In special sections of interval tunnels, such as collecting wells, lining rings that need to be opened or sections that are expected to bear special loads, steel or cast iron segments are generally used. Segment types and their characteristics see Table 1-5.

表 1-5 不同管片特点

管片名称	优　点	缺　点
钢筋混凝土管片	①成本低、应用广泛； ②耐久性好	①厚度大，掘削面大； ②重量大，运输、组装需要手工操作，易损伤
球墨铸铁管片	①强度好、耐久性好，制作精度高； ②与钢筋混凝土管片相比，重量轻、掘削面小； ③承受特殊荷载处可选用特殊构造； ④耐久性好	①成本高； ②焊接困难
钢管片	①重量轻、组装运输容易； ②加固容易； ③中小盾构隧道中使用多	①容易变形； ②耐腐蚀性差
复合管片	管片由混凝土和钢板有效复合构造，与钢筋混凝土管片相比厚度小	①钢板的抗腐蚀性差； ②接头构造复杂

Table 1-5　Characteristics of different segments

Segment name	Characteristics	Problems
reinforced concrete segment	① Low cost, widely; ② Good durability	① Large thickness, large cutting face; ② Heavy weight, transportation and assembly by manual, easy to damage
ductile iron segment	① Good strength, good durability and high precision; ② Compared with reinforced concrete segment, it has light weight and small cutting face; ③ Special structures can be selected under special loads; ④ Good durability	① High cost; ② Welding difficulty
steel segment	① Light weight, easy assembly and transportation; ② Easy reinforcement; ③ Widely used in medium and small shield tunnels	① Easily deformed; ② Poor corrosion resistance
composite segment	The segment is composed of concrete and steel plate, which is smaller in thickness than the reinforced concrete segment	① Poor corrosion resistance of steel plate; ② Complex joint structure

按管片螺栓手孔大小,可将管片分为箱型和板型两类,如图 1-34 和图 1-35 所示。

According to the size of bolt holes, segments can be divided into box segments and plate segments, as shown in Figure 1-34 and Figure 1-35.

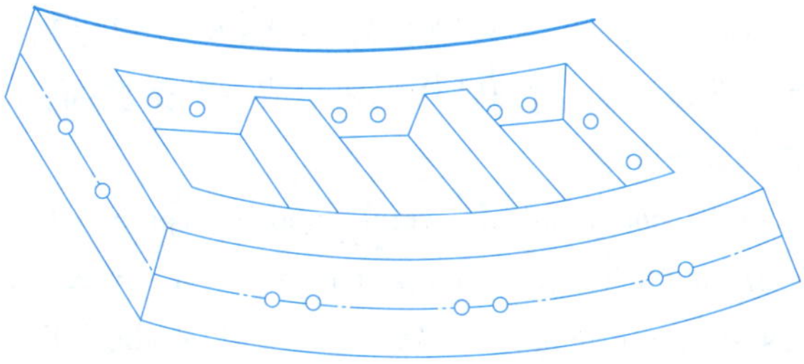

图 1-34　箱型管片

Figure 1-34　Box segment

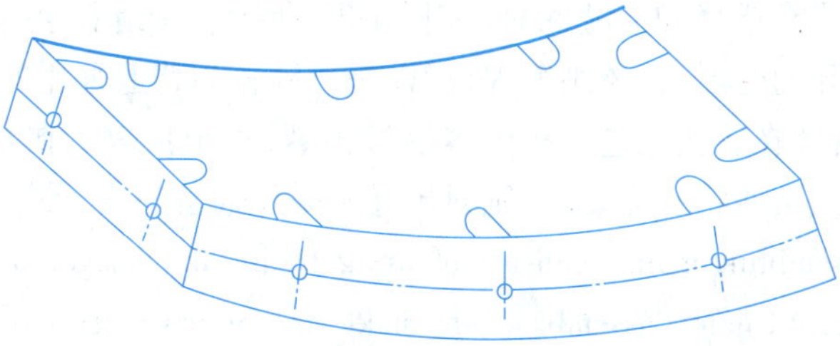

图 1-35　板型管片

Figure 1-35　Plate segment

箱型管片是指因手孔较大而呈肋板型结构,手孔较大不仅方便了接头螺栓的穿入和拧紧,而且也节省了材料,使单块管片重量减轻,便于运输和拼装。但因截面削弱较多,在盾构千斤顶推力作用下容易开裂,故只有强度较大的金属管片才采用箱型结构。直径和厚度较大的钢筋混凝土管片也有采用箱型结构,在箱型管片中纵向加劲肋是传递千斤顶推力的关键部位,一般沿衬砌环向等距离布置。

Box segment refers to the ribbed plate structure with large bolt holes, which not only facilitates the penetration and tightening of joint bolts, but also saves materials, reduces the weight of a single segment, and is convenient for transportation and assembly. However, due to the weakening of cross-section, it is easy to crack under the thrust of the shield jack, so only the metal segments with high strength can adopt the box structure. Reinforced concrete segments with large diameter and thickness also adopt box structure. In the box segment, the longitudinal stiffening rib is the key part to transmit the jack thrust, which is generally arranged at equal distance along the lining ring direction.

板型管片是指因螺栓手孔较小或无手孔而呈曲板型结构的管片,由于管片截面削弱少或无削弱,故对盾构千斤顶推力具有较大的抵抗力,对通风的阻力也较小。钢筋混凝土管片多采用板型结构。

Plate segment refers to the curved plate structure with small or no bolt hole. Due to little or no weakening of segment section, it has greater resistance to the thrust of shield Jack and less resistance to ventilation. Reinforced concrete segments are mostly of plate structure.

衬砌环的组成,一般有两种方式:一种是有若干标准管片(A)、两块相邻管片(B)和一块封顶管片(K)组成;另一种是由若干块 A 型管片,一块 B 型管片和一块 K 型管片构成,如图 1-36 所示。相邻管片一端带坡面,封顶管片则两端或一端带坡面,从方便施工、提高衬砌环防水效果角度看,第一种方式较好。

The lining ring is generally composed of several standard segments (A), two adjacent segments (B) and one seal roof segment (K); The other is composed of several segments A, one segment B and one segment K, as shown in Figure 1-36. One end of the adjacent segment is provided with a slope surface, and the seal roof segment is provided with a slope surface at both ends or one end. From the perspective of the construction and waterproof of lining rings, the first method is better.

衬砌环的拼装形式有错缝和通缝两种,如图 1-37 所示。错缝拼装可使接缝分布均匀,减少接缝以及整个衬砌环的变形,整体刚度大,所以是一种较为普遍采用的拼装形式。但当管片制作精度不够高时,管片在盾构推进过程中容易被顶裂,甚至顶碎。在某些场合,例如需要拆除管片修建旁通道处或某些特殊需要时,则衬砌通常采用通缝拼接形式,以便施工。

The lining ring assembling mainly consists of straight joint and staggered joint method, as shown in Figure 1-37. Staggered joint assembly can make the joints evenly distributed, reduce the deformation of the joints and the whole lining ring, and have stong integral stiffness. Therefore, it is a commonly used assembly method. However, when the accuracy of segments does not meet the requirements, segments are easy to be cracked or even broken during shield driving. In some cases, such as when it is necessary to dismantle segments to build side channels or when there are special needs, the lining is usually assembled by straight joint method.

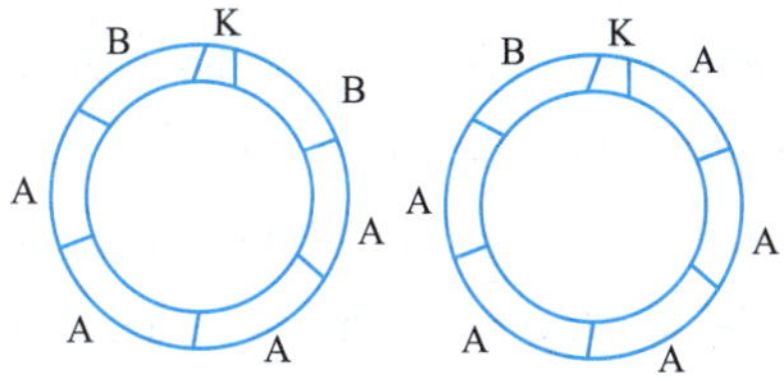

图 1-36 管片分块

Figure 1-36 Segment division

（a）通缝
Straight joint

（b）错缝
Staggered joint

图 1-37 管片拼缝形式

Figure 1-37 Segment assembling methods

（2）双层衬砌

(2) Double lining

为防止隧道渗水和衬砌腐蚀，修正隧道施工误差，减少噪声和振动以及作为内部装饰，可以在装配式衬砌内部再做一层整体式混凝土或钢筋混凝土内衬。根据需要，还可以在装配式衬砌与内层之间敷设防水隔离层。国内外在含地下水丰富和含有腐蚀性地下水的软土地层内的隧道，大都选用双层衬砌，即在隧道衬砌的内侧再附加厚 250 ~ 300 mm 的现浇钢筋混凝土内衬，主要解决隧道防水和金属连接杆件防蚀问题，也可使隧道内壁光洁，减少空气流动阻力。

In order to prevent water seepage and lining corrosion of the tunnel, correct tunnel construction errors, reduce noise and vibration, and serve as internal decoration, a layer of integral concrete or reinforced concrete lining can be applied inside the fabricated lining. According to needs, waterproof isolation layer can also be laid between the prefabricated lining and the inner layer. Double lining is mostly adopted in the tunnels in soft soil layer with rich groundwater and corrosive groundwater at home and abroad. The cast-in-situ reinforced concrete lining with a thickness of 250 - 300 mm is added inside the tunnel lining, which mainly solves the problems of tunnel waterproof and metal rod corrosion, and also makes the inner wall of the tunnel smooth to reduce air flow resistance.

（3）挤压混凝土整体式衬砌

(3) Extruded concrete integral lining

挤压混凝土整体式衬砌就是随着盾构向前推进，用衬砌施工设备在盾尾同步灌注的混凝土或钢筋混凝土整体式衬砌，其灌注后即承受盾构千斤顶推力的挤压作用。挤压混凝土整体式衬砌可以是素混凝土或是钢筋混凝土，但应用最多的是钢纤维混凝土。

Extrusion concrete integral lining is a concrete or reinforced concrete integral lining that is synchronously poured at the shield tail by lining construction equipment as the shield advances. It bears the squeezing effect of shield jack thrust after pouring. Extruded concrete integral lining can be made of plain concrete, reinforced concrete, and steel fiber concrete.

挤压混凝土整体式衬砌一次成型，内表面光滑，衬砌背后无空隙，故无须注浆，且对控制地层移动特别有效。但因挤压混凝土整体式衬砌需要较多的施工设施，且混凝土制备、配送、钢筋骨架等工艺较为复杂，在渗透性较大的土层中要达到防水要求有困难，故挤压混凝土整体式衬砌的应用范围不广泛。

The extruded concrete lining is molded in one time, with smooth inner surface and no gap behind the lining. The method can control the ground movement effectively without grouting. However, extruded concrete integral lining requires more construction facilities, and the concrete preparation, distribution, reinforcement framework and other processes are more complex, so it is difficult to meet the waterproof requirements in the permeable soil layer, so the extruded concrete integral lining has not been widely used.

(4)联络通道

(4) Connecting passage

《地铁设计规范》要求，两条单线区间隧道之间，当隧道连贯长度大于600 m时，应设置联络通道，并在通道两端设双向开启的甲级防火门。联络通道的位置一般处于各段区间隧道的中间段，由于地铁建设常常采用“高站位，低区间”的方法，中间段通常也为线路最低处。在实际工程中，常将其与地下泵站合并建设，如图1-38所示。

According to *Code for Design of Metro*, when the continuous length of two single line section tunnels is greater than 600 m, a connecting passage with Class A fire doors of two-way opening at both ends shall be set. The connecting passage is generally located in the middle of each section. In the subway construction, the method of “high station, low section” is often adopted, so the middle section is usually the lowest part of the line. In practical engineering, the connected aisle and the underground pump station are often constructed together, as shown in Figure 1-38.

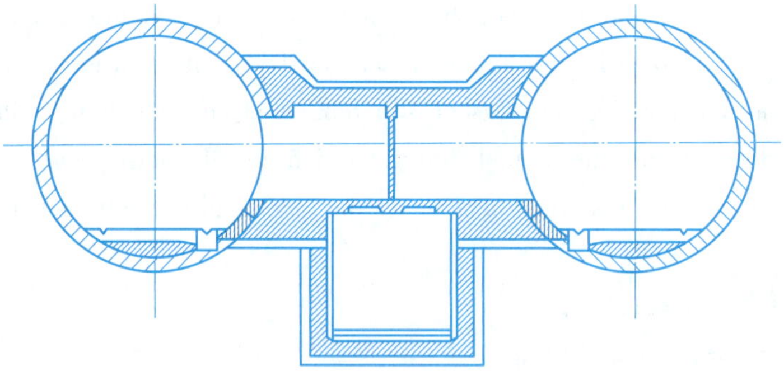

图1-38　联络通道与泵站合建结构

Figure 1-38　Structure of connecting passage and underground pump station

4. 沉管法隧道结构

4. Tunnel structures by immersed tube method

地下铁道穿越江、河、湖、海时，往往采用预制沉管法施工。这一方法的要点是先在干船坞或船台上分段制作隧道结构，然后放入水中，浮运至设计位置，逐段沉入水底预先挖好的沟槽内，处理好各阶段的接缝，将其连接成一个整体贯通隧道。

When the underground railway crosses rivers, lakes and seas, the precast immersed tube method is often used for construction. This method is to make the tunnel structure in sections on the dry dock or slipway, then put the sections into the water, transport them to the design position, immerse them into the dredged trench at the bottom of water one by one, seal the joints and connect them into a whole tunnel.

沉管结构横断面有圆形和矩形两大类,断面形状要从空间的充分利用和结构受力合理两方面综合考虑,如图1-39所示。当隧道位于深水中(大于45 m),管段承受较大的水压时,其相应的内力较大,采用圆形或接近圆形的断面比矩形断面更为有利;当水深在35 m之内时,可用矩形断面;水深介于35~45 m时,要进行详细对比予以选择。

The cross-section of immersed tube structure can be divided into circular and rectangular. The determination of cross-section should be based on the comprehensive consideration of full utilization of space and reasonable structure stress, as shown in Figure 1-39. When the tunnel is located in deep water (more than 45 m), the internal force of tube is large under high water pressure, so a circular or near circular section is better than a rectangular section; When the water depth is within 35 m, a rectangular section can be used. When the water depth is between 35 m and 45 m, a detailed comparison should be made to select it.

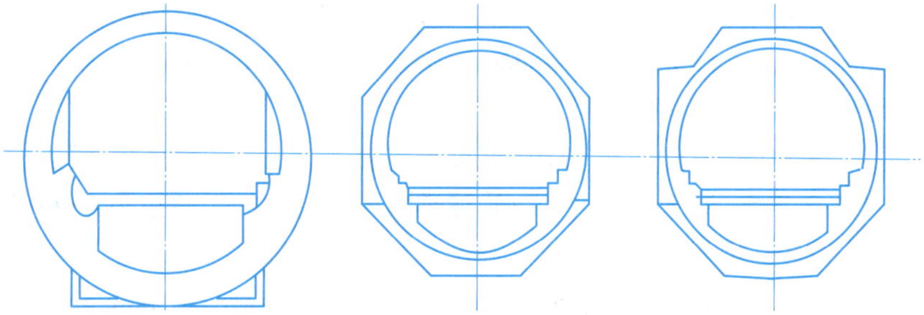

(a) 圆形
Circular

(b) 八角形
Octagon

(c) 花篮形
Flower basker shaped

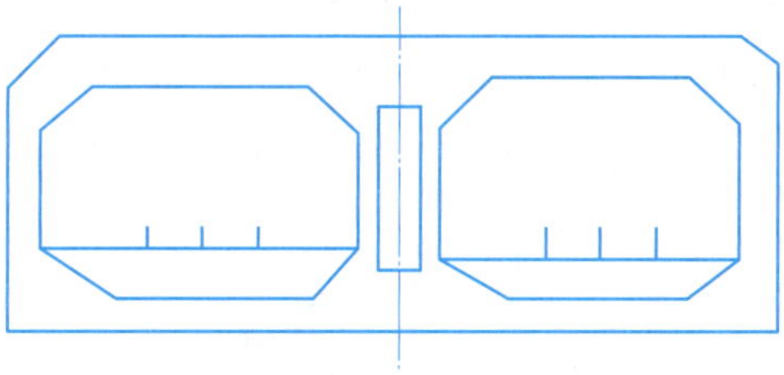

(d) 矩形
Rectangular

图1-39 沉管法隧道结构

Figure 1-39 Tunnel structures by immersed tube method

每节沉管的长度依据所在水域的地形、地质、航运、航道、施工方法等方面的要求等确定,一般为60~140 m,多数在100 m左右。断面尺寸根据使用要求、埋深、地质条件、施工方法等确定。管段结构构造除满足受力要求外,还应考虑管段浮运、沉没、波浪力、基础形式及地基性质的影响。

The length of each immersed tube is determined according to the terrain, geology, navigation, navigation channel, construction method and other factors of the water. It's generally 60 - 140 m, most of which are about 100 m. The section size shall be determined according to the use requirements, burial depth, geological conditions, construction methods, etc. When determining the tube structure, not only load-bearing, but also floating, sinking, wave force, foundation types and soil conditions should be considered.

沉管段结构的外轮廓尺寸除满足抗浮设计要求外,还要保证一定的干舷和安全系数。沉管结构混凝土等级一般为 C30 ~ C50,不容许出现通透性裂缝,非通透性裂缝的开展宽度应控制在 0. 15 ~0. 2 mm。

In addition to meeting the requirements of anti floating design, the outer contour of immersed tube structure should also ensure a certain freeboard and safety factor. The concrete grade of immersed tube structure is generally C30 - C50. Penetrating cracks are not allowed, and the width of non penetrating cracks shall be controlled within 0. 15 - 0. 2 mm.

当隧道的跨度较大,或者水、土压力较大(300 ~400 kPa)时,顶、底板受到的弯矩和剪力都很大,也可采用预应力结构。一般为简化施工,尽量采用普通钢筋混凝土结构。

When the tunnel has a large span and suffers high water or earth pressure (300 - 400 kPa), the bending moment and shear force on the top and bottom slabs are so large that the prestressed structure shall be used. Generally, in order to simplify the construction, reinforced concrete structure shall be adopted as far as possible.

沉管段连接均在水下进行,一般有水中混凝土连接和水压压接两种方式。按变形状况可分为刚性接头和柔性接头,对于地震区的沉管隧道宜采用特殊的柔性接头,这种接头即能适应线位移和角变形,又具有足够的轴向抗拉、抗压、抗剪和抗弯强度。

The immersed tube sections are connected underwater, generally including underwater concrete connection and hydraulic pressure connection. It can be divided into rigid joints and flexible joints according to the deformation. For immersed tube tunnels in earthquake areas, special flexible joints should be used, which can not only adapt to linear displacement and angular deformation, but also have sufficient strength of axial tensile, compressive, shear and bending.

1. 3. 4 隧道防水要求

1. 3. 4 Requirements of tunnel waterproofing

1. 地下结构防水要求

1. Waterproofing requirements for underground structures

渗漏水会影响结构的耐久性,导致结构产生不均匀沉降,危及行车安全,影响设备的正常使用,因此,防水对于地下工程非常重要。地铁养护单位在日常工作中遵循“逢漏必堵,逢损必固,逢沉必注”的指导原则。

Water leakage will affect the durability of the structure, lead to uneven settlement of the structure, endanger the safety of driving, and affect the normal use of equipment. Therefore, waterproof is very important for underground engineering. The metro maintenance unit shall block every leakage, reinforcement every damage, and grout in case of settlement in daily work.

目前,我国地下工程防水等级分四级,见表 1-6,地铁工程防水按二级防水要求执行。

At present, the waterproofing of underground works in China is divided into four grades see Table 1-6, and the waterproofing of subway structure is carried out according to the requirements of Grade Ⅱ.

表 1-6 地下工程的防水标准

防水等级	防水标准
一级	不允许渗水,结构表面无湿渍
二级	不允许漏水,结构表面可有少量湿渍; 工业与民用建筑:总湿渍面积不应大于总防水面积(包括顶板、墙面、地面)的 1‰;任意 100 m^2 防水面积上的湿渍不超过 2 处,单个湿渍的最大面积不大于 0.1 m^2; 其他地下工程:总湿渍面积不应大于总防水面积的 2‰;任意 100 m^2 防水面积上的湿渍不超过 3 处,单个湿渍的最大面积不大于 0.2 m^2;隧道工程还要求平均渗漏量不大于 0.05 L/(m^2·d),任意 100 m^2 防水面积上的渗水量不大于 0.15 L/(m^2·d)
三级	有少量漏水点,不得有线流和漏泥沙; 任意 100 m^2 防水面积上的漏水或湿渍点数不超过 7 处,单个漏水点的最大漏水量不大于 2.5 L/d,单个湿渍的最大面积不大于 0.3 m^2
四级	有漏水点,不得有线流和漏泥沙; 整个工程平均漏水量不大于 2 L/(m^2·d);任意 100 m^2 防水面积上的平均漏水量不大于 4 L/(m^2·d)

Table 1-6 Waterproofing standards for underground works

Waterproofing grade	Waterproofing standard
Grade Ⅰ	Water seepage is not allowed, and there is no wet spot on the surface of the structure
Grade Ⅱ	Water leakage is not allowed, and there may be a small amount of wet stains on the surface of structure; Industrial and civil buildings: the total wet area shall not be greater than 1‰ of the total waterproof area (including roof, wall and floor); there shall be no more than 2 wet stains on any 100 m^2 waterproof area, and the maximum area of a single wet stain shall not be greater than 0.1 m^2; Other underground works: the total wet area shall not be more than 2‰ of the total waterproof area; there shall be no more than 3 wet stains on any 100 m^2 waterproof area, and the maximum area of a single wet stain shall not be more than 0.2 m^2. Among them, the average leakage of tunnel engineering is required to be no more than 0.05 L / (m^2·d), and the leakage of any 100 m^2 waterproof area is required to be no more than 0.15 L / (m^2·d)
Grade Ⅲ	There is a small amount of water leakage, without line flow and mud and sand leakage; The number of water leakage or wet stains on any 100 m^2 waterproof area shall not more than 7, the maximum water leakage of a single position shall not be greater than 2.5 L/d, and the maximum area of a single wet stain shall not be greater than 0.3 m^2
Grade Ⅳ	If there is water leakage, there shall be no line flow and mud and sand leakage; The average water leakage of the whole project is not more than 2 L/(m^2·d); The average water leakage on any 100 m^2 waterproof area is not more than 4 L/(m^2·d)

不同的场所适用不同的防水等级见表 1-7。设计规范规定,地下车站、行人通道和机电设备集中区段的防水等级应为一级;区间隧道及连接通道等附属的隧道结构防水等级应为二级。根据不同的施工方法,其防水措施不尽相同。

Different waterproof grades are applicable to different places see Table 1-7. According to the design specification, the underground station, pedestrian passage and electromechanical equipment section shall be designed as Waterproofing Grade I; The section tunnel and connecting passage shall be designed as Waterproofing Grade II. The waterproof measures are different according to different construction methods.

表 1-7 不同防水等级的适用范围

防水等级	适用范围
一级	人员长期停留的场所;因有少量湿渍会使物品变质、失效的贮物场所及严重影响设备正常运转和危及工程安全运营的部位;极重要的战备工程和地铁车站
二级	人员经常活动的场所;在有少量湿渍情况下不会使物品变质、失效的贮物场所及基本不影响设备正常运转和工程安全运营的部位;如重要的战备工程
三级	人员临时活动的场所和一般战备工程
四级	对渗漏水无严格要求的工程

Table 1-7 Application scope of different waterproofing grades

Waterproofing grade	Application scope
Grade Ⅰ	Places where people stay for a long time; places where goods will deteriorate and fail due to wet stains; places that seriously affect the normal operation of equipment and the safe operation of critical projects; extremely important war preparedness projects and subway stations
Grade Ⅱ	Places where people often move, places where goods will not deteriorate or fail in case of wet stains; places where normal operation of equipment and safe operation of engineering will not be affected; important war preparedness projects
Grade Ⅲ	Places for temporary activities of personnel, not important war preparedness projects
Grade Ⅳ	Projects without strict requirements for water leakage

2. 明挖法隧道结构防水

2. Waterproofing of open cut tunnel structure

采用明挖法的结构防水,一般由结构自防水和附加防水层所组成。附加防水层可以用卷材、防水涂料或水泥基防水材料等做成。通常防水层都设在主体结构外侧(迎水面),且要求与结构的表面黏结良好。

The structural waterproofing with open cut method is generally composed of structural self waterproofing and additional waterproof layer. The additional waterproof layer can be made of coiled material, paint or waterproof mortar. Generally, the waterproof layer is set outside the main structure (upstream), and it is required to bond well with the surface of the structure.

(1)主体结构防水层施工

(1) Waterproof layer construction of main structure

① 卷材防水。

① Coiled material waterproof.

根据基坑支护方法,选择不同的卷材防水做法。对于敞口放坡法施工的结构,先在垫层上铺贴底层卷材、四周留出接头,待底板混凝土和立面混凝土浇筑完毕,将立面卷材防水层直接铺设在防水结构的外墙外表面。对于桩支护法施工的结构,先浇筑混凝土垫层,在垫层上将永久性保护墙全部砌好,抹水泥砂浆找平层,将卷材防水层直接铺贴在垫层和永久性保护墙上。明挖结构防水构造如图 1-40 所示。

Different construction methods of coiled material waterproof are applied according to the foundation pit support types. For the structure constructed by the open sloping method, the bottom coiled material shall be paved on the cushion, and the joints shall be left around. After the bottom slab concrete and the facade concrete are poured, the facade coiled material waterproof layer shall be directly laid on the outer surface of the waterproof structure. For the structure constructed by pile support, pour concrete cushion first, build all the permanent protective walls on the cushion, plaster the cement mortar leveling layer, and directly lay the coiled material waterproof layer on the cushion and the permanent protective wall. The waterproofing of open cut structure is shown in Figure 1-40.

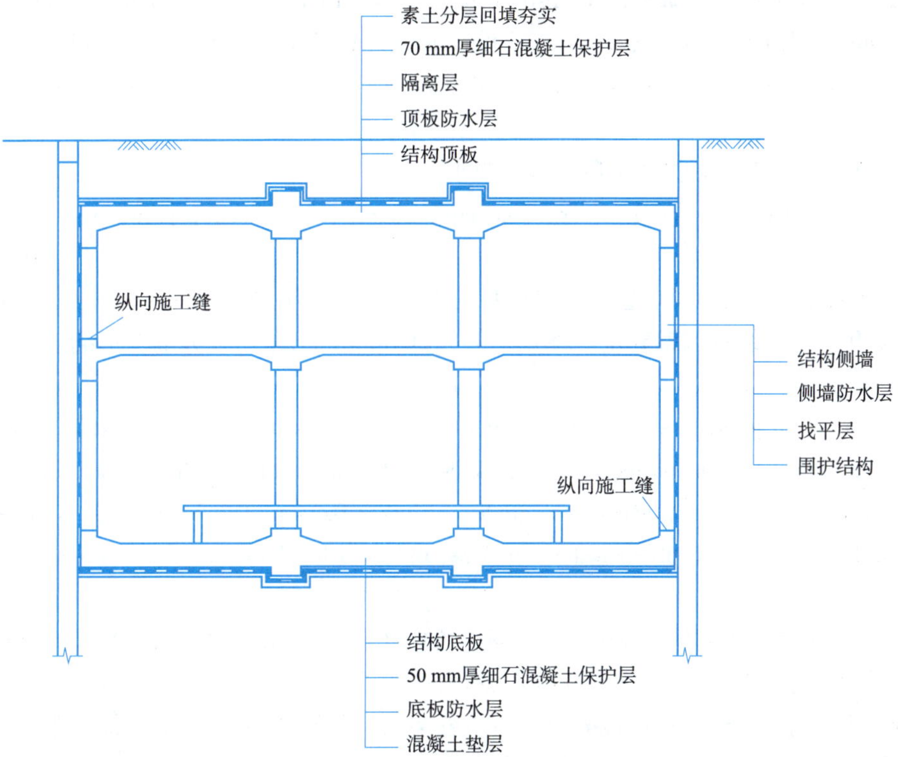

图 1-40　明挖结构防水构造示意图

Figure 1-40　Schematic diagram of open cut structure waterproof

素土分层回填夯实：plain soil by layering backfill and compaction

70 mm 厚细石混凝土保护层：70 mm thick fine stone concrete protective layer

隔离层：isolation layer　　顶板防水层：roof waterproof layer

结构顶板：structural roof　　纵向施工缝：longitudinal construction joint

结构侧墙：structural side wall　　侧墙防水层：side wall waterproof layer

找平层：screed course　　围护结构：enclosure structure　　结构底板：structural floor

50 mm 厚细石混凝土保护层：50 mm thick fine stone concrete protective layer

底板防水层：bottom waterproof layer　　混凝土垫层：concrete cushion

防水卷材要求有良好的耐水性和对温度变化的稳定性（高温下不流淌、不起泡、不滑动；低温下不脆裂），有一定的机械强度、延伸性和抗断裂性，要有一定的柔韧性和抗老化性等。

Waterproof coiled materials are required to have good water resistance, stability to temperature changes (no flowing, bubbling, stirring under high temperature; no embrittlement under low temperature), certain mechanical strength, extensibility, fracture resistance, flexibility and aging resistance.

② 涂层防水。

② Waterproof coating.

在明挖结构中也可采用大面积的涂层防水,但要注意保证涂层防水厚度的均匀一致。因卷材在基面复杂部位不易施工,故采用涂层防水。

Large area waterproof coating can also be used in open cut structures, but attention should be paid to ensuring that the coating waterproof thickness is uniform. In the parts with complex base surface, it is more convenient to use coating for waterproofing because the coiled material is not easy to construct.

(2)变形缝、后浇缝等防水构造和施工要求

(2) Waterproof structure and construction requirements of deformation joint, post pouring joint, etc.

① 变形缝:变形缝防水构造形式和材料应根据工程特点、地基和主体结构变形情况以及水压、水质和防水等级等因素确定。缝宽一般为 20 ~ 30 mm,水压较大的变形缝通常采用埋入式橡胶止水带。

① Deformation joint: the waterproof structure form and material of deformation joint shall be determined according to the project characteristics, deformation of foundation and main structure, water pressure, water quality, waterproof grade and other factors. The joint width is generally 20-30 mm, and the embedded rubber waterstop is usually used for deformation joints under large water pressure.

② 后浇缝:后浇缝应在其两侧结构混凝土的龄期达 6 周以后再施工;施工前应将接缝处的混凝土凿毛,清洗干净,保持润湿并刷水泥浆,或凿毛清洗后等其干燥,在其结构断面中部附近安放遇水膨胀腻子条;用补偿混凝土将后浇缝注满,其强度等级和抗渗等级均不低于两侧主体结构混凝土;养护时间不小于 28 天。

② Post pouring joint: the post pouring joint shall be constructed after the age of structural concrete on both sides reaches 6 weeks; before construction, the concrete at the joints shall be roughened, cleaned, kept wet and brushed with cement slurry, or dried after roughening and cleaning, and the water swelling putty strip shall be placed near the middle of the structural section; fill the post pouring joint with compensating concrete, and its strength grade and impermeability grade are not lower than the main structure concrete on both sides; the curing time shall not be less than 28 d.

③ 施工缝:凿毛清洗干净后,在结构断面中部附近放置遇水膨胀腻子条。也可采用橡胶或塑料止水板等,但施工比较麻烦。

③ Construction joint: after roughening and cleaning the structure, place a water swelling putty strip near the middle of the structural section. Rubber or plastic water stop plates can also be used, but the construction is relatively troublesome.

④ 穿墙管:穿墙管应在浇筑混凝土前埋设,并加止水环,环与主管要满焊。

④ Wall through pipe: the wall through pipe shall be buried before concrete pouring, and water stop ring shall be added. The ring and main pipe shall be fully welded.

3. 盖挖法隧道结构防水

3. Waterproofing of tunnel structure with cover excavation method

盖挖法修建的地下铁道结构,其侧墙有两种形式:一种是地下连续墙或桩墙和内衬所组成的复合墙;另一种是只有地下连续墙的单层墙。无论是哪种构造形式,侧墙以及侧墙和板接缝处的防水问题都是技术上的难题。

The side walls of subway structures built by cover excavation method have two forms: one is the diaphragm wall or the composite wall composed of pile wall and lining; the other is the single layer wall with only the diaphragm wall. No matter what kind of structure, the waterproof problem of side wall and the joint between side wall and slab is a technical problem.

盖挖法结构防水除采用结构自防水外(抗渗标号不低于P8),并应增设附加防水层组成的多道防线,连续墙附加防水层按不同结构形式采用两种不同的方法。

In addition to structural self waterproofing (impermeability mark is not lower than P8), multiple lines of defense composed of additional waterproof layers shall be added for structural waterproofing by cover excavation method. Two different methods shall be adopted for additional waterproof layers of continuous walls according to different structural forms.

(1)夹层式防水结构

(1) Sandwich waterproof structure

夹层式防水结构,即在复合墙的地下连续墙与内衬之间设置防水隔离层。实践证明,这种防水结构不仅防水效果好,而且可消除连续墙对现浇混凝土内衬收缩的约束作用,减少内衬的收缩裂缝。

The sandwich waterproof structure, that is, a waterproof isolation layer is set between the diaphragm wall and the lining of the composite wall. The practice proves that this waterproof structure not only has good waterproof effect, but also can eliminate the constraint of continuous wall on the shrinkage of cast-in-situ concrete lining and reduce the shrinkage cracks of the lining.

夹层式防水结构的施工方法和矿山法复合衬砌的相同。

The construction method of sandwich waterproof structure is the same as that of composite lining in mining method.

(2)涂抹式防水结构

(2) Coating waterproof structure

涂抹式防水结构,即在单层墙的内表面(经处理过的),涂抹一层防水砂浆或其他防水涂料的刚性防水层。防水砂浆可以是用普通硅酸盐水泥为基料,也可以用膨胀水泥为基础配制成。防水涂料种类很多,其中以高效渗透型水泥密封剂效果较好,因为这种涂料在一定时间可渗混凝土表面下50 mm,并在混凝土的孔隙中产生一种不溶解的结晶,堵塞毛细水的渗漏通道。

The coating waterproof structure is a rigid waterproof layer coated with a layer of waterproof mortar or other waterproof coatings on the inner surface (treated) of a single wall. Waterproof mortar can be prepared with ordinary Portland cement as the base material or expansion cement as the basis. There are many kinds of waterproof coatings, among which the effect of efficient permeable cement sealant is better, because this coating can penetrate 50 mm below the concrete surface in a certain time, and produce an insoluble crystal in the concrete pores, blocking the capillary water leakage channel.

4. 矿山法隧道结构防水

4. Waterproofing of tunnel structure by mining method

(1)复合式衬砌防水系统

(1) Composite lining waterproof system

复合式衬砌防水系统由三道防水防线构成:初期支护结构(钢筋格栅+喷射混凝土);防水层(柔性外包防水);二次衬砌结构(钢筋骨架+模筑防水混凝土)。三者相辅相成,同时加上施工缝、变形缝等防水,共同形成了矿山法复合式衬砌防水体系。

The composite lining waterproof system consists of three waterproof lines: initial support structure (reinforcement grid + shotcrete); waterproof layer (flexible outer waterproof); Secondary lining structure (reinforcement skeleton + formwork waterproof concrete). The three complement each other, and together with waterproofing of construction joints and deformation joints, they form a composite lining waterproofing system for mining method.

(2)柔性外包防水层(夹层防水层)

(2) Flexible outer waterproof layer(sandwich waterproof layer)

柔性外包防水层,作为地下车站结构的"辅助防水层",设置在初期支护结构内表面,包裹在二次衬砌结构的外表面。

The flexible outer waterproof layer, as the "auxiliary waterproof layer" of the underground station structure, is set on the inner surface of the initial support structure and wrapped on the outer surface of the secondary lining structure.

柔性外包防水层不仅能起到防水作用,而且对初期支护喷射混凝土和二次衬砌的模筑混凝土来说,起到隔离和润滑作用;可以改善模筑混凝土的施工条件,有利于保证模筑混凝土的施工质量;可以避免或减缓混凝土硬化过程中的应力效应,减少防水混凝土产生裂缝的概率;可以保护和发挥二次衬砌结构的防水作用,有利于延长二次衬砌结构的寿命。

The flexible outer waterproof layer not only plays a waterproof role, but also plays an isolation and lubrication role for the initial support of sprayed concrete and the secondary lining of the formwork concrete. It can improve the construction conditions of the molded concrete and ensure its construction quality of. It can avoid or slow down the stress effect in the process of concrete hardening, and reduce the probability of cracks in waterproof concrete. It can protect and play the waterproof role of the secondary lining structure, which is conducive to extending the service life of the secondary lining structure.

复合式衬砌的柔性外包防水一般为:在初期支护混凝土表面铺设缓冲层(土工布或聚乙

烯泡沫塑料卷材)和导水的垫层,再采用无钉孔铺设法施作防水板(橡胶沥青类、合成橡胶类、塑料类等防水隔离层材料)。柔性外包防水层结构如图 1-41 所示。

The flexible outer waterproof of composite lining is generally to lay a buffer layer (geotextile or polyethylene foam plastic coiled material) and a water guiding cushion on the surface of the initial supported concrete, and then use non nail hole paving as a waterproof board (rubber asphalt, synthetic rubber, plastic and other waterproof isolation layer materials). The structure of flexible outer waterproof is shown in Figure 1-41.

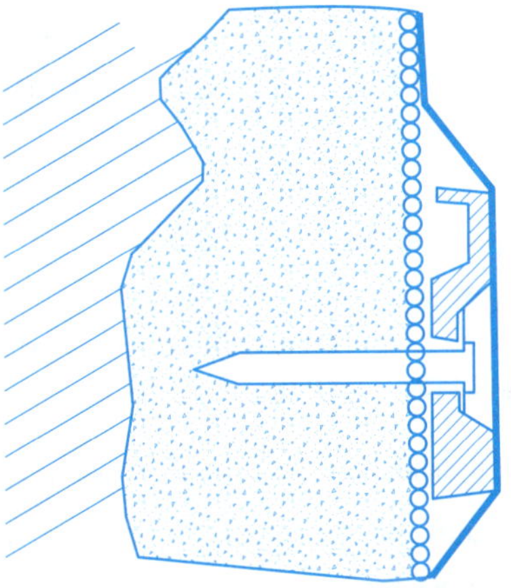

图 1-41　柔性外包防水层结构

Figure 1-41　The structure of flexible outer waterproof

5. 盾构法隧道结构防水

5. Waterproof system of shield tunnel

在一定的水压作用下,不仅盾构管片能够防水抗渗,而且管片环纵缝在预定张开量下也具有防水能力。因此,盾构隧道结构防水采用"自身防水为主,多道防线,综合处理"的原则。

Under a certain amount of water pressure, not only can the shield tunnel segment be waterproof and impermeable, but the longitudinal joints of the segment ring also have waterproof ability under a predetermined opening amount. Therefore, the shield tunnel waterproofing system includes self waterproofing, multiple defense and comprehensive treatment.

盾构隧道的防水体系由管片自防水、管片外防水防腐涂层和管片接缝处理组成。管片防水构造如图 1-42 所示。

The waterproof system of shield tunnel is composed of segment self-waterproof, segment external waterproof and anti-corrosion coating and segment joint treatment. The segment waterproof structure is shown in Figure 1-42.

(1)管片自防水

(1) Segment self-waterproof

管片自防水是首选的防水措施,主要通过采用防水混凝土及严密的施工工艺来保证管片质量,以达到防水效果。管片混凝土强度等级为 C50 ~ C55,抗渗标号可达 P8 ~ P12 以上。

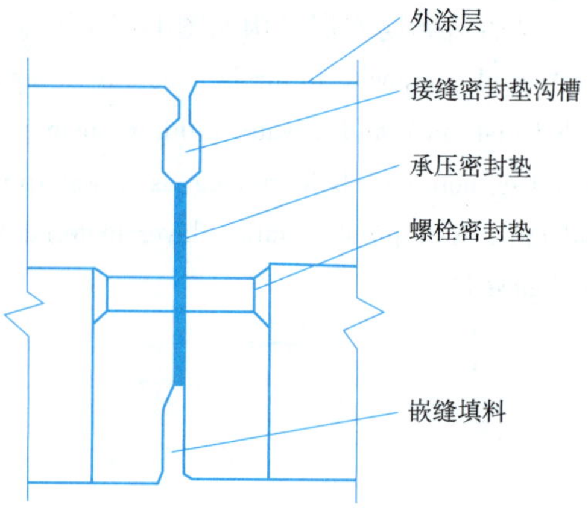

图 1-42 管片防水构造

Figure 1-42 Segment waterproof structure

外涂层:external coating 接缝密封垫沟槽:joint gasket groove
承压密封垫:pressure bearing gasket 螺栓密封垫:bolt gasket 嵌缝填料:caulking filler

Segment self-waterproof is the first choice of waterproof measures, through waterproof concrete and strict construction to ensure the quality of segments, in order to achieve the waterproof effect. The strength grade of segment concrete is C50 - C55, and the impermeability grade can reach above P8 - P12.

(2)管片外防水防腐涂层

(2) Waterproof and anticorrosive coating outside segment

管片外防水防腐涂层需根据管片材质而定,凡有较深裂纹的管片一般都要增加外防水涂层。施涂工作在管片预制厂进行。技术要求如下:

The outer arc surface of the segment is coated with two-component polyurethane coating for waterproof and anti-corrosion. The coating work is carried out in the segment prefabrication plant. Technical requirements:

① 涂层在盾尾密封圈钢丝刷与钢板的挤压磨损下不损坏、不渗水。

① The coating has no damage and water seepage under the extrusion wear of steel wire brush and steel plate of shield tail sealing ring.

② 在管片弧面的混凝土裂缝宽度达到 0.3 mm 时,仍能抗 0.8 MPa 水压。

② When the concrete crack width of segment arc surface reaches 0.3 mm, it can still resist 0.8 MPa water pressure.

③ 涂层的耐腐蚀性、耐侵蚀性、耐久性好。

③ The coating has good corrosion resistance, corrosion resistance and durability.

④ 涂层具有防迷流的功能。

④ The coating can prevent stray current.

⑤ 除管片背面外,还应涂抹于接缝环形密封圈外侧的混凝土上。

⑤ In addition to the back of the segment, it shall also be applied to the concrete outside the ring seal of the joint.

管片外防水防腐涂层,除应涂抹于管片背面外,还应涂抹在环、纵面橡胶密封条外侧的混凝土上。但应指出,若管片制作质量高,采用抗侵蚀水泥,可不做外防水层。

The waterproof and anticorrosive coating outside the segment should not only be applied to the back of segment, but also to the concrete on the outer side of the ring and longitudinal rubber sealing strip. However, it should be pointed out that if the quality of segment is high and corrosion-resistant cement is used, the external waterproof layer may not be used.

(3)管片接缝处理

(3) Segment joint treatment

管片接缝防水是盾构法隧道防水的核心,分为密封、嵌缝和螺栓孔防水三种。根据使用目的不同,有时只采用密封,有时三种措施同时采用。

Waterproofing of segment joint is the core of waterproof of shield tunnel, which is divided into three types: sealing, caulking and bolt hole waterproof. According to different purposes of use, sometimes only sealing is used, sometimes three measures are used at the same time.

① 密封防水。

① Sealing waterproof.

密封防水是在管片接头表面进行喷涂或粘贴胶条的方法,胶条一般是橡胶止水带。橡胶止水带通常有遇水膨胀型和弹性密封型及两者结合型三种。遇水膨胀橡胶带是由可遇水膨胀的脂与合成橡胶混合而成,止水带与水接触后膨胀,填满管片间隙,并压紧管片,从而密封止水。弹性密封垫则是利用氯丁橡胶及三元乙丙等硬质橡胶制成,依靠本身的弹性密封止水。

Sealing waterproof refers to the method of spraying or pasting adhesive strips on the surface of segment joints. The adhesive strips are generally rubber waterstops. There are generally three types of rubber waterstops: water expansion type, elastic seal type and combination type. The water expansion rubber belt is composed of the grease that can expand in contact with water and synthetic rubber. The water stop belt expands after contacting with water, fills the gap between segments, and compresses the segments to seal the water stop. The elastic sealing type waterstop is made of neoprene, EPDM and other hard rubber and relies on its own elastic sealing.

② 嵌缝防水。

② Caulking waterproof.

对管片接缝部位施作嵌缝,特别是在止水条失效的部位施作嵌缝,是盾构法施工隧道防水有效而实用的一种办法。嵌缝防水指预先在管片的内侧边缘留有嵌缝槽,以后用嵌缝材料填塞。

It is an effective and practical method to caulk the segment joints, especially at the places where the waterstop bar fails. Caulking waterproof refers to reserving caulking groove at the inner edge of segment in advance, and then filling with caulking material.

嵌缝槽的形状要考虑拱顶嵌缝时,不致使填料堕落、流淌,其通常深度为20 mm、宽度为12 mm。嵌缝材料应具有良好的水密性、耐侵蚀性、收缩复原性、硬化时间短、收缩小、便于施工等特性。满足上述要求的材料有以环氧类、聚硫橡胶类、尿素树脂类为主的材料。

The shape of the caulking groove shall consider that the caulking of the vault will not cause the filler to fall and flow, and its depth is generally 20 mm and width is 12 mm. The caulking material shall have good water tightness, corrosion resistance, shrinkage recovery, short hardening time, small shrinkage, easy construction and other characteristics. The materials meeting the above requirements are mainly epoxy, polysulfide rubber and urea resin.

③ 螺栓孔与压浆孔防水。

③ The waterproof of bolt hole and grouting hole.

螺栓与螺栓孔或压浆孔之间的装配间隙是渗水的重要通道,所采取的防水措施就是用塑性(合成树脂类、石棉沥青或铅)和弹性(橡胶或聚氨酯水膨胀橡胶等)密封圈垫在螺栓和螺孔口之间,在拧紧螺栓时,密封圈受挤压变形充填在孔壁之间,达到止水效果。另一种防水方法是采用塑料螺栓孔套管,浇筑在混凝土预埋管片内,与密封圈结合起来使用,防水效果更佳,见图 1-43。

The assembly clearance between the bolt and the bolt hole or grouting hole is an important channel for water seepage. The waterproof measure taken is to use plastic (synthetic resin, asbestos asphalt or lead) and elastic (rubber or polyurethane water expansion rubber, etc.) sealing rings to pad between the bolt and the screw hole opening. When tightening the bolt, the sealing ring is squeezed and deformed and filled between the hole walls to achieve the water stop effect. Another waterproof method is to use plastic bolt hole casing, which is poured in the concrete embedded segment and used together with the seal ring, so the waterproof effect is better. See Figure 1-43.

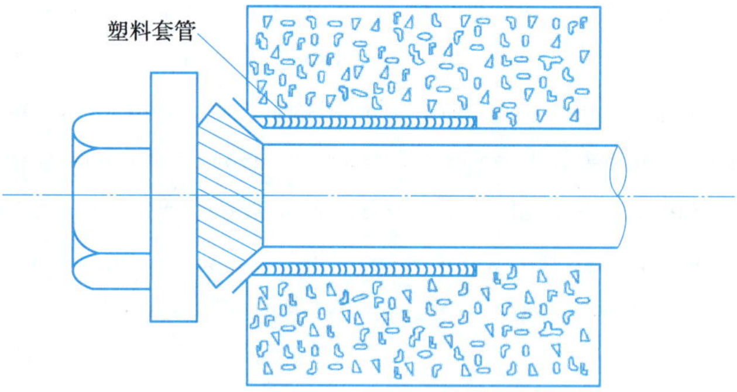

图 1-43 螺栓孔与压浆孔防水

Figure 1-43 Waterproofing of bolt hole and grouting hole

塑料套管:plastic bushing

密封圈应具有良好的伸缩性、水密性、耐螺栓拧紧力、耐老化等。为了提高防水效果,螺丝孔口可做成喇叭状。由于螺栓垫圈会产生蠕变而松弛,为了提高止水效果,有必要对螺栓进行二次拧紧。

The sealing ring shall have good scalability, water tightness, bolt tightening resistance, aging resistance, etc. In order to improve the waterproof effect, the screw hole can be made into a trumpet shape. As the bolt washer will creep and relax, it is necessary to tighten the bolt again to improve the water stop effect.

施工时螺栓位置偏于一边的现象经常发生,应予以充分的注意,必要时也可对螺栓孔进行注浆。

During construction, the phenomenon that the bolt position deviates to one side often occurs, which should be paid full attention to. If necessary, the bolt hole can also be grouted.

6. 联络通道的防水设计

6. Waterproof design of connecting passage

联络通道的防水措施如下:加强钢筋混凝土结构的抗裂、防渗能力,进一步提高其耐久性;以施工缝等接缝防水为重点,辅以附加防水层加强防水;允许对渗漏水进行引排。

Waterproof measures for connecting passage: Strengthen the crack resistance and seepage resistance of reinforced concrete structure, and improve its durability and self-waterproof; Focus on waterproof of construction joints and other joints, and add waterproof layer to strengthen waterproof; Drain the leakage water.

(1)混凝土自防水

(1) Self waterproofing of concrete

混凝土自防水要求采用高性能混凝土,混凝土抗渗等级应根据联络通道的具体埋深,按有关规定选定。暗挖法通道拱顶部分的混凝土浇筑困难,且浇筑结束后无法振捣,因此,在工程实践中,除了通过补注浆外,施工单位多采用无振捣(或自流平)混凝土。

High performance concrete is required to be used for self-waterproofing of concrete. The impermeability grade of concrete shall be determined according to the specific burial depth of connecting passage and relevant regulations. It is difficult to pour and vibrate the concrete at the arch crown of covered-excavation tunnel. Therefore, in engineering practice, in addition to supplementary grouting, non-vibrating (or self-leveling) concrete is mostly used by the construction organization.

(2)附加防水层

(2) Additional waterproof layer

塑料防水板加土工布(滤除泥沙)制成的外侧缓冲层与内侧保护层,组成外包复合防水层,如图 1-44 所示。在卷材内侧应预留疏水盲管,引流由于塑料防水板局部破损造成的渗漏水,避免对内衬结构造成损害。

The outer buffer layer and inner protective layer made of plastic waterproof board and geotextile (to filter sediment) form an outer composite waterproof layer, as shown in Figure 1-44. A drain blind pipe shall be reserved at the inner side of coiled material to drain the water leakage caused by the local damage of the plastic waterproof board, so as to avoid damage to the lining structure.

(3)联络通道的接缝防水

(3) Joint waterproofing of connecting passage

联络通道的施工缝防水关键是在通道结构与隧道钢管片之间的接缝。由于通道结构的钢

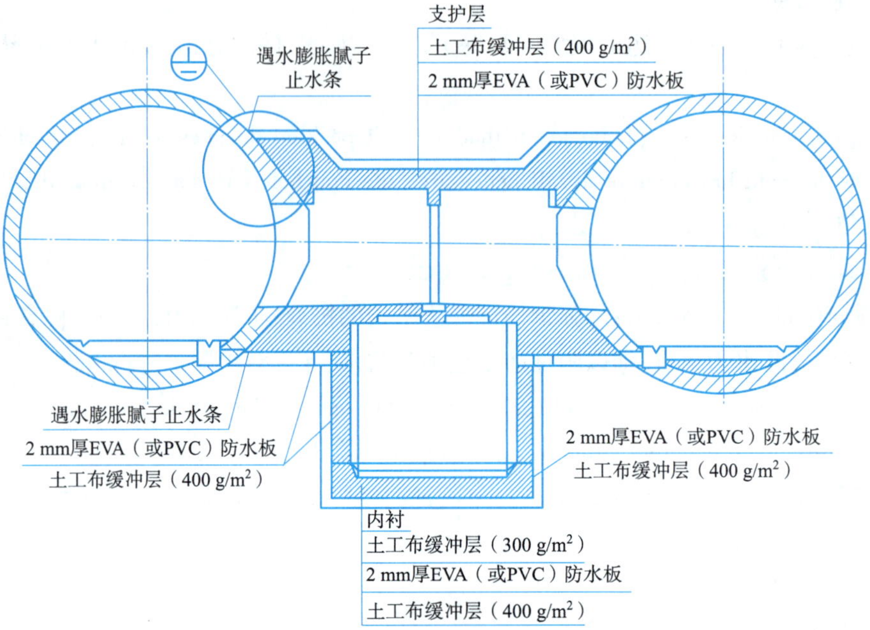

图 1-44　外侧全包防水示意图

Figure 1-44　Schematic diagram of outer all inclusive waterproofing

遇水膨胀腻子止水条:putty type Water swelling water stop strip

支护层:support layer

土工布缓冲层(400 g/m^2): geotextile buffer layer (400 g/m^2)

2 mm 厚 EVA(或 PVC) 防水板:2 mm thick EVA (or PVC) waterproof board

内衬:lining

筋与钢管片焊接连接,可以不考虑结构的变形,故可采用预埋注浆管,待结构稳定后,灌注亲水性环氧浆液止水防漏,同时也可补强结构。通道的初次衬砌钢管片的接缝也要采取防水措施,否则一旦渗漏,会给内衬结构的施工带来不良影响。这道止水仅为施工阶段服务,因此,采用遇水膨胀止水条或密封胶即可,如图 1-45 所示。

The key of construction joint waterproofing is connecting passage is the joint between passage structure and tunnel steel segment. The reinforcement and steel segment of passage structure are welded, the structure deformation can be ignored, so the embedded grouting pipe can be used. After the structure becomes stable, the hydrophilic epoxy slurry can be poured to prevent water leakage, and the structure can be reinforced at the same time. Waterproof measures should also be taken for the joints between primary lining steel segments of passage, or once the water leakage occurs, it will bring adverse effects to the lining structure construction. As a temporary waterproof measure during construction, the water swelling waterstop or sealant can be used, as shown in Figure 1-45.

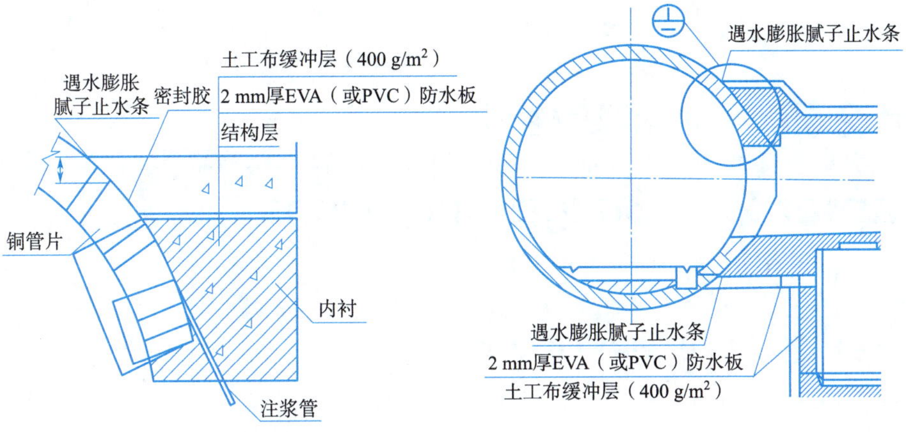

图 1-45　联络通道的接缝防水示意图

Figure 1-45　Schematic diagram of joint waterproofing of cross passage

密封胶：sealant　结构层：structural layer　钢管片：steel segment　注浆管：grouting pipe

课后练习
Exercises

1. 简述车辆限界、设备限界和建筑限界之间的关系。
1. Briefly describe the relationship between vehicle gauge, equipment gauge and construction gauge.
2. 桥隧限界多久检查一次？
2. How often is the bridge and tunnel gauge checked?
3. 简述桥梁的基本组成。
3. Briefly describe the basic composition of bridge.
4. 如何按受力体系划分桥梁类型？
4. How to divide the types of bridges based on the structural system?
5. 简述桥梁支座的作用。
5. Briefly describe the function of bridge bearings.
6. 隧道施工方法有哪些？
6. What methods are used for tunnel construction?
7. 简述隧道复合式衬砌的构造及各组成部分的作用。
7. Briefly describe the structure of tunnel composite lining and the function of each component.
8. 简述明挖法隧道结构的防水措施。
8. Briefly describe the waterproof measures of tunnel structure with open cut method.

第2章 桥梁作业

Chapter 2 Bridge Operations

学习目标 (Learning Objectives)

1. 能力目标

1. Capability objectives

(1)能够对桥梁设施常见病害的成因进行分析。

(1) Be able to analyze the causes of common diseases of bridge facilities.

(2)能够进行桥梁维修作业,并达到验收标准。

(2) Be able to carry out bridge maintenance operations and meet the acceptance standards.

2. 知识目标

2. Knowledge objectives

(1)掌握桥梁设施常见病害及成因。

(1) Master the common diseases of bridge facilities, and their causes.

(2)掌握桥梁维修作业操作流程及验收标准。

(2) Master the process and acceptance standards of bridge maintenance operations.

(3)熟悉桥梁维修养护管理的工作内容。

(3) Be familiar with the work contents of bridge maintenance management.

3. 素质目标

3. Quality objectives

(1)具有发现问题、解决问题的能力以及创新实践能力。

(1) Have the ability to find and solve problems as well as the ability to innovate and practice.

(2)遵守劳动纪律,具备质量意识、安全意识、团队精神和工匠精神。

(2) Abide by labor discipline and have quality awareness, safety awareness, team spirit and craftsmanship spirit.

(3)具备良好的身体素质,吃苦耐劳的工作态度以及忠于职守的工作作风。

(3) Have good physical quality, hard-working working attitude and loyal working style.

2.1 桥梁常见病害
2.1 Common diseases of bridge

2.1.1 伸缩缝的病害及成因
2.1.1 Diseases and causes of expansion joint

伸缩缝由于设置在梁端部构造薄弱部位，直接承受车辆荷载的反复作用又暴露于自然环境下，损坏原因可分为设计原因、施工原因、外部原因和养护原因，见表 2-1。

Expansion joint are set in the weak parts of beam ends, they directly suffer repeated vehicle loads and are exposed to natural environment. There are design causes, construction causes, external causes and maintenance causes, see Table 2-1.

表 2-1 伸缩缝损坏原因

类 别	描 述
设计原因	桥面板端部刚度不足； 伸缩缝装置本身刚度不足； 伸缩缝装置锚固构件的强度不够； 伸缩缝伸缩计算量错误； 后浇筑材料选择有误； 较大跨度桥梁或斜、弯桥梁的伸缩缝结构形式、固定方式与梁不吻合
施工原因	桥面板间伸缩间距的施工误差； 伸缩缝装置安装质量不好； 后浇筑材料施工质量不良； 桥面板施工质量不好； 伸缩缝安装时坑槽处理、清洗不彻底
外部原因	车轮荷载反复的冲击作用； 交通量增加、车辆荷载增大； 伸缩缝本身材料的老化及后浇筑材料老化； 接头前、后桥面凹凸不平； 支座、桥墩异常； 火灾、地震等异常事态的发生
养护原因	没有经常清除缝内的垃圾，养护不及时

Table 2-1 Damage causes of expansion joint

Category	Description
Design causes	The rigidity of the deck end is insufficient; The rigidity of the expansion joint device is insufficient; The anchor member strength of the expansion joint device is insufficient; Expansion calculation amount of expansion joint is wrong; Post pouring materials are incorrectly selected; The structural form and fixing method of expansion joint on large-span bridges or inclined and curved bridges are not consistent with the beams

continued

Category	Description
Construction causes	Construction error of expansion spacing between bridge decks; Poor installation quality of expansion joint device; Poor construction quality of post pouring materials; Poor construction quality of bridge deck; The pit treatment and cleaning are not thorough during the installation of expansion joint
External causes	Repeated impact of wheel load; Increase in traffic volume and vehicle load; Material aging of expansion joint itself and post pouring material; The bridge decks on both sides of the joint are uneven; Abnormal bearing and pier; Occurrence of abnormal events such as fires and earthquakes
Maintenance causes	The garbage in the joint is not regularly removed and the maintenance is not timely

伸缩缝的损坏形式见表2-2。

The damage forms of expansion joint see Table 2-2.

表2-2 伸缩缝的损坏形式

类　型	损坏形式
锌铁皮伸缩缝	① 软性防水材料，如沥青砂或聚氯乙烯胶泥等老化、脱落； ② 伸缩缝凹槽填入其他硬物，不能自由变形； ③ 锌铁皮上压填的铺装层如水泥混凝土或沥青混凝土等断裂、剥离； ④ 伸缩缝上后铺压填部分发生沉陷，高低不平； ⑤ 由于墩台下沉，出现异常的伸缩，车辆行驶时出现冲击及噪声
钢板伸缩缝	① 角钢与钢筋混凝土锚固不牢，使钢板松动，在车辆行驶时受到冲击振动，更加速了它的破损； ② 缝内塞进石块或铁夹物，使伸缩缝接头活动异常，不能自由变形； ③ 排水管发生破坏损坏或被土砂堵塞； ④ 表面钢板焊接部位破坏损伤； ⑤ 梳形钢板伸缩缝在梳齿与承托板的焊接处出现裂缝，更严重者出现剪断现象
橡胶伸缩缝	① 橡胶条破坏损伤； ② 橡胶条剥离； ③ 在橡胶嵌条连接部位漏水； ④ 锚固构件破损、锚固螺栓松脱； ⑤ 伸缩缝构造部位下陷或凸出； ⑥ 车辆行驶时不适，发生噪声

Table 2-2 Damage forms of expansion joint

Types	Damage forms
Zinc iron sheet expansion joint	① Soft waterproof materials such as asphalt sand or PVC mortar age and fall off; ② The grooves of expansion joint are filled with other hard objects and cannot be freely deformed; ③ The paving layer pressed on the zinc iron sheet, such as cement concrete or asphalt concrete, is broken and peeled off; ④ Settlement and unevenness of the back paving and filling part on expansion joint occurs; ⑤ Due to the sinking of piers, abnormal expansion and contraction appears, and impact and noise occurs when the vehicle is running.

continued

Types	Damage forms
Steel plate expansion joint	① The angle steel and reinforced concrete are not firmly anchored, which makes the steel plate loose. The vehicle is subjected to shock and vibration when driving, which accelerates its damage. ② Stones or iron inclusions get into joint, and the expansion joint cannot move normally and deform freely. ③ Drain pipes are damaged or blocked by soil and sand; ④ The welded part of steel plate surface is damaged; ⑤ The expansion joint of comb shaped steel plate is cracked or even cut at the weld between comb teeth and support plate
Rubber expansion joint	① Damage of rubber strips; ② Peeling of rubber strips; ③ Water leakage at the connection of rubber joint strip; ④ Damage of anchoring members and loosening of anchoring bolt; ⑤ Sinking and protruding of structural parts of expansion joint; ⑥ Noise caused by uncomfortable driving

2.1.2　支座的病害及成因
2.1.2　Diseases and causes of bearings

桥梁支座的病害包括支座本身的病害和支座垫块(板)的病害。

The diseases of bridge bearings mainly come from bearings itself and the bearing pads (plates).

1. 桥梁支座本身的病害
1. Diseases of bridge bearings

各种形式的支座,其本身状况不同,病害也不相同。

Various types of bearings have different diseases based on their different conditions.

① 钢支座的滑动面磨耗大、不平整,钢轴承有裂纹或切口,滚轴有偏移和下降。

① The sliding surface of the steel bearing is worn and uneven, the steel bearing has cracks or notches, and the roller has offset and descent.

② 支座螺母松动或螺栓脱落,支座地脚螺栓剪断。

② The nut is loose or the bolt falls off, and the anchor bolt is cut off.

③ 固定支座的固定锚栓剪断。

③ The fixed anchor bolt of the fixed bearing is cut off.

④ 活动支座不灵活或实际位移不正确。

④ The movable bearing is not flexible or the actual displacement is incorrect.

⑤ 钢辊轴式支座辊轴的实际纵向位移偏大或发生横向位移。

⑤ The actual longitudinal displacement of the roller shaft of the steel roller bearing is too large or lateral displacement occurs.

⑥ 橡胶支座出现橡胶老化、变质现象,梁丧失自由伸缩能力。

⑥ The bearing rubber is aged and deteriorated, and the beam loses free expansion and contraction capacity.

⑦ 橡胶支座纵向剪切变形或转角位移过大,超出最大规定值,支座损坏。

⑦ The longitudinal shear deformation or angular displacement of the rubber bearing is too large and exceed the maximum specified value, so that the bearing is damaged.

⑧ 支座脱空,尤其是板梁或异性板的橡胶支座脱空,造成脱空支座的偏移和梁体受力不均。

⑧ Bearing disjoint, especially the rubber bearing of plate beam or anisotropic plate, causes the deflection of the void bearing and uneven stress of the beam body.

⑨ 聚四氟乙烯支座或盆式橡胶支座的聚四氟乙烯板滑出支座,支座滑动干涩。

⑨ The PTFE plate of the PTFE bearing or the pot rubber bearing slides out of the bearing, and the bearing is hard to slide.

2. 桥梁支座垫块(板)的病害

2. Diseases of bridge bearing pads (plates)

① 桥梁支座的底板翘起、扭曲或者断裂。

① The bottom plate of the bridge bearing is warped, twisted or broken.

② 支座砂浆垫块裂缝。

② The mortar cushion block of the bearing cracks.

③ 桥梁支座座板混凝土压坏、剥离、掉角等。

③ The concrete of the bridge bearing plate is crushed, peeled off, and corner failure occurs.

桥梁支座损坏的原因是多方面的,既有设计方面的原因,也有施工缺陷、维修养护不够等原因,见表 2-3。

There are many causes for the damages of bridge bearings, including design causes, construction defects, insufficient maintenance and other reasons, see Table 2-3.

表 2-3 桥梁支座损坏原因一览表

损坏原因	具体内容
设计时缺乏足够的考虑	形式的选定与布置错误; 材料选定错误,或者施工没有按要求执行; 支座边缘距离不够; 支座支承垫块加强钢筋不足; 对螺栓、螺母等的脱离估计不够
施工制作时不完备	铸件等材料质量较差; 金属支座的油漆、防腐防锈处理不可靠; 砂浆填充不可靠,或者水泥砂浆强度不足
维修、养护、管理不善	滑动面、滚动面夹杂尘埃、异物; 因防水、排水装置的缺陷,向支座漏、溢水,使支座锈蚀; 螺母、螺栓松动、脱落,又没有及时修理
其他因素	桥台、桥墩产生的不均匀沉陷、倾斜与水平变位以及上部结构位移,影响支座的正常使用

Table 2-3 Damage cause of bridge bearings

Damage causes	Specific contents
Lack of adequate consideration in design	The selection and arrangement of bearing is improper; The material is wrongly selected, or the construction is not carried out as required; The bearing edge distance is insufficient; The reinforcing steels in the bearing pad are insufficient; The separation of bolts and nuts is not fully considered
Incomplete construction	Poor quality of castings and other materials; The paint, anti-corrosion and anti-rust treatment of metal bearings are unreliable; Mortar filling is not full, or the strength of cement mortar is insufficient
Poor repair, maintenance, management	The sliding surface and rolling surface is mixed with dust and foreign objects; Due to the defects of waterproof and drainage devices, water seeps into bearings, which results in the bearing corrosion; The nuts and bolts are loose and fall off, and can not be repaired in time
Other factors	The uneven subsidence, inclination and horizontal displacement of bridge abutments and piers, as well as the superstructure displacement, affect the normal use of bearings

2.1.3 混凝土梁的病害及成因

2.1.3 Diseases and causes of concrete beams

混凝土梁式桥的主要病害表现为混凝土梁体式桥裂缝和钢筋锈蚀。混凝土的缺陷最主要的是裂缝,同时还包括蜂窝、麻面、孔洞、露筋、剥落、白化、层析、保护层厚度不够等表层缺陷。钢筋锈蚀则主要是普通钢筋锈蚀、预应力钢筋锈蚀和预应力锚具锈蚀等。

The common diseases of concrete beam bridges are the cracks of concrete beams and the corrosion of steel bars. The main defects of concrete are cracks, but also surface defects such as voids, pits, holes, reinforcement exposure, spalling, efflorescence, delamination and insufficient thickness of protective layer. The corrosion of steel bars mainly comes from ordinary steel bars, prestressed steel bars and prestressed anchor.

混凝土梁式桥长期暴露在自然环境中,受各种因素的影响,病害逐步产生和发展。人为因素主要是超高车辆或船只撞击主梁、超载造成主梁产生裂缝;自然环境中的酸性废气、二氧化碳、较大的湿度和的雨水等造成混凝土的退化和钢筋的锈蚀。

Concrete beam bridges are exposed to the natural environment for a long time. Under the influence of various factors, diseases are gradually generated and developed. Human factors include over-high vehicles or cracks in the main beam caused by ships hitting and overloading. Besides, acid waste gas, carbon dioxide, high humidity and excessive rain in the environment cause concrete degradation and steel corrosion.

导致混凝土梁式桥产生缺陷的原因不是单一的,而是由一个因素诱发、多个因素促进发展的过程。同时,各种病害相互影响、相互促进、共同伴生。在发现混凝土梁式桥出现缺陷后,必须及时对缺陷进行调查研究,分析缺陷产生的原因、现状、发展趋势,以及桥梁遭受破坏的程度,对运营使用的影响等,以便及时采取相应措施。

The reason for concrete beam bridge defects is not single, but a process induced by one factor and promoted by multiple factors. At the same time, various diseases interact, promote and coexist with each other. After discovering defects in concrete bridges, it is necessary to investigate and study the defects in time, and analyze the causes, status, trends of defects, the damage degree to the bridges, and the impact on operation, so as to take corresponding measures.

钢筋混凝土及预应力混凝土桥的各种病害表现有：

Various diseases of reinforced concrete and prestressed concrete bridges are as follows:

① 裂缝。

① Cracks.

② 钢筋及预应力钢筋锈蚀。

② Corrosion of steel bars and prestressing bars.

③ 混凝土剥落、剥离。

③ Concrete spalling and peeling.

④ 混凝土层析。

④ Concrete delamination.

⑤ 混凝土蜂窝。

⑤ Concrete voids.

⑥ 混凝土白化(钙化)。

⑥ Concrete efflorescence (calcification).

⑦ 保护层厚度不足。

⑦ Insufficient protective layer thickness.

⑧ 混凝土碳化。

⑧ Concrete carbonization.

⑨ 膨胀性集料反应。

⑨ Expansive aggregate reaction.

⑩ 构件撞损。

⑩ Damaged components.

⑪ 梁体变位与变形。

⑪ Beam displacement and deformation.

在上述病害现象中，裂缝及钢筋锈蚀以目视检测为主，其中，裂缝是导致构件失效的主要特征。检测时，可依据裂缝类型及尺寸(结合历史记录的对比结果)，大略了解构件退化的原因及程度。当难以用目视判断原因时，可利用非破坏性检测或其他方法进一步诊断。钢筋锈蚀将造成钢筋断面减少、强度降低并伴随混凝土体积膨胀，最终导致混凝土产生裂缝并将减少钢筋与混凝土间的握裹力。

Among the above-mentioned diseases, cracks and steel corrosion is mainly detected by visual inspection, and cracks are the main feature leading to component failure. During inspection, the cause and degree of component degradation can be roughly understood based on the type and size of cracks (combined with the comparison results of historical records). When it is difficult to determine the cause visually, non-destructive testing or other methods can be used for further diagnosis. Reinforcement corrosion will reduce the section and strength of reinforcement and accompany with the volume expansion of concrete, which will eventually lead to cracks in the concrete and reduce the bond stress between steel bars and concrete.

1. 混凝土表层病害

1. Diseases of concrete surface

对于混凝土桥梁,某一缺陷在各种因素的影响下会日益恶化,如蜂窝、麻面,由于水的渗入,出现混凝土材料恶化,引起钢筋锈蚀,见表 2-4。在产生钢筋锈蚀物过程中伴随体积膨胀,又导致混凝土表面产生锈蚀裂缝,形成恶性循环。

For concrete bridges, a certain defect will deteriorate under the influence of various factors. Take voids and pits as an example, water seeps into the concrete and makes concrete deterioration and reinforcement corrosion, as shown in Table 2-4. In the process of producing rebar rust, the volume expansion will lead to corrosion cracks on the concrete surface, and finally form a vicious cycle.

表 2-4　混凝土表层病害一览表

病害形式	具体内容
蜂窝	混凝土局部疏松,砂浆少,石子多,石子之间出现空隙,形成蜂窝状孔洞
麻面	混凝土表面局部缺浆、粗糙,或有许多小凹坑,但无钢筋外露现象
孔洞	混凝土内部有空隙,局部没有混凝土,蜂窝特别大的现象常发生在钢筋密集处或预留孔洞和预埋件处
露筋	主梁受到意外撞击造成混凝土崩落,使得钢筋外露
剥落	混凝土表面水泥砂浆流失,造成粗集料外露的现象,严重者造成粗集料松脱,一般发生在混凝土表层品质较差的部位,一般不会很深
白化	又称为游离石灰,是由内部渗出、附在混凝土构件表面的附着物,通常为呈白色的石灰类附着物
层析	构件受氯气或盐水侵袭,构件内的钢筋锈蚀体积膨胀,导致钢筋与外层钢筋附近的混凝土分离

Table 2-4　Diseases of concrete surface

Types of diseases	Specific contents
Voids	Concrete is locally loose with less mortar and more stones, and voids appear between stones and look like honeycomb holes
Pits	The concrete surface is partially lack of grout and rough, or there are many small pits, but no reinforcement is exposed
Holes	There are voids in the concrete, and there is even no concrete in some parts. The honeycomb is particularly large at the places where the reinforcement is closely spaced or at the reserved holes and embedded parts
Reinforcement exposure	Accidental impacts on the main beam cause the collapse of concrete, leaving the steel bars exposed
Spalling	The loss of cement mortar on the concrete surface causes the exposure of coarse aggregates, and in severe cases, the coarse aggregates are loosened, which generally occurs on the concrete surface of poor quality

continued

Types of disease	Specific contents
Efflorescence	Also known as free lime, it is an attachment that seeps out from the interior and adheres to the concrete member surface, usually a white lime attachment
Delamination	Under the attack of chlorine or salt water, the reinforcement in the member is corroded and expanded, which breaks the bonding between the steel and surrounding concrete

2. 混凝土梁式桥典型裂缝

2. Typical cracks in concrete beam bridges

混凝土梁式桥损伤开裂的原因复杂多样。一是混凝土材料退化损伤引起的裂缝,如混凝土碳化、有害物质的侵蚀、碱集料反应、钢筋锈蚀等原因引起混凝土开裂;二是施工过程中引起的裂缝,如混凝土水化热产生的温度应力,混凝土结硬过程中的收缩、干缩,支架不均匀沉降,模板变形,原材料质量及施工质量问题;三是设计方法及构造上的不合理引起的裂缝,如结构计算内力与实际内力不符,构造设计不合理,计算荷载考虑不全面,设计与施工方法综合考虑不周等原因;四是使用阶段引起的裂缝,由于超载运营、车辆撞击、桥梁维护不当等原因引起混凝土的开裂。

The reasons for damage cracking of concrete beam bridges are complex and diverse. Reason 1: Cracks as a result of concrete deterioration, such as concrete carbonization, erosion of harmful substances, alkali-aggregate reaction, corrosion of steel bars, etc. Reason 2: Cracks during construction, such as temperature stress caused by heat of hydration in concrete, shrinkage and drying shrinkage during concrete hardening, uneven settlement of support, formwork deformation, bad quality of raw materials and poor construction. Reason 3: Cracks as a result of bad design detailing, such as discrepancy between the calculated internal force of structure and the actual internal force, lack of comprehensive consideration for calculated loads, design without full consideration of construction methods. Reason 4: Cracks in use: overloaded operation, vehicle collisions, and improper bridge maintenance, etc.

混凝土开裂原因总结归纳如下:

The reasons for concrete cracking are summarized as follows:

① 车辆超载而产生梁体底部弯曲开裂和剪切开裂。

① Bending cracks and shear cracks at the bottom of the beam due to vehicle overload.

② 墩台的不均匀沉陷所引起的裂缝。

② Cracks caused by uneven settlement of piers.

③ 支座失效引起梁的附加应力,由此产生裂缝。

③ Cracks caused by the additional stress of beam which comes from the bearing failure.

④ 混凝土施工养护不善而引起的干缩开裂或层裂。

④ Shrinkage cracking or spalling caused by poor concrete construction and maintenance.

⑤ 水灰比和振捣不实而产生的梁体收缩裂缝。

⑤ Shrinkage cracks in beams caused by improper water-cement ratio and vibration.

⑥ 温度变化或者冻融效应产生的裂缝。

⑥ Cracks caused by temperature changes or freeze-thaw effects.

⑦ 大体积混凝土浇筑时,水泥水化反应导致的自体收缩裂缝。

⑦ Self-shrinkage cracks caused by cement hydration reaction during large-volume concrete pouring.

⑧ 施工接缝处混凝土龄期不同产生的裂缝。

⑧ Cracks caused by different ages of concrete at construction joints.

⑨ 强风或地震等外在环境冲击力导致的裂缝。

⑨ Cracks caused by external environment impact such as strong wind or earthquake.

⑩ 钢筋锈蚀膨胀导致裂缝。

⑩ Cracks caused by corrosion and expansion of steel bars.

⑪ 预应力锚固区的局部高应力产生的裂缝。

⑪ Cracks caused by local high stress in the prestressed anchorage area.

⑫ 在徐变等材料本质特性的共同作用下，混凝土的拉力与剪力和钢筋握裹力抵消后的净拉力或剪切作用力大于混凝土材料的抗拉力或抗剪强度所致。

⑫ Under the combined action of the material essential characteristics, such as creep, when the net tension or shear force offset by the tensile force of concrete, shear force and steel bond strength is greater than the tensile or shear strength of concrete, cracking occurs.

⑬ 梁刚度不足，产生过大挠度，引起裂缝。

⑬ The excessive deflection owing to the insufficient beam rigidity cause cracking.

裂缝类型可以分为结构裂缝与非结构裂缝两种。

There are two types of cracks: structural cracks and non-structural cracks.

(1)结构裂缝

(1) Structural cracks

结构裂缝由静荷载及活荷载所造成。结构裂缝的类型包括弯曲裂缝及剪力裂缝。剪力裂缝一般发生于主梁支点附近的梁腹底部；弯曲裂缝发生于构件最大拉应力区，呈垂直状，往压力区发展。一般在构件跨中底部，如梁底或桥面板底，或连续梁在桥墩处的梁体上部，最易发现弯曲裂缝。

Structural cracks are caused by static and live loads. Types of structural cracks include bending cracks and shear cracks. Shear cracks generally occur at the bottom of beam web near the main beam support. Bending cracks occur in the maximum tensile stress zone of member, which is vertical and develops to the pressure zone. Generally, bending crack is most easily found at the mid-span bottom of members, such as beams or decks, or in the upper part of continuous beams at the pier.

(2)非结构裂缝

(2) Non-structural cracks

非结构裂缝虽不影响构件的安全，但如果裂缝深入构件内部，也可能损及构件。非结构裂缝类型有：

They will not affect the safety of members, but if the crack penetrate into the member, it may damage the member. The types of non-structural cracks are as follows:

① 温度裂缝。温度高低变化引起的热胀冷缩裂缝。

① Temperature cracks. Thermal expansion and contraction cracks caused by changes in temperature.

② 干缩裂缝。混凝土养护期间造成的收缩，一般发生于预应力梁的梁腹。

② Shrinkage cracks. Due to shrinkage during concrete curing, generally occurs in the web of prestressed beams.

③ 大体积裂缝。浇筑大体积混凝土后，混凝土内外部温差造成的裂缝。

③ Cracks in mass concrete. Cracks caused by the difference in temperature between inside and outside of concrete after pouring mass concrete.

④ 施工缝裂缝。施工缝是混凝土施工无法避免的情形，施工缝处裂缝将随时间增加而使钢筋锈蚀，并扩大裂缝。施工缝附近，因混凝土龄期不同或不等量收缩，使此处密实性较差，腐蚀因子较易侵入，扩大缝隙。施工缝裂缝一般为应力裂缝，造成钢筋锈蚀范围也较广，也可能造成构件退化。常见施工缝裂缝之处，有预应力梁与现浇桥面板间，桥梁护栏与桥面板间，箱梁底板与腹板间，预制预应力梁与现浇横隔梁间。

④ Construction joint cracks. Construction joints are unavoidable in concrete construction. Cracks at construction joints will increase over time, causing steel corrosion and expand cracks. Due to the different age of concrete or unequal shrinkage, the concrete in the vicinity of construction joint is not well compacted, and corrosives are easy to invade into it and make crakes bigger. The cracks of construction joints are generally stress cracks, which cause a wide range of steel corrosion and may also cause component degradation. Construction joint cracks often occur at these junctions, such as prestressed beams and cast-in-situ bridge decks, bridge guardrails and bridge decks, box girder bottom plates and webs, prefabricated prestressed beams and cast-in-situ diaphragms.

⑤ 钢筋锈蚀裂缝。钢筋生锈后体积膨胀，推挤混凝土，产生裂缝或扩大裂缝。

⑤ Steel corrosion cracks. The volume expansion of the steel after rusting will push the concrete to produce cracks or expand cracks.

混凝土板桥常在跨中出现横向裂缝，支点附近出现斜向裂缝，板底出现纵向裂缝。产生裂缝的原因是正应力、剪应力和横向应力过大。整体式板桥横向配筋少是导致板底出现纵向裂缝的主要原因。装配式空心板桥由于横向铰缝构造薄弱，在车辆荷载反复作用下造成铰缝破坏，形成单板受力状态。由于板的跨中正应力和支点附近的剪应力过大，导致混凝土开裂，如图 2-1 所示。

Concrete slab bridges often have transverse cracks in the mid-span, oblique cracks near the fulcrum, and longitudinal cracks at the bottom of slab. Excessive normal stress, shear stress and transverse stress causes cracks. The lack of transverse reinforcement in the integral slab bridge results in the longitudinal cracks at the bottom of slab. Due to the weak structure of the transverse hinge joints on fabricated hollow slab bridges, the hinge joints are damaged at the effect of repeat traffic loading, forming single slab bearing. Concrete cracks due to excessive mid-span normal stress of slab and excessive shear stress near the support, as shown in Figure 2-1.

装配式混凝土肋梁桥常出现跨中梁底横向裂缝和支点附近斜向裂缝，而梁片间横向连接薄弱导致单梁受力是出现受力裂缝的主要原因。

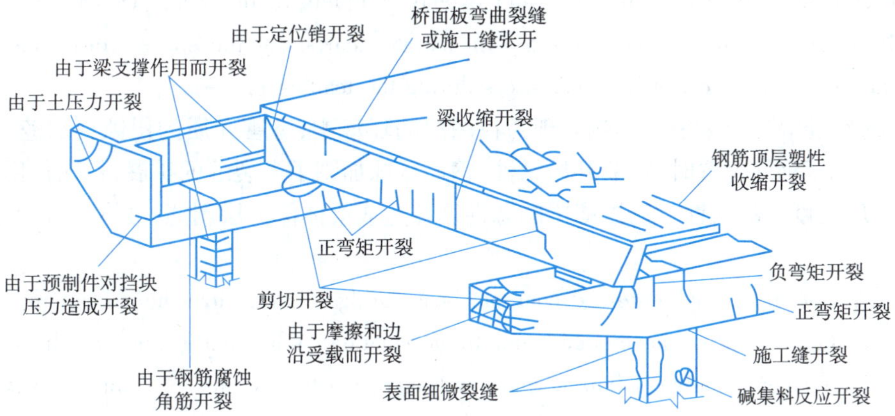

图 2-1　混凝土桥梁的各种裂缝形态

Figure 2-1　Cracks of concrete bridges

由于土压力开裂:cracking due to earth pressure

由于梁支撑作用而开裂:cracking due to supporting the beam

由于定位销开裂:cracking due to dowel pin

桥面板弯曲裂缝或施工缝张开:bending cracking of bridge deck or construction join to opening

梁收缩开裂:shrinkage cracking of beam

钢筋顶层塑性收缩开裂:plastic shrinkage cracking in the top layer of reinforcement

由于预制件对挡块压力造成开裂:cracking of stops due to the pressure from prefabricated parts

由于钢筋腐蚀角筋开裂:cracking of corner bars due to steel corrosion

剪切开裂:shear cracking

由于摩擦和边沿受载而开裂:cracking due to friction and edge loading

表面细微裂缝:fine cracks on the surface

负弯矩开裂:cracking due to negative moment

正弯矩开裂:cracking due to positive moment

施工缝开裂:cracking due to construction joints

碱集料反应开裂:cracking due to alkali aggregate reaction

The transverse cracks at the beam bottom of midspan and the oblique cracks near the support often occur in prefabricated concrete rib bridges. The weak transverse connection between beams leads to the single beam bearing and causes cracks.

混凝土箱梁桥常在桥跨跨中附近的腹板出现竖向裂缝并沿底板横向扩展;在桥跨支点附近,腹板出现45°方向的斜裂缝并沿顶板横向扩展。在跨中梁段范围内,顶板底面出现相互平行的纵向裂缝;底板内侧靠近腹板处出现纵向裂缝并向腹板斜向扩展。引起箱梁各部位开裂的主要原因就是箱梁空间应力状态分析不准确、设计存在缺点,箱梁受载过程中局部应力过大引起混凝土开裂。

For concrete box girder bridges, vertical cracks often appear in the web near the mid span and spread transversely along the bottom plate. Near the support of girder, 45° inclined cracks appear in the web and extend transversely along the top plate. Within the midspan beam segment, longitudinal cracks parallel to each other appear on the bottom of top plate, and longitudinal cracks appear at the inner side of bottom plate near the web and extend obliquely to the web. The main reasons for various cracks of box girder components are inaccurate analysis of the space stress state and bad design detailing, and the excessive local stress during the loading process.

裂缝对钢筋混凝土梁桥的影响表现为在潮湿的环境中,有害介质的侵蚀会加速混凝土的碳化。当碳化至钢筋位置时,钢筋开始锈蚀,钢筋锈蚀加剧了微裂缝的扩展,长期作用下,降低了梁的强度、刚度及耐久性。锈蚀膨胀的恶性循环造成梁体保护层剥落,最终导致梁体的彻底破坏。

The effect of cracks on reinforced concrete beam bridges is that in a humid environment, the erosion of harmful media will accelerate concrete carbonation. When carbonation reach the depth of the steel reinforcement, the steel bars corrode and aggravate the expansion of micro-cracks, which reduces the strength, stiffness and durability of the beam under long-term action. The vicious cycle of corrosion and expansion causes the beam protective layer to peel off, which eventually leads to total destruction.

裂缝对预应力混凝土桥梁危害更大,我国相关规范规定,全预应力混凝土桥梁不允许带裂缝工作。预应力混凝土梁桥中的预应力钢筋处于高应力工作状态。当长期暴露于大气环境中,在一定的温度、湿度及有害介质的作用下,极易在钢筋的表面发生电化学反应,在一定环境条件下可能发生应力腐蚀,在有氢离子的参与下发生氢脆现象,从而导致预应力钢筋在低应力状态下发生脆断,造成混凝土桥梁结构突然破坏,且破坏前无任何征兆,危害性极大。

Cracks are more harmful to prestressed concrete bridges. According to relevant regulations of China, fully prestressed concrete bridges are not allowed to work with cracks. The prestressed reinforcement in the prestressed concrete beam bridge is in a high stress working state. When it is exposed to the atmospheric environment for a long time, electrochemical reaction is easily produced on the reinforcement surface under the actions of certain temperature, humidity and harmful media, stress corrosion may occur under specific circumstances, and hydrogen embrittlement may occur in the presence of hydrogen ions. As a result, the prestressed steel bars are brittle under low stress conditions and lead to sudden failure of concrete bridge structure. For there is no sign before the destruction, it is extremely dangerous.

因此,裂缝对混凝土梁式桥的影响体现在两个方面:一是对桥梁使用性能的影响。开裂使桥梁刚度降低,变形增大,跨中挠度超标,继而影响桥梁的正常使用,严重的开裂问题导致桥梁承载力下降,直至影响桥梁的安全使用。二是对桥梁的耐久性及使用寿命的影响。裂缝会加速混凝土碳化和钢筋锈蚀,钢筋锈蚀又加速了裂缝的进一步扩展,造成桥梁使用性能趋于恶化,耐久性下降,使用寿命缩短。

Therefore, Cracks have two effects on concrete beam bridges. First, cracks have an effect on the service performance of bridges. Cracking reduces the rigidity, increases the deformation, and make the mid-span deflection exceed the standard, which in turn affects the normal use of bridge. The serious cracking even leads to a decrease in the bearing capacity of the bridge and affects the safe use of bridge. Second, cracks have an effect on the durability and service life of bridge. Cracks will accelerate the carbonization of concrete and the corrosion of steel bars. The corrosion of reinforcement accelerates the further expansion of cracks, resulting in the deterioration of bridge performance, durability and service life.

3. 钢筋及预应力钢筋的锈蚀病害

3. Corrosion of steel bars and prestressed bars

对于预应力混凝土构件,一般要求正常运营状态下不出现裂缝,钢筋和预应力钢筋一般不易锈蚀,但是由于施工和严重超载,锈蚀也会发生但不易发现,一旦发现锈蚀时,则该构件已呈严重损坏状态。所以在桥梁检测时,钢筋锈蚀为检测重点之一,需要进行较为详细的记录。

For prestressed concrete components, it is generally required that no cracks appear under the normal operation. Steel bars and prestressed steel bars are generally not easy to corrode. However, due to construction and severe overloading, corrosion will also occur but it is not easy to find. Once corrosion is found, the component has been severely damaged state. Therefore, during the inspection, steel bars corrosion is one of the key points, and it is necessary to record in more detail.

钢筋锈蚀使混凝土因承受拉力而裂开,钢筋暴露于大气中,又加速了生锈,进而造成外层混凝土剥落。受力主筋锈蚀后,钢筋横断面积减少,主梁的承载能力急剧下降,严重影响结构物的安全。

Steel bar corrosion causes the concrete cracks due to the tensile force. The steel bar is exposed to the atmosphere, which accelerates rusting and in turn causes the outer concrete to peel off. After the main reinforcement is corroded, the cross-sectional area of the reinforcement decreases, which makes the bearing capacity of main beam decrease sharply and affects the structure safety seriously.

综上所述,造成钢筋锈蚀的主要内在原因有:一是钢筋受湿气及氧气的作用;二是混凝土中性化;三是钢筋表面氯离子含量高。造成钢筋锈蚀的主要外在原因有:一是混凝土构件开裂;二是主梁受损,混凝土剥落;三是施工时预留保护层太薄,混凝土碳化深度较大;四是后张预应力的灌浆和封锚不合格,导致锚下积水或空洞。

To sum up, the main internal reasons for steel bar corrosion are: first, moisture and oxygen; second, neutralization of concrete; third, high chloride ion on the steel bar surface. The main external reasons for steel bar corrosion are: first, cracking of concrete components; second, damage of main beam and spalling of concrete; third, thin reserved protective layer during construction and great carbonization depth of concrete is large; fourth, unqualified grouting and anchor sealing, which results in water accumulation or voids under the anchor.

钢筋锈蚀可分为两种情况:一种是混凝土开裂后导致的钢筋锈蚀,即先裂后锈;一种是因为保护层太薄或露筋而引起的钢筋锈蚀。钢筋锈蚀体积膨胀导致混凝土开裂或表面混凝土成块脱落,即先锈后裂。主梁一般先裂后锈,混凝土保护层保护作用失去后,锈蚀很容易发展。而先锈后裂的情况较少,常出现在附属结构上,如防撞墙等。

Steel bar corrosion can be divided into two cases. One is the steel corrosion caused by concrete cracking, that is, first cracking and then rusting; One is steel corrosion caused by too thin protective layer or exposed reinforcement. Volume expansion of corroded steel bars cause concrete cracking or falling off of surface concrete in blocks, that is, first rusting and then cracking. Generally, the main beam cracks before rusting, and the rust is easy to develop after losing the protective effect of concrete protective layer. However, there are few cases of rust before cracking, which often occur in ancillary structures, such as anti-collision walls.

梁体混凝土在二氧化碳、氧气、湿度、温度、有害气体、化学侵蚀、物理作用等因素的影响下,首先使混凝土发生碳化,导致保护层破坏,水汽侵入,进而造成钢筋的锈蚀,而钢筋锈蚀又会造成混凝土的劣化与开裂,使梁体结构产生病害,影响桥梁结构的耐久性和使用寿命。随着桥梁结构损伤程度的不断发展,最终导致桥梁结构的整体破坏。

Under the influence of carbon dioxide, oxygen, humidity, temperature, harmful gas, chemical erosion, physical action and other factors, the concrete of beam is first carbonized, which leads to the destruction of protective layer and the intrusion of water vapor, and in turn causes the corrosion of steel bars. It will cause the deterioration and cracking of the concrete, make the beam structure suffer from disease, and affect the durability and service life of bridge structure. With the development of bridge structure damage, it will eventually lead to the overall damage of bridge structure.

2.1.4 钢结构锈蚀

2.1.4 Corrosion of steel structure

钢梁、钢塔架、钢拱肋、人行道支架、限高防护架等都应进行保护涂装,防止钢结构锈蚀。钢结构涂装失效后,应对钢结构表面进行重新涂装或维护性涂装,延长使用寿命。钢结构保护涂装在钢桥维修中占有重要地位,特大桥钢梁的保护涂装工作,一般要占全部维修工作量的50%左右。

Steel beams, steel towers, steel arch ribs, sidewalk supports, height-limiting protective frames, etc. should be protected and painted to prevent corrosion of steel structures. After the failure of steel structure coating, the steel structure surface should be re-painted or maintenance-painted to prolong its service life. Steel structure protective coating plays an important role in the maintenance of steel bridges. The steel girder protective coating of long-span bridges generally accounts for about 50% of the total maintenance work.

1. 钢结构锈蚀的原因

1. Causes of steel structure corrosion

钢结构锈蚀主要是钢铁受到大气中所含的氧气、水分、盐类、二氧化碳、二氧化硫、氮的氧化物等酸性物质及具有化学活泼性物质的作用,发生化学的或电化学作用的结果。这种现象,我们称为钢铁的腐蚀。这些变化在钢铁表面产生的松散堆积物[Fe_2O_3、$Fe(OH)_3$],通常叫作铁锈。

Steel structure corrosion is mainly the result of chemical or electrochemical action when steel suffers oxygen, moisture, salt, carbon dioxide, sulfur dioxide, nitrogen oxides and other acidic substances and chemically active substances contained in the atmosphere. We call this phenomenon steel corrosion. These changes produce loose deposits [Fe_2O_3、$Fe(OH)_3$] on the steel surface, which is commonly called rust.

钢铁腐蚀分为两种:化学性腐蚀和电化学腐蚀。

Steel corrosion is divided into two types: chemical corrosion and electrochemical corrosion.

2. 钢结构锈蚀的危害性

2. Harmfulness of steel structure corrosion

钢结构锈蚀的危害性主要表现在以下几方面:

Steel structure corrosion has the main following dangers:

① 钢梁杆件断面削弱。

① The section of steel beam member is weakened.

② 钢结构联结松弛。

② Connection of steel structure is loosened.

③ 降低钢结构的承载能力。

③ The bearing capacity of steel structure is reduced.

④ 缩短钢结构的使用年限。

④ The service life of steel structure is shortened.

⑤ 钢结构锈蚀严重者,将危及行车安全。

⑤ The steel structures which are seriously corroded will endanger the driving safety.

3. 钢梁容易锈蚀的部位

3. Parts of steel beam easy to rust

① 有氧化皮处。

① Parts with scales.

② 钢梁上盖板。

② Cover plates on steel beam.

③ 缝隙及角落隐藏处。

③ Hidden places such as gaps and corners.

④ 有害气体及电解溶液反复侵蚀处。

④ Places repeatedly eroded by harmful gas and electrolytic solution.

⑤ 易积水和污物处。

⑤ Ponding and dirty places.

⑥ 已有锈蚀处。

⑥ Places where there is existing rust.

⑦ 施工不良处。

⑦ Places with construction defects.

4. 防止钢结构锈蚀的主要方法

4. Main methods to prevent steel structure corrosion

防止钢结构锈蚀的方法,目前广泛采用的是喷涂油漆。有时也配合以喷镀金属(如喷锌)或磷化处理(磷酸盐保护膜)等,以增强其防护能力。油漆防锈的基本原理,是使钢料与气体和水分等介质隔绝,避免化学腐蚀和电化学腐蚀的产生,从而达到防锈的目的。

The method to prevent steel structure corrosion is currently widely used by spraying paint. Sometimes it is also combined with metal spray coating (such as zinc spraying) or phosphating treatment (phosphate protective film) to enhance its protective ability. The paint will prevent the steel from gas and moisture and other media to avoid chemical corrosion and electrochemical corrosion, so as to achieve the purpose of rust prevention.

此外,防止钢梁锈蚀的方法还有:选择耐候、耐腐蚀的合金钢;钢料表面喷镀锡、铭、铝等金属;用化学处理钢料表面,如氧化、铭化等;钢料表面喷镀塑料、搪瓷;采用阳极保护等。但这些方法有的价格昂贵,有的施工复杂,对桥梁这样的大型建筑物是不适宜的。

In addition, the methods to prevent the steel beam corrosion include: selecting weather-resistant and corrosion-resistant alloy steel; spraying tin, inscription, aluminum and other metals on the steel surface; chemical treatment of steel surface, such as oxidation, inscription, etc.; spraying steel surface with plastic or enamel; anodized protection. However, some of these methods are expensive, and some are complicated to operate, which are not suitable for large buildings such as bridges.

5. 漆膜失效状态及检查鉴定方法

5. Paint failure state and identification methods

漆膜粉化、露底、裂纹、剥落、吐锈等都是失效的现象。漆膜失效的检查鉴定方法如下:

Chalking, exposure bottom, cracks, flaking, rust, etc. are all failure phenomena. The inspection and identification methods of paint failure are as follows:

(1)肉眼观察

(1) Visual observation

明显的面漆粉化、露底或龟裂、起泡、剥落、锈蚀等是容易发现的,但细小的裂纹及针尖状的吐锈等不容易被发现,可借助放大镜检查。另外,如漆膜表面有不正常的鼓起(角落部位用光照射有凹凸不平时),下面可能有锈蚀。

Obvious topcoat chalking, exposed bottom or crazing cracks, blistering, flaking, rust, etc. are easy to inspect. However, for fine cracks and needle-like rust which is not easy to find can be inspected with a magnifying glass. In addition, if there are abnormal bulges on the paint surface (the corners are uneven when irradiated with light), there may be rust below.

(2)用手触摸

(2) Touch by hand

用手指揩擦漆膜表面,如有粉末沾手,表示漆膜粉化。对角落隐蔽部位如手摸感到粗糙,凹凸不平,可能有锈蚀存在。

Wipe the paint surface with fingers. If there is powder on your hands, it means that the paint is chalked up. If the corners and hidden parts feel rough and uneven, they may be rust.

(3)刮膜检验

(3) Inspection by scraping

对有怀疑的部位,铲除表面漆膜检查钢料是否锈蚀;对有脱皮处,可用刮刀检查其失效范围。如用刮刀铲起漆膜,漆膜成刨花状卷起、底漆色泽鲜艳,说明漆膜良好;如漆膜用刮刀一触即碎或呈粉末状，底漆色泽暗淡，或一并带起，说明漆膜已经失效或接近失效。

For uncertain parts, remove the paint surface to check whether the steel is rusty; For places with flakes, use a scraper to check the failure range. If the paint shoveled rolls up in the shape of shavings and the color of primer is bright, it indicates that the paint is good. If the paint is broken or powdery at the touch of a scraper, the color of primer is dull, or it is brought up together, it indicates that the paint has failed or is close to failure.

(4)滴水检验

(4) Drip test

在漆膜表面喷水，如水珠很快流淌，无渗透现象，则漆膜完好；如水很快往里渗透或扩散，则表示漆膜粉化，渗水的深度即为漆膜失效的厚度。

Spray water on the paint surface. If the water drops flow quickly and there is no penetration, the paint is intact; If the water penetrates or diffuses quickly, it indicates that the paint film is chalked, and the depth of water penetration is the thickness of invalid paint.

2.2　桥面作业
2.2　Bridge deck operation

2.2.1　桥面检查
2.2.1　Bridge deck inspection

桥面检查包括初始检查、定期检查、临时检查和专项检查。

Bridge deck inspection includes initial inspection, regular inspection, temporary inspection and special inspection.

各项检查必须建立相应考核制度，保证各项检查工作的落实。各工区应建立检查记录簿，并按规定认真填写，保证数据准确可靠，为状态分析评定和编制维护工作计划提供依据。为保证检查的精度，应配备必要的检查工具和仪器。

Corresponding assessment system must be established for all inspections to ensure their implementation. Each working section shall establish an inspection record book, which shall be carefully filled in according to the regulations to ensure the accuracy and reliability of the data, so as to provide a basis for condition analysis and maintenance work plan preparation. For the accuracy of inspection, necessary inspection tools and instruments should be equipped.

对桥隧设备状态变化较快和直接影响行车安全的部位应经常检查。对桥面所有设备进行添乘巡视，每月一遍，及时发现不安全因素。此外，对桥面声屏障进行专项巡查，每月一遍。

The parts where the status of bridge and tunnel changes rapidly and directly affect the running safety should be checked frequently. Inspect all facilities on the bridge deck once a month to discover unsafe factors in time. In addition, a special inspection of sound barrier on the bridge deck is carried out once a month.

对普通桥梁桥面进行检查，至少每月一次，主要检查桥面铺装是否完好；泄水孔有无堵塞；

钢梁上盖板是否锈蚀;电缆沟盖板是否损坏缺失;栏杆是否锈蚀或损坏;桥面伸缩缝止水带是否脱落破损;声屏障和立柱有无锈蚀,连接件有无锈蚀、松动或脱落,屏体有无损坏;装饰板有无锈蚀、损坏、脱落等。

Examine the ordinary bridge deck at least once every month, mainly including: whether the deck pavement is in good condition; whether the drain hole is blocked; whether the cover plate of steel girder is corroded; whether the cover of cable trench is damaged or missing; whether the railing is corroded or damage; whether the waterstop of expansion joint on the bridge deck has fallen off and damaged; whether sound barriers and their columns are rusted; whether the fittings are rusted, loose or falling off; whether the screens are damaged; whether decorative boards are rusted, damaged, or falling off, etc.

在秋季应对桥梁设施进行全面检查,据以评定桥梁设备技术状态,拟订病害整治措施,安排设备改善计划,确保行车安全。对桥梁设备各部分的技术状态,应按相关规定进行全面细致的检查,必要时用仪器检测或试验,以查明各种病害情况。桥梁维护部根据秋检结果,填写桥梁建筑物状态评定明细表,并汇总填写桥梁建筑物状态评定表,提出病害发生原因、增减情况等状态分析报告。

In autumn, a comprehensive inspection of bridge facilities should be carried out to assess the technical status of bridge, draw up disease control measures, and arrange improvement plans to ensure running safety. The each part technical status of bridge should be examined comprehensively and meticulously in accordance with the related standard. Use instruments to detect or test when necessary to find out various diseases. According to the autumn inspection results, maintenance department fills in the detail list of bridge status assessment, summarizes and fills in the bridge status assessment form, and proposes a status analysis report such as the causes, increase and decrease of bridge diseases.

临时检查是当设备遭受地震、洪水、台风、火灾和车船撞击等紧急情况或发生突发性严重病害时,为及时掌握结构物状态而进行的检查。临时检查由工班组织进行,必要时由公司组织进行。

When earthquakes, floods, typhoons, fires, vehicle and ship collisions, or sudden serious diseases occur, temporary inspection shall be organized to grasp the structure condition in time by the gang, if necessary, by the company.

专项检查是指包括挠度、拱度和横向振幅测量、墩台变形和基础病害检查、声屏障安全检测在内的针对特定项目的检查。

Special inspections refer to inspections for specific items including deflection, camber and lateral amplitude, pier deformation, foundation disease, and sound barrier safety.

凡跨度在 40 m 及以上的钢梁,至少每三年测量一次挠度和拱度(固定测点位置)。对有病害的钢梁、钢筋混凝土梁和预应力混凝土梁挠度、拱度和跨中横向振幅的测定至少每年测量一次。挠度测量时,可先测动荷载所产生的挠度,必要时再复测静荷载所产生的挠度。

For steel girder with a span of 40 m and above, the deflection and camber should be measured at least once every three years (fixed measuring points). For diseased steel girder, reinforced concrete beams, and prestressed concrete beams, the deflection, camber, and mid-span transverse amplitude shall be measured at least annually. When measuring the deflection, the deflection caused by the dynamic load can be measured first, and then the deflection caused by the static load can be re-measured if necessary.

特大桥及病害严重的桥梁,对其墩台均应进行下沉或位移的观测。为求得各墩台位移和下沉的绝对值,墩台标高应与桥梁附近国家水准点相联系,基准线在观测区以外应有控制系统。观测工作一般每年一次,经多年观测位移和下沉基本稳定时,可每隔若干年观测一次。历年观测资料应妥善保存,绘制出汇总后的图表,以分析了解其变化趋势。

For large-span bridges and bridges with serious diseases, the subsidence or displacement of piers and abutments should be observed. In order to obtain the absolute value of displacement and subsidence of each pier and abutment, the pier and abutment elevation should be related to the national benchmark near the bridge, and the reference line which is outside the observation area should have a control system. The observation is generally carried out once a year, or once every several years when the displacement and subsidence reaches to good numerical stability after many years. The observational data over the years should be properly preserved, and the summarized charts should be drawn to analyze its changing trend.

声屏障投入使用后,应间隔一定时间对立柱垂直度、立柱整体直线度等结构构造和力学性能进行检测,对立柱和底板构件、锚固螺栓锈蚀情况,以及立柱和底板涂层厚度、风化程度等涂层防护状况进行检测,对基础混凝土强度、抽检螺母拧紧扭矩值和锚固螺栓抗拉拔强度值等的强度进行检测。

After sound barriers go into service, the items need to be tested including: the structural and mechanical properties of columns; corrosion of components and bolts; coating thickness and weathering degree of columns and baseplates; concrete foundation strength, nut tightening torque and bolt tensile.

2.2.2 桥面找平作业

2.2.2 Leveling operation of bridge deck

桥面找平是指按照设计的桥面纵横坡度做桥面铺装层,适用于轨道交通桥梁混凝土结构基面上的找坡施工。

Leveling operation of bridge deck refers to making the pavement of bridge deck according to the designed vertical and horizontal slope of the bridge deck, which is suitable for the construction of slope leveling on the concrete structure base of rail transit bridges.

1. 材料及工器具

1. Materials and tools

每平方米的桥面找平作业,大约需要界面剂 0.25 kg、42.5R 硅酸盐水泥 50 kg、中砂 100 kg 和钢筋网 1.1 m^2。所需的工器具主要有激光投线仪、高压风机和高压水枪。

For each square meter's bridge deck leveling, about 0.25 kg of interface agent, 50 kg of portland cement, 100 kg of medium sand and 1.1 m^2 of reinforcing mesh are required. The tools mainly include Laser Levels, high-pressure fans and high-pressure water guns.

2. 操作要求

2. Operation requirements

① 桥面坡度需符合设计要求;增铺部分应根据桥面荷载进行核算。

① The deck slope shall meet the design requirements; the additional paving shall be calculated according to the deck loads.

② 凿毛时,注意操作安全,应确保基层坚硬、清洁、干燥、无油脂。

② When roughening, pay attention to the operation safety and ensure that the base coarse surface is hard, clean, dry and free of grease.

③ 水泥砂浆配比准确,找平施工时符合坡度要求。

③ During leveling construction, the cement mortar mixing ratio is accurate and the slope meets requirements.

④ 找平后应进行洒水养护。

④ Sprinkling water curing shall be carried out after leveling.

⑤ 正确使用工器具,施工最低气温不得低于 5 ℃。

⑤ Use tools and appliances correctly, and the minimum construction temperature shall not be lower than 5 ℃.

3. 操作步骤

3. Operation steps

步骤 1:定坡设计。

Step 1: design slope.

① 根据积水面积、现场既有坡度情况,确定找坡坡度。

① Determine the falling gradient according to ponding areas and gradients of existing slopes on site.

② 现场进行坡度标记。根据设计的坡度,计算出横截面上桥面中点与边缘的高度,然后在对应位置立上短钢筋(或砖块等)到计算高度,并拉线作为标记。也可使用激光投线仪。

② Slope marking on site. According to the designed gradient, calculate the heights of the midpoint and edge of the bridge deck on the cross section, and then erect short steel bars (or bricks, etc.) at the corresponding position to the calculated height, and draw a thread as a marker. Laser level can also be used.

步骤 2:基面凿毛。

Step 2: make the base surface rough.

① 维修区域边缘部位垂直切割,使垂直边缘至少有 1 cm 的接触边界。

① Cut the maintenance area edge vertically, so that the vertical edge has at least 1 cm contact boundary.

② 维修区域表面凿毛。

② Chisel the surface of maintenance area.

③ 用高压风机冲洗凿毛界面。

③ Rinse the roughing interface with a high-pressure fan.

步骤 3：布设钢钉、钢丝网。

Step 3: lay out steel nails and reinforcing mesh.

① 在处理清洁的界面上布设钢钉，用锤子直接将 2.5 cm 长的钢钉打入 1.5 cm，钢钉横竖间隔 10 cm。

① Lay steel nails on the cleaned interface, directly hammer 2.5 cm long steel nails into 1.5 cm, with an interval of 10 cm horizontally and vertically.

② 待基层彻底干燥后，用滚筒在界面上涂刷界面剂；对高吸收的基层可以涂刷两遍。

② After the base layer is completely dry, use a roller to brush the interface agent on it; for the base layer with high absorption, brush the agent twice.

③ 立即铺设钢丝网，铺设面积大于找坡面积的 3/5，使其与界面剂充分接触。

③ Immediately lay the reinforcing mesh on greater than 3/5 of the slope area, and make it fully contact with the interface agent.

④ 待表面风干即可进行下道工序的施工。

④ Carry out the next process after the surface is air-dried.

步骤 4：找坡施工。

Step 4: leveling construction.

① 配制 1:2 水泥砂浆。

① Prepare 1:2 cement mortar.

② 用泥刀将修补砂浆涂抹到已处理完毕的待修界面上，施工时应用力压抹，确保完全黏结，防止出现蜂窝和孔洞。

② Press mortar to the treated interface with a trowel to ensure complete bonding and prevent voids and holes.

③ 对垂直边缘的边角用泥刀将砂浆批向中心，并在初凝时，用干净的泥刀按要求获得相应的排水坡度。

③ Scrape mortar from the vertical edge corner toward center with a clean trowel, and reach the required falling gradient during initial setting.

步骤 5：成品养护。

Step 5: cure slope.

确保在 3 天内进行适当的浇水养护。

Ensure proper wet curing within 3 days.

4. 质量控制要求

4. Quality control requirements

① 施工最低气温不得低于 5 ℃。

① The minimum construction temperature shall not be lower than 5 ℃.

② 避免雨天、烈日下施工。

② Avoid constructing in rainy days and blazing sunshine.

5. 作业验收

5. Operation acceptance

① 界面清洁凿毛时,基层应达到坚硬、清洁、干燥、无油脂等。

① When the interface is cleaned and chiseled, the base layer shall be hard, clean, dry, and free of grease.

② 垫层抹平无坑洼,与原混凝土结构联牢。

② The cushion layer is smooth without potholes, and bonded with the original concrete structure firmly.

③ 防水层平顺密实,与边墙及泄水孔衔接严密,无渗漏现象。

③ The waterproof layer is smooth and compact, and tightly connected with the side wall and the drain hole without leakage.

④ 保护层厚度不小于 30 mm,坡度不小于 3%,压实抹平,无裂损和空鼓。

④ For protective layer, the thickness is not less than 30 mm; the gradient is not less than 3%, and it is compacted and smoothed without cracks and hollows.

2.2.3 桥面防水涂料施工

2.2.3 Construction of waterproof paint for bridge deck

在大规模桥面铺装时,常见的防水涂料有:JBS 环保型桥梁防水涂料,SBS 改性沥青桥面防水涂料和 FYT-1 改进型沥青防水涂料等。

In large-scale bridge deck paving, the common waterproof paint includes: JBS environmentally friendly bridge waterproof paint, SBS modified asphalt bridge deck waterproof paint and FYT-1 improved asphalt waterproof paint, etc.

1. 防水涂料涂刷前应做好基层处理

1. Base course should be treated before painted

① 基层表面应压实平整,采用水泥砂浆找平层时,必须充分养护,不得有松动、起沙、起皮现象,应符合设计要求。

① The base-layer surface should be compacted and leveled. When cement mortar screed-coat is adopted, it must be fully maintained and meet the design requirements without cracking, sanding, or peeling.

② 为提高防水层和沥青混凝土的铺装层同混凝土面板之间抗剪切强度,混凝土面板需进行拉毛处理,以提高它们的截面嵌锁力和摩阻力,从而使桥面在车辆行驶后长时间不出现起皱、裂缝。

② In order to improve the shear strength between waterproof layer, asphalt concrete pavement and the concrete panel, the concrete panel needs to be roughened to improve the interlocking force and frictional resistance of combined section, so that bridge deck does not appear wrinkled or cracked for a long time after the vehicle runs.

③ 桥面必须清理干净,不得有杂物和灰尘,以免影响黏结强度。

③ Bridge deck must be cleaned without debris and dust, so as not to affect the bonding strength.

④ 防撞墙拆模后,应彻底清除防撞墙和混凝土桥交接部位的钢筋、铁丝等杂物。

④ After removing the anti-collision wall formwork, the steel bars, iron wires and other debris at the junction of the anti-collision wall and the concrete bridge should be completely cleaned up.

⑤ 桥面含水率不应大于 10%。

⑤ The bridge deck's moisture content should not be greater than 10%.

2. 防水涂料施工的注意事项

2. The precautions for waterproof paint construction

① 施工前应将棕刷、毛刷充分浸润,使其柔软涂刷流畅。

① Before construction, fully soak the brush and make it soft and smooth.

② 气温低于 0 ℃或高于 35 ℃不得施工(应避免高温施工)。

② No construction is allowed when the temperature is below 0 ℃ or higher than 35 ℃ (Construction under high temperature should be avoided).

③ 储运温度 5 ℃ ~35 ℃为宜。

③ The storage and transportation temperature should be 5 ℃ -35 ℃.

④ 应选择 4 h 内无雨雪天气施工。

④ Construct without rain or snow in 4 hours.

⑤ 涂膜未干燥或未铺装沥青混凝土前,严禁踩踏和汽车行驶。

⑤ Before coating is dry or asphalt concrete is not paved, it is strictly forbidden to step on and drive.

⑥ 施工工具用完后马上用水冲洗干净,以备再用。

⑥ Wash the tools with water immediately after use for reuse.

2.2.4 桥面防水层作业

2.2.4 Construction of waterproof layer for bridge deck

目前,城轨桥隧建筑普遍采用冷作防水层。冷作防水层通常有两种结构的规格,一种为“二布三涂”,另一种为“薄膜加筋”。“二布三涂”为由两层中碱玻璃纤维布和三层再生橡胶沥青防水涂料组合而成。冷作防水层使施工现场减少了熬制沥青的工序,改善了环境和工人的劳动条件,加快了施工进度。

At present, the construction of urban rail bridges and tunnels generally adopts cold-worked waterproof layers. The cold-worked waterproof layer usually has two structural specifications, one is “two-cloths and three-coatings”, and the other is “film reinforcement”. “Two-cloth and three-coating” is a combination of two layers of medium-alkali glass fiber cloth and three layers of recycled rubber asphalt waterproof coating. The cold-worked waterproof layer reduces the process of making asphalt at the construction site, improves the environment and the working conditions of workers, and speeds up the construction progress.

针对局部桥面防水层破损、空鼓等,需进行重新铺装作业。

For partial waterproof layer damage and hollowing on the bridge deck, it is necessary to re-pave.

1. 操作要求

1. Operation requirements

① 铺设防水层前对桥面应实施找平。

① The bridge deck should be leveled before laying the waterproof layer.

② 防水层施工前基面清理需平整干净、无污物。

② Before the construction of the waterproof layer, the base surface should be clean and free of dirt.

③ 防水层选择需符合现场实际情况,涂层必须均匀。

③ The selection of the waterproof layer must conform to the actual situation on site, and the coating must be uniform.

④ 在涂层干燥前不得踩踏碰擦,涂后要进行喷水养护。

④ Do not step on and rub the coating before drying, and spray water for curing after coating.

⑤ 正确使用工器具。

⑤ Use tools correctly.

2. 操作步骤

2. Operation steps

步骤1:选定作业区域,一般为包含破损位置的矩形区域,然后对桥面的基面进行清理。

Step 1: select the working area, generally a rectangular area containing the damaged position, and then clean the base surface of the bridge deck.

步骤2:如基面不平整需进行找平作业。

Step 2: if the base surface is uneven, leveling operation is required.

步骤3:铺装防水层。

Step 3: lay the waterproof layer.

步骤4:适当洒水养护。

Step 4: properly sprinkle water for conservation.

步骤5:工完场清。

Step 5: clean up the site after work.

3. 作业验收

3. Operation acceptance

① 界面清洁凿毛时,基层应达到坚硬、清洁、干燥、无油脂等。

① When the interface is cleaned and chiseled, the base layer should be hard, clean, dry, and free of grease.

② 垫层抹平无坑洼,与原混凝土结构联牢。

② The cushion layer is smoothed without potholes, and is firmly connected with the original concrete structure.

③ 防水层平顺密实,与边墙及泄水孔衔接严密,无渗漏现象。

③ The waterproof layer is smooth and compact, tightly connected with the side wall and the drain hole, and there is no leakage.

④ 保护层厚度不小于 30 mm,坡度不小于 3%,压实抹平,无裂损和空鼓。

④ The thickness of the protective layer is not less than 30 mm, the gradient is not less than 3%, and it is compacted and smoothed without cracks and hollows.

2.2.5 桥面铺装层养护

2.2.5 Maintenance of bridge deck pavement layer

在城轨桥梁上,水泥混凝土铺装较为普遍,其耐磨性能好,适合重载交通,但也有养护期长,修补麻烦的缺点。其中,裂纹最为常见,可分为大面积裂纹和局部裂纹两类。

On urban rail bridges, cement concrete pavement is more common for its favorable abrasive resistance and strong adaptability to heavy traffic. However, it also has the shortcomings of long maintenance period and troublesome repair. Among them, cracks are the most common, which can be divided into large-area cracks and local cracks.

大面积裂纹一般呈均匀分布的龟状细裂缝,通常是在水泥混凝土板铺装过程中,由于表面整修收水不当、气温较高、养护不周等原因,导致混凝土板表面因失水过快而引起的表面收缩裂缝,这种裂缝一般只是深入混凝土表面几毫米,不会随时间延长而发展。另外,由于混凝土材料的不稳定,如碱集料反应等原因,也会引起铺装层大面积的开裂,裂缝呈不规则状况,有些会引起翘曲等。

Large-area cracks are generally uniformly distributed tortoise-like fine cracks in the process of cement concrete slab paving. Due to improper water collection on the repair surface, high temperature, poor maintenance and other reasons, excessive water loses on the concrete slab surface, the resulting surface shrinkage cracks generally only penetrate a few millimeters into the concrete and will not develop over time. In addition, due to the instability of concrete, such as the alkali-aggregate reaction, it will also cause large-scale cracking of the pavement layer. The cracks are irregular, and some may even cause warpage.

局部裂纹一般分施工时产生的初期裂缝和使用后产生的纵横向裂缝、板角裂缝及结构附近裂缝等几种。纵横方向和板角处的裂缝均为贯通裂缝。初期裂缝产生的原因一般是水泥混凝土硬化过程中表面砂浆沉降开裂及早期混凝土塑性收缩而产生的开裂,其长度一般为数厘米到数十厘米。

Local cracks are generally divided into initial cracks generated during construction, longitudinal and transverse cracks, plate corner cracks and cracks adjacent to the structure, which generate after use. The longitudinal and transverse cracks and plate corner cracks are through. The initial cracks are generally caused by the settlement cracking of surface mortar and the plastic shrinkage of early concrete during cement concrete hardening, and the length is generally several centimeters to tens of centimeters.

当水泥混凝土铺装层出现磨光、脱皮、露骨或破裂等缺陷出现,通常可采用如下方法进行维修。

When the cement concrete pavement has defects such as polishing, peeling, exposed or cracked, it can usually be repaired by the following methods.

① 原结构凿补。将原水泥混凝土铺装层的表面凿毛,并尽可能深一些,使骨料露出,用清水冲洗干净并充分湿润,再涂刷上同强度等级的水泥砂浆(或其他黏结材料),最后铺筑一层4~5 cm厚的水泥混凝土铺装层(在桥梁荷载能力容许的前提下)。

① The original structure is chiseled and repaired. Chisel the surface of original cement concrete pavement as deep as possible to make the aggregate exposed, rinse it with clean water and fully wet it, and then apply the cement mortar (or other bonding material) of the same strength grade. Lay cement concrete pavement with a thickness of 4 - 5 cm (on the premise that the load capacity of the bridge allows).

② 全部凿除,重筑铺装层。桥面铺装层如已严重损坏,可采用全部凿除,重筑铺装层的方法修补。新铺面层可采用普通水泥混凝土,也可采用钢筋混凝土等其他材料。对于钢筋混凝土桥,一般宜用标号为C30的混凝土;对于预应力桥,一般宜用标号为C40的混凝土。桥面重新铺装的铺装层厚度宜10~12 cm。

② The original structure is all chiseled off, and the pavement is rebuilt. If the bridge deck pavement has been seriously damaged, it can be repaired by chiseling off and rebuilding. The new pavement can be made of ordinary cement concrete or other materials such as reinforced concrete. For reinforced concrete bridges, C30 concrete should be generally used; for prestressed bridges, C40 concrete should be generally used. The thickness of re-paving pavement should be 10 - 12 cm.

2.2.6 桥面伸缩缝养护

2.2.6 Maintenance of expansion joint on the bridge deck

1. 伸缩缝的日常检查

1. Daily inspection of expansion joint

桥面伸缩缝是最容易遭到破坏而又相对难以修复的部位。严重时,会影响交通,甚至会危及行车安全。因此,必须做好日常检查,及时修补或更换破损的伸缩缝。

The bridge deck expansion joint is the most easily damaged and relatively difficult to repair. If the damage is serious, it will affect the traffic and even endanger the driving safety. Therefore, daily inspection must be conducted and damaged expansion joint must be repaired or replaced in time.

日常检查工作主要包括:伸缩缝是否堵塞、挤死、失效;各部分的构件是否完好;锚固连接是否牢固,连接件是否松动;有无局部破损;密封橡胶带是否老化、失去弹性、异常变形或开裂;伸缩缝是否有不正常的响声或异常的伸缩量;伸缩缝各基本单元间隙是否均匀;钢构件是否锈蚀、变形;伸缩缝处是否平整等。

The daily inspection mainly includes: whether expansion joint is blocked, squeezed, or invalid; whether components of each part are in good condition; whether anchor connections are firm; whether connectors is loose; whether there are local damages; whether sealing rubber belts are aging, loss of elasticity, abnormally deformed or not cracked; whether there is abnormal noise or unusual expansion and contraction in expansion joint; whether the gap between basic units of the expansion joints are uniform; whether steel members are corroded or deformed; whether expansion joints are flat, etc.

为便于养护维修,对检查应做好记录,建立检查记录档案。

For the convenience of maintenance and repair, records of inspections should be kept and inspection record files should be established.

2. 伸缩缝的养护

2. Maintenance of expansion joint

日常养护工作的主要内容有:清除碎石、泥土等杂物;拧紧螺栓,并涂油保护;修理个别损坏部分等。若有损坏或功能失效要及时修理或更换。

The main content of daily maintenance work includes: removing debris such as gravel and soil; tightening the bolts and apply oil for protection; repairing individual damaged parts, etc. If there is damage or functional failure, it should be repaired or replaced in a timely manner.

伸缩装置更换要选型合理,以满足桥跨结构对于温度、混凝土收缩和混凝土徐变的需要,使行车平稳,不漏水。

The replacement of expansion device shall be reasonably selected to meet the needs of bridge span structure for temperature, concrete shrinkage and concrete creep, so as to ensure smooth driving and no water leakage.

2.2.7　桥面排水设施养护维修

2.2.7　Maintenance and repair of bridge deck drainage facilities

桥面排水设施的常见缺陷有:桥面积水管、泄水管堵塞,泄水管被截断导致水流方向改变等。对于钢筋混凝土桥梁,桥面积水将使雨水渗入混凝土的细小裂缝中,会使混凝土产生破坏而缩短使用寿命,同时水分还会使钢筋锈蚀;对于钢桥,桥面积水将会加速对梁体表面的侵蚀。

Common defects of bridge deck drainage facilities include: catchment pipes and drain pipes on bridge decks are blocked, and the water flow direction is changed due to the truncation of drain pipes. For reinforced concrete bridges, the ponding on bridge decks will make rainwater to penetrate into the small concrete cracks, which will damage the concrete and shorten its service life. For steel bridges, the ponding on bridge decks will accelerate the erosion of beam surface.

1. 排水设施检查

1. Inspection of drainage facilities

应经常检查桥面是否有坑槽,是否有积水;泄水管是否完好、畅通;泄水管的盖板是否损坏、丢失;管口是否被杂草或石块堵塞;管体有无脱落;出水口是否畅通;桥头排水功能是否完好等。

It is necessary to frequently check whether there are pits or ponding on bridge decks; whether the drain pipes are in good condition and unblocked; whether the cover plates of drain pipes are damaged or lost; whether the pipe inlets are blocked by weeds or stones; whether some pipes falls off; whether water outlet are unblocked; whether the drainage system at the bridge head is in good condition, etc.

2. 排水设施养护

2. Maintenance of drainage facilities

① 经常清扫桥面,使其保持整洁。桥面不得有凹凸不平,如发现桥面有坑槽,应及时进行修补,避免积水。

① The bridge deck should be cleaned regularly to keep it clean. The bridge deck shall not be uneven. If there are pits on the bridge deck, it shall be repaired in time to avoid ponding.

② 泄水管盖板(进水管口处)上的杂物应及时清除,避免杂物掉入管内堵塞管道而影响排水。

② The debris on the drain pipe cover plates (at the drain pipe inlets) should be removed in time to avoid the debris falling into pipes to block pipes and affects drainage.

③ 若发现泄水管出水口处有泥石杂物堆积,应及时清除。

③ If debris accumulation is found at the outlet of the drain pipe, it should be removed in time.

④ 泄水管应经常进行疏通。

④ Drain pipes should be dredged frequently.

⑤ 当发现泄水管损坏时应及时修补,接头不牢已掉落的应重新安装接上,损坏严重的应予以更换。

⑤ When drain pipes are damaged, they should be repaired in time. If joints are not firm and has fallen, it should be re-installed and connected. If they are seriously damaged, they should be replaced.

3. 桥面排水作业

3. Drainage operation of bridge deck

桥面排水作业,一般采用"排管引流法",主要适用于轨道交通桥梁道床积水整治的施工作业,通过在桥面上开洞并排设引流管将水引至既有落水管的一种排水作业方法。所需的工器具主要有钻孔机和电锤。

The drainage operation of bridge deck generally adopts the "drainage method of setting pipes", which is mainly suitable for the treatment to pondings in the track bed of rail transit bridges. It is a kind of drainage method that leads the water to the existing downspouts by making holes in the bridge deck and setting drainage pipes side by side. The tools required are mainly drills and electric hammers.

"排管引流法"的操作程序为

The operation procedure of the "drainage method of setting pipes" is as follows:

(1)钻孔位置确定

(1) Determination of drilling position

① 分析积水现场,寻找积水最深区域或找平层放坡最低点。

① Analyze ponding sites to find the deepest ponding area or the lowest point of leveling layer.

② 根据梁体外侧落水口具体位置,在先前选定区域确定钻孔泄水位置。

② According to the specific positions of water outlets on the outside beam, determine the boreholes' position for drainage in the previously selected area.

(2)桥下脚手架搭设

(2) Erection of scaffold under bridge

① 结合桥面所确定的钻孔位置,进行桥下脚手架的搭设。

① Combined with the drilling position determined by the bridge deck, the scaffold under the bridge is erected.

② 脚手架搭设必须安全牢固。

② The scaffold should be set up safely and firmly.

(3)钻孔泄水

(3) Drilling and draining

① 结合桥面所确定的钻孔位置,用钻孔机进行梁体钻孔,开孔在直径 110 mm 左右,方便后续落水管埋设。

① Combined with the drilling position determined by the bridge deck, the beam is drilled with drills, and the diameter of the holes is about 110 mm, which is convenient for the subsequent embedding of downpipes.

② 钻孔时,利用钢筋探测器探测钻孔处钢筋位置,钻孔尽量避免损坏梁体钢筋。

② When drilling, use the steel detector to detect the position of steel bars at the drilling, and try to avoid damaging the steel bars in the beam.

③ 钻孔后进行桥面泄水,清空桥面积水。

③ After drilling, the water shall be discharged from the bridge deck and the pondings shall be emptied.

(4)引流管排设

(4) Arrangement of drainage tubes

① 钻孔后,在洞口埋设直径 110 mm PVC 管,并对洞口接管进行密封处理。

① After drilling, the PVC pipe with a diameter of 110 mm shall be buried at the opening, and the nozzle at the opening shall be sealed.

② 朝着既有落水管的方向,排设引流管道。PVC 抱箍固定于梁体上,固定时尽量避开梁体钢筋位置。

② Drainage pipes shall be arranged in the direction of the existing downpipes. The PVC hoops are fixed on the beam, avoiding steel bars as far as possible.

③ 将引流管接入既有落水管,并做好管口密封处理。排管时要注意适当放坡,引流管放坡坡度应大于 3%。

③ Connect drainage pipes to existing downpipes and seal orifices. Pay attention to sloping when arranging the drainage pipe, and the gradients of drainage pipes should be greater than 3%.

"排管引流法"的质量控制要求有:

The quality control requirements of "drainage method of setting pipes" are as follows:

① 桥面钻孔区域确定时,先利用积水深浅判别坡度方向,若积水不明显可用水平尺测量,推断找平层放坡方向并确定一个或多个钻孔区域。区域选择必须满足桥面积水排放的需求,尽量做到开孔后可完全排空积水。

① When determining the drilling area of bridge deck, the ponding depth is used to determine the slope direction. If the ponding is not obvious, it can be measured with a level ruler, so that the grading direction of the leveling layer can be inferred and one or more drilling areas can be determined. The selected areas must meet the demands for water discharge, and the pondings can be completely drained after opening as far as possible.

② 桥下钻孔时,注意钻孔位置的选择,避免因钻孔,导致梁体产生裂缝。

② When drilling under the bridge, pay attention to the drilling locations, avoid cracking in the beam due to drilling.

③ 安装 PVC 管道时,洞口处与接头处注意密封处理,防止泄水过程中产生滴漏。

③ When laying PVC pipes, pay attention to the sealing treatment at openings and joints to prevent dripping during water discharge.

④ 钻孔洞口密封后,对洞口周边做适当养护,提高洞口密封效果。

④ After holes are sealed, proper maintenance should be performed around the holes to improve the sealing effect.

2.2.8 作业通道及栏杆

2.2.8 Operating passages and railings

1. 作业通道及栏杆检查、养护

1. Inspection and maintenance of operating passages and railings

① 人行道各部尺寸符合设计要求,钢支架的铆接、栓接、焊接及涂装质量符合有关规定。

① The each part dimension of the sidewalk meet the design requirements, and the quality of riveting, bolting, welding and painting for steel brackets meets the relevant regulations.

② 步行板四角整平,各部尺寸和制作质量符合要求,连接牢固。钢筋混凝土板平整无裂无损,边缝堵塞饱满;木板无腐朽断裂,防腐处理良好;钢质板除锈彻底,涂漆均匀,无漏涂、流淌。钢质、橡胶步板等应与人行道托架有防止移动、脱落的扣系。

② The four corners of walking boards are leveled, the dimensions and production quality of each part meet the requirements, and the connections are firm. The reinforced concrete slabs are smooth without cracks and damage, the side seams are fully blocked. The wood boards have no decay and fracture with good anti-corrosion treatment. The steel plate shall be thoroughly derusted, evenly painted without leakage. Steel or rubber step boards should be fastened with the sidewalk bracket to prevent movement and falling off.

③ 步行板铺设平直,边缘成一直线。

③ The walking boards are laid straight and the edges are in a straight line.

④ 人行道栏杆平直,连接牢固,无扭曲,10 m 弦矢度小于 20 mm。梁端断开,活动端处能与梁体共同移动。

④ The sidewalk railing is straight, the connection is firm, and there is no twist, and the chord vector of 10 m is less than 20 mm. Beam ends are disconnected, and the movable ends can move together with the beams.

2. 栏杆涂油作业

2. Oiling the railings

(1)作业程序

(1) Operating procedures

① 除锈及涂油。为使边缘整齐,可事先划线,应先上后下,先难后易。

① Derusting and oiling. In order to make edges neat, the lines can be drawn in advance. It should be up to down, and difficult before easy.

② 对附着牢固的锈块,可用小锤轻轻敲击。将锈粒打碎后再行铲刮,并用钢丝刷清除残留的氧化皮,至露出银灰色钢面。

② For the firmly attached rust block, tap lightly with a small hammer. After breaking the rust particles, scrape them with a shovel, and use a wire brush to remove the remaining oxide scale until the silver-gray steel surface is exposed.

③ 除锈完毕用砂布打磨,再用干油刷和棉纱头先后清除表面灰尘,如当天不能涂红丹底漆时,可用棉纱头蘸少量稀料(豆麻仁油或清油)涂刷钢面。

③ After rust removal, use emery cloth to polish railings, and then use dry oil brush and cotton yarn to remove surface dust successively. If you cannot apply red lead primer on the same day, you can use a cotton yarn head to dip a small amount of thinner (bean sesame oil or clear oil) to brush the steel surface.

④ 进行第二度油漆前须用砂布将旧油漆表面轻轻打磨一遍后再用棉纱头揩拭表面灰尘。

④ Before the second paint, the old paint surface must be lightly polished with an emery cloth, and then the dust on the surface should be wiped off with a cotton yarn end.

(2)技术标准

(2) Technical standards

① 失效面漆及底漆、铁锈、污垢均应清除彻底,边缘整齐。

① The failed topcoat and primer, rust and dirt should be thoroughly removed, and the edges should be neat.

② 铲锈后涂底漆及面漆各 2 度。

② After removing rust, apply two coats of primer and topcoat respectively.

③ 灰面漆粉化处加盖灰面漆 2 度。

③ Two coats of grey topcoat shall be applied to the powdered part of grey topcoat.

④ 仅个别处生锈而大部分面漆完好者采用小补修油漆方法修理。

④ If only a few parts are rusted and most of the topcoat is intact, use the small touch-up paint method to repair.

⑤ 部分生锈而大部分面漆失效者,则采用小补修油漆和加盖 2 度灰面漆方法修理。

⑤ If part of the rust is rusted and most of the topcoat fails, it should be repaired with a small paint and covered by two coats of gray topcoat.

⑥ 所涂底、面漆允许边缘压住 1 日漆 3 ~5 mm。

⑥ The applied primer and topcoat allow the edge to be covered by the 1st paint of 3 -5 mm.

2.3 桥跨作业
2.3 Bridge span operation

2.3.1 桥下检查
2.3.1 Inspection under bridge

桥下检查制度主要为定期检查。各工区应建立检查记录簿，并按规定认真填写，保证数据准确可靠，为状态分析评定和编制维护工作计划提供依据。为保证检查的精度，应配备必要的检查工具和仪器。

The inspection regulation under bridge mainly refers to regular inspection. Each working section shall establish an inspection record book, which shall be carefully filled in according to the regulations to ensure the accuracy and reliability of the data, so as to provide a basis for condition analysis and maintenance work plan preparation. To ensure the accuracy of inspection, the necessary inspection tools and instruments should be equipped.

对普通桥梁桥下部进行检查，每半年一次，主要检查圬工梁体或墩台有无裂纹或裂纹有无发展；钢梁是否锈蚀；跨路跨河桥的限高防护架或防撞设施是否变形或损坏；泄水管有无损坏缺失；外装饰板有无损坏、脱落等。对特殊桥梁（如钢梁桥、组合梁桥、系杆拱桥、斜拉桥、经常被社会车辆撞击的桥梁等）的桥下每月均检查一遍。

The under bridge parts of ordinary bridges are inspected once every six months, mainly to check whether cracks appear or develop in the masonry beams or piers; whether steel girders are corroded; whether the height-limiting protective frames or anti-collision facilities of road or river crossing bridge are deformed or damaged; whether drain pipes are damaged or missing; whether outer decorative plates are damaged or fallen off, etc. The under bridge parts of special bridges (such as steel girder bridges, composite girder bridges, tied arch bridges, cable-stayed bridges, bridges frequently hit by social vehicles, etc.) are inspected once a month.

在秋季应对桥梁进行全面检查，据以拟定病害整治措施，安排设施改善计划，确保行车安全。

In autumn, a comprehensive inspection of bridge facilities should be carried out to assess the technical status of bridge, draw up disease control measures, and arrange improvement plans to ensure running safety.

2.3.2 混凝土梁整修
2.3.2 Renovation of concrete beam

1. 整修方法
1. Renovation methods

① 对梁的弯曲裂缝或沿预应力筋的纵向裂缝，可采用粘贴钢板法、粘贴纤维复合方法，也可采用增大截面法加固。

① For the beam bending cracks or the longitudinal cracks along the prestressed tendons, the bonding steel plate method, bonding fiber composite method, or section enlargement method can be used for reinforcement.

② 对于腹板上斜裂缝,可在与裂缝反向并近似于水平线成 45°角,大致正交于斜裂缝的方向粘贴钢板或纤维复合材料;当梁高度低、钢板或纤维锚固长度不足时,可粘贴成沿梁底的 U 形箍或加压条的形式。

② For inclined cracks on the web, the steel plates or fiber composite materials can be pasted in the direction opposite to cracks and approximately at an angle of 45° to the horizontal line, roughly perpendicular to the inclined cracks; when the beam height is low and the steel plate or fiber anchorage length is insufficient, it can be pasted in U-shaped hoops or by adding battens along the beam bottom.

③ 对腹板上的收缩裂缝和锚固区的裂缝,可视裂缝小采用环氧树脂胶封闭或灌浆处理。

③ For shrinkage cracks on the web and cracks in anchoring area, if the cracks are small, epoxy resin glue is used for sealing or grouting.

④ 对桥面纵向裂缝及横隔板裂缝,一般可通过加大横隔板解决。

④ For the deck longitudinal cracks and the diaphragm cracks, they can generally be solved by enlarging the diaphragm.

⑤ 对于梁体病害严重,加固不能满足使用要求时,可考虑换梁。

⑤ When the beam is seriously damaged and the reinforcement cannot meet the use requirements, the beam should be replaced.

2. 裂缝嵌补

2. Crack filling

(1)作业程序

(1) Operating procedures

① 根据需要搭设脚手架,检查裂纹宽度,确定凿缝长度(要大于裂纹长度)。

① Set up scaffolding as needed, check the crack width and determine the chisel length (larger than the crack length).

② 凿缝并将缝内碎渣粉尘清擦干净。

② Chisel the seam and wipe off the debris in it.

③ 拌和环氧树脂砂浆。按比例拌和细填充料并加入细砂,稀释环氧树脂,加入硬化剂,可加热但温度不得超过 65 ℃。

③ Mix the epoxy resin mortar. Mix the fine filler in proportion and add fine sand, dilute the epoxy resin and add the hardener. It can be heated but the temperature should not exceed 65 ℃.

④ 拌和砂浆。应在浅盘中拌制,一次拌和不得过多,以能在半小时内用完为度,各种材料加入后,必须迅速搅拌均匀。

④ Mix mortar. Mortar should be mixed in a shallow dish, and the mixing should not be too much at one time, so that it can be used up within half an hour. After adding various materials, it must be stirred quickly and evenly.

⑤ 在凿成的槽内涂环氧树脂涂料一层,厚度约 0.2 mm。

⑤ Apply a layer of epoxy resin coating in the chiseled groove with a thickness of about 0.2 mm.

⑥ 勾缝。填满砂浆,压实、抹光。

⑥ Jointing, Fill mortar in the groove, compact and trowel mortar.

⑦ 拆除脚手架,清洗工具、容器。

⑦ Remove scaffolding, clean tools and containers.

(2)技术标准

(2) Technical standards

① 材料配合比、工艺符合要求;槽宽度误差不超过 ±5 mm,深度不超过 8 mm。

① The material mix ratio and process meets the requirements; the groove width error does not exceed ±5 mm, and the depth does not exceed 8 mm.

② 勾缝平实,凹凸不超过 ±3 mm,与圬工结合牢固、压实、平顺、光滑、无断道、色泽均匀、协调。

② The joint shall be flat and the unevenness shall not exceed ±3 mm. It shall be firmly combined with the masonry work, and compacted, smooth, without any breakage, and have a uniform and coordinated color.

3. 裂缝注浆

3. Crack grouting

(1)作业程序

(1) Operating procedures

① 搭设好安全可靠的脚手架。

① Set up safe and reliable scaffolding.

② 检查裂纹、布置压浆嘴。一般情况下,不论是竖直缝、水平缝,压浆嘴的间距按裂纹密度确定。裂纹两端应布置压浆嘴,如圬工体的两侧裂纹贯通,其两侧应错开布嘴。

② Check cracks and arrange grout nipples. In general, whether it is a vertical seam or a horizontal seam, the grout nipple spacing is determined according to crack density. Grout nipples should be arranged at both crack ends. If cracks on both sides of masonry run through, the grout nipples should be staggered on both sides.

③ 清洗基面。用小锤、刮锈刀、钢丝刷将裂纹两侧 100 mm 范围内的混凝土表面的碎屑、浮渣、污垢等清理干净。在打磨整平后,用棉纱蘸无水乙醇或丙酮擦洗,同时注意不堵塞压浆嘴部位的裂隙。

③ Clean the surface. Clean the debris, scum and dirt on the concrete surface on both crack sides of 100 mm with small hammers, rust scrapers and steel wire brushes. After polishing and leveling, wipe with cotton yarn dipped in absolute ethanol or acetone, and pay attention not to block the cracks at the grout nipples.

④ 固定注浆嘴。用自黏性胶带将注浆嘴固定在规定位置,注浆嘴间距根据裂缝宽度来确

定(宽度0.05~0.3 mm,间距为100~150 mm;宽度0.3~1 mm,间距为150~250 mm;宽度1~3 mm及以上时,间距250~400 mm)。每条裂缝至少在两端各粘贴一个注浆嘴。

④ Fix grout nipples. Fix grout nipples at the specified positions with self-adhesive tapes, and the spacing of grout nipples is determined according to the crack width (width 0.05 - 0.3 mm, spacing 100 -150 mm; width 0.3 -1 mm, spacing 150 -250 mm; width 1 -3 mm and above, spacing 250 -400 mm). At least grout nipples shall be pasted at both ends of each crack.

⑤ 封缝作业。裂缝两侧100 mm范围内均匀涂刷两道薄薄的底层涂料,待第一道底层涂料不粘手后,再涂刷第二道底层涂料,待第二道底层涂料不粘手后用油灰刀刮抹密封封闭涂料。每层厚度0.8~1 mm,总厚度2.5~3 mm。

⑤ Sealing operation. Evenly apply two thin primers within 100 mm on both crack sides. After the first primer is not sticky, apply the second primer. Until the second primer is not sticky, use a putty knife to scrape the sealant paint. The thickness of each layer is 0.8 -1 mm, and the total thickness is 2.5 -3 mm.

⑥ 试压。用手压注浆泵或风动压浆罐将无水乙醇或丙酮压注入裂缝中,检查注浆嘴粘贴和裂缝封闭的质量,看是否存在漏浆现象。同时估算注浆量,确定注浆压力。

⑥ Pressure test. Inject anhydrous ethanol or acetone into cracks by a hand pressure grouting pump or a pneumatic grouting tank, check the quality of grouting nozzle paste and crack sealing, and make sure if there is any leakage. At the same time, estimate the grouting amount and determine the grouting pressure.

⑦ 吹干。用空气压缩机风力把每个注浆嘴通气15分钟以上,把裂缝中的水分和溶剂吹干。

⑦ Drying. Use the air compressor to ventilate each grouting nozzle for more than 15 min, and dry the moisture and solvent in the cracks.

⑧ 压力注浆。同一裂缝各注浆嘴应同时注浆,每个注浆孔注浆时间不少于40 min,以确保浆液渗入细微的裂缝深处。

⑧ Pressure grouting. All grout nipples in the same crack should be grouted at the same time, and each grouting hole should be grouted for no less than 40 min to ensure that the grout penetrates into the fine crack.

⑨ 铲嘴整平。注浆后第二天(相隔10 h以上),将注浆嘴逐个铲除,不平处用封闭材料刮抹平整。

⑨ Shovel nipples and leveling. On the second day after grouting (more than 10 h apart), remove grouting nipple one by one, and use sealing material to scrape the uneven places.

⑩ 注浆记录。将工程地点、结构物名称、裂缝编号、长度、注浆材料、气候情况、注浆嘴编号、间距、注浆量、压力及时间记录在表格中。

⑩ Grouting record. Record the project location, structure name, crack number, length, grouting materials, weather conditions, grouting nipple number, spacing, grouting amount, pressure and time in the table.

(2)技术标准

(2) Technical standards

① 浆液配合比、水灰比符合要求。

① The grout mixing ratio and water-cement ratio meet the requirements.

② 封闭裂纹要严密,压浆嘴位置布置合理:一般为200~400 mm,裂纹窄,间距宜小些,反之应大些。缝端应设嘴。

② The cracks should be sealed tightly, and the grouting nipple positions should be reasonable: generally at the interval of 200-400 mm, the spacing should be smaller for fine cracks, otherwise it should be larger. The nipple should be set at the end of seams.

③ 缝内压浆饱满,与圬工结合牢固。

③ The grouting in the seam is full and is firmly combined with masonry.

(3)作业要点

(3) Operational standards

① 检查圬工表面损坏部位,画好标记。

① Check the damaged parts of masonry surface and draw marks.

② 凿除破损部分和损坏的旧混凝土,对外露钢筋要除锈,清除表面遗留灰屑。对旧缝用钢丝刷除去碎粉尘,用水冲洗干净。

② Chisel the damaged parts and old concrete, remove the rust of exposed steel bars and the ash left on the surface. Use a steel wire brush to remove fine dust from old cracks and rinse the cracks with water.

③ 拌合环氧黏结剂、环氧混凝土或水泥砂浆和砂子。

③ Mix epoxy binder, epoxy concrete, or cement mortar and sand.

④ 补修破损表面。将凿除的表面,先涂一层约0.2 mm的黏结剂后用环氧混凝土补平压光,如补修较大面积的破损可立模板,以防止环氧混凝土下坠,模板表面涂一层二丁酯以便拆模。

④ Repair damaged surfaces. First coat the chiseled surface with a adhesive layer of about 0.2 mm, and then use epoxy concrete to trowel and calender. If repairing a large area of damage, the formwork can be erected to prevent epoxy concrete from falling, whose surface is coated with a layer of dibutyl ester for form removal.

(4)技术标准

(4) Acceptance criteria

① 材料配合比符合要求。

① The material mix ratio meets the requirements.

② 补修圬工联结牢固,表面补修平整,新旧接茬密实,无飞边断裂、无空响。

② The repaired masonry shall firmly connect with each other, the surface shall be repaired and leveled, the joints of old and new parts shall be compacted with no flash fracture and empty sound.

③ 补修平整,有排水坡度。

③ Repair and level with drainage slope.

2.3.3 钢结构整修

2.3.3 Renovation of steel structure

1. 锈蚀等级和除锈等级

1. Rust grades and derusting grades

为了确保新涂漆膜对钢梁表面或旧漆膜间的附着力，提高油漆质量，延长钢结构的使用寿命，在涂装底层涂料前，应将钢料表面的污泥、油垢、铁锈、旧涂膜和氧化皮彻底清除干净，清除方法可采用喷砂、喷丸、手工清理和化学除锈，严禁使用腐蚀性物质清理钢表面。

In order to ensure the adhesion of the newly coated paint film to the steel beam surface or to the old paint films, improve the paint quality and prolong the service life of steel structure, the sludge, oil dirt, rust, old film and mile scale on the steel surface shall be completely removed before coating the primer. The removal methods includes sand blasting, shot blasting, manual derusting and chemical derusting, but corrosive substances are forbidden to clean the steel surface.

(1)锈蚀等级

(1) Rust grades

通常钢材表面锈蚀可分为 A、B、C 和 D 4 个等级。

Generally, the steel surface rust can be divided into four grades A, B, C and D.

① 锈蚀等级 A: 全面地覆盖着氧化皮而几乎没有铁锈的钢材表面。

① Rust Grade A: steel surface covered completely with adherent mill scale and with little if any rust.

② 锈蚀等级 B: 已发生锈蚀，并且部分氧化皮已经剥落的钢材表面。

② Rust Grade B: steel surface which has begun to rust and from which the mill scale has begun to flake.

③ 锈蚀等级 C: 氧化皮已因锈蚀而剥落，或者可以刮除，并且有少量点蚀的钢材表面；

③ Rust Grade C: steel surface on which the mill scale has rusted away or from which it can be scraped, but with little pitting visible to the naked eye.

④ 锈蚀等级 D: 氧化皮已因锈蚀而全面剥离，并且已普遍发生点蚀的钢材表面。

④ Rust Grade D: steel surface on which the mill scale has rusted away and on which considerable pitting is visible to the naked eye.

(2)除锈等级

(2) Derusting grades

钢材表面除锈等级以代表所采用的除锈方法的字母(“Sa”“St”“Fl”)表示。如果字母后面有阿拉伯数字，则表示清除氧化皮、铁锈和油漆涂层等附着物的程度等级。

The derusting grade of steel surface is indicated by the letters “Sa”, “ST” or “FL” representing the derusting method adopted. If the letter is followed by a numeral, it indicates the removal degree of mill scale, rust, paint coating and other attachments.

① 喷射或抛射除锈。

① Spray or projectile derusting.

喷射或抛射除锈以字母“Sa”表示。喷射或抛射除锈前,应铲除厚的涂层,清除可见的油脂和污垢。喷射或抛射除锈后,应清除钢材表面的浮灰和碎屑。

Spray cleaning or shot blasting is indicated by the letters “Sa”. Before spray cleaning or shot blasting, remove thick coating, visible grease and grime. After spraying or blasting, the surface should be free of floating ash and debris.

喷射或抛射除锈过的钢材表面处理是根据以下质量标准进行的。

The surface treatment is performed by spray cleaning or shot blasting according to the following quality standards.

Sa1 级:轻度的喷射或抛射除锈。钢材表面应无可见的油脂和污垢,并且没有附着不牢的氧化皮、铁锈和油漆涂层等附着物。

Sa1 Grade: mild spray cleaning or shot blasting. The surface should be free of visible grease, dirt, weakly attached scale, rust, paint coating, and impurities.

Sa2 级:彻底的喷射或抛射除锈。钢材表面应无可见的油脂和污垢,并且氧化皮、铁锈和油漆涂层等附着物已基本清除,其残留物应是牢固附着的。

Sa2 Grade: thorough spray cleaning or shot blasting. Derusting surface should be free of visible grease, dirt, mile scale, rust, paint coating, and impurities, and the residue should be firmly attached.

Sa2. 5 级:非常彻底的喷射或抛射除锈。钢材表面应无可见的油脂、污垢、氧化皮、铁锈和油漆涂层等附着物,任何残留的痕迹应仅是点状或条纹状的轻微色斑。

Sa2. 5 Grade: very thorough spray cleaning or shot blasting. Rust removal surface should be free of visible grease, dirt, mile scale, rust, paint coating, and impurities, and the residue traces only show slight spots or streaks.

Sa3 级:使钢材表观洁净的喷射或抛射除锈。钢材表面应无可见的油脂、污垢、氧化皮、铁锈和油漆涂层等附着物,该表面应显示均匀的金属色泽。

Sa3 Grade: spray cleaning or shot blasting to the clean surface. The steel surface should be free of visible grease, dirt, mile scale, rust, paint coating, and impurities, and the surface has a uniform metallic color.

② 手工或动力除锈。

② Manual or mechanical derusting.

用手工和动力工具,如用铲刀、手工或动力钢丝刷、动力砂纸盘或砂轮等工具除锈,以字母“St”表示。手工或动力工具除锈前,应铲除厚的涂层,清除可见的油脂和污垢。手工或动力工具除锈后,钢材表面应清除浮灰和碎屑。

Derusting with hand and power tools, such as a spatula, hand or power steel wire brush, power sandpaper disc or grinding wheel, is indicated by the letters “St”. Before derusting by hand and power tools, a thick coating, visible grease and grime should be removed. After de-rusting by hand or power tools, the steel surface should be free of ash and debris.

对于手工或动力工具除锈过的钢材表面,有以下两个除锈等级:

For the steel surface that has been derusted by hand or power tools, there are the following two derusting grades.

St2 级:钢材表面应无可见的油脂和污垢,并且没有附着不牢的氧化皮、铁锈和漆涂层等附着物。

St2 Grade: the steel surface should be free of visible grease, dirt, weakly attached mile scale, rust, paint coating, and impurities.

St3 级:钢材表面应无可见的油脂和污垢,并且没有附着不牢的氧化皮、铁锈和油漆涂层等附着物。除锈应比 St2 级更为彻底,底材显露部分的表面应具有金属光泽。

St3: the steel surface should be free of visible grease, dirt, weakly attached mile scale, rust, paint coating, and impurities. Derusting should be more thorough than St2 Grade, and the exposed surface of substrate has metallic luster.

2. 钢结构表面清理

2. Surface cleaning of steel structure

涂装前钢表面处理是涂装体系中非常重要的环节。只有钢表面处理达到标准,才能保证涂料与钢表面有良好的附着力,保证涂层与钢表面的整体性。目前,常用的方法有手工除锈和喷砂除锈。

The steel surface preparation before painting is an important part of the painting system. Only when the steel surface treatment meets the standard, can the coating and steel surface have good adhesion and integrity. At present, manual derusting and sandblasting are the commonly used methods.

(1)手工除锈

(1) Manual de-rusting

常用工具及操作方法:

Common tools and operation methods:

① 刮刀。

① scraper.

刮刀由弹簧钢、工具钢或合金钢头加工锻制而成。两端或一端弯成直角,薄刃,其长度、宽窄根据需要而确定。

Machined and forged with spring steel, tool steel or alloy steel heads. Both ends or one end is bent at a right angle, with a thin blade, and its length and width are determined according to needs.

使用时,手持刮刀腰部,刀刃与工作物成 30°~50°角。当使用一端弯成半圆形的刮刀时,手稍许放平些,由前方向胸前拉或一手压住刮刀前端,一手向胸前拉(刮铆钉头时用)。

When using, hold the scraper waist, and the blade is at an angle of 30°-50° with the working object. When using a scraper with one end bent into a semicircle, put your hand slightly flat, pull it from the front to the chest, or press the scraper front end with one hand and pull it towards the chest with the other hand (for scraping rivet heads).

② 除锈锤。

② Scaling hammer.

用弹簧钢或普通钢加工锻制。一头尖形,另一头平形,或两头均为平形。尖头为敲除表面不平凹陷处,平头为敲除平面锈层严重处所。敲击锈块的尖头以钝为宜,防止击伤钢板。

Processed and forged with spring steel or ordinary steel. One end is pointed, the other end is flat, or both ends are flat. The sharp end is used to knock out the uneven surface, while the flat end is used to knock out the serious plane rust layer. The tip used for knocking rust blocks should be blunt to prevent damaging steel plates.

③ 钢丝刷。

③ Steel wire brush.

一般采用4～6行的钢丝刷。钢丝刷有平把、翘把、直把等形式，使用翘把钢丝刷最为方便。在除锈和铲除漆皮或氧化皮后，用钢丝刷清除钢板上残留杂质和氧化皮，直到除净为止。

Generally, 4-6 rows of steel wire brushes are selected. The steel wire brush has flat handle, warped handle and straight handle, among which the warped handle steel wire brush is the most convenient. After removing scale, rust, or paint coating, the residual impurities and scale on steel plate shall be removed with a steel wire brush until they are completely removed.

手工除锈具有工具简单、不受条件限制、施工方便等优点，但劳动强度大、工作效率低、除锈不易彻底、质量较难保证。一般均在工作量不大，或局部除锈作业时采用。

Manual derusting has the advantages of simple tools, no restriction and convenient construction, but it is difficult to remove rust completely and ensure the quality. Due to high labor intensity and low work efficiency, it is generally adopted for small workload or local rust removal.

（2）喷砂除锈

(2) Sandblasting derusting

喷砂除锈方法，有干喷砂和湿喷砂两种。利用压缩空气将砂粒送至专用喷嘴，以高速度喷射于钢板表面，借助砂粒的冲击和摩擦，将旧漆膜、污垢、铁锈、氧化皮等全部除去。

The two general sandblasting methods are wet sandblasting and dry sandblasting. The sand is sent to the special nozzle by compressed air, and sprayed on the steel surface at a high speed. With the help of the impact and friction of sand, the old paint film, dirt, rust, scale are all removed.

① 常用机具。

① Common equipments.

a. 动力设备：空气压缩机（内燃或电动，3 m^3/min 以上）、贮风桶（风包或分配器）、送风管路（把风送到喷砂器）。

a. Power equipments: air compressor (internal combustion or electric, more than 3 m^3/min), air storage bucket (air bag or distributor), air supply pipeline (to send air to sandblaster).

b. 备砂机具：筛砂机、运砂小车、储砂库。

b. Sand preparation equipment: sand screening machine, sand transport trolley, sand storage warehouse.

c. 喷砂机具：ϕ25 mm 压力橡胶皮管、油水分离器、贮风桶、盛砂设备、喷砂器、喷砂嘴及连接器、喷砂衣及其他劳动防护用品、ϕ8 mm 供风管（供工人呼吸用）、工具袋（内装面罩、备用玻璃、喷嘴、铁线、电工刀、活口扳手、克丝钳）等。

c. Sandblasting equipments: ϕ25 mm pressure rubber hose, oil-water separator, air storage bucket, sand holding equipment, sandblaster, sandblasting nozzle and connector, sandblasting clothing and other labor protection articles, ϕ8 mm air supply pipe (for workers to breathe), tool bag (including mask, glass, nozzle, iron wire, electrician's knife, open-ended wrench and wire clamp for standby), etc.

d. 喷砂用砂子的技术条件。

d. Technical conditions of sand for blasting.

喷砂用的砂子以洁净干燥、呈锐角颗粒的石英河砂为最好,加工筛选后颗粒为 0.5 ~ 2.5 mm 的河砂,这种砂在喷射时尘雾少且效率高。

The best sand used for sandblasting is clean and dry quartz river sand with sharp-angle particles. After processing and screening, river sand with a particle size of 0.5 to 2.5 mm has less dust and mist and high efficiency during spraying.

② 操作方法。

② Operation method.

a. 准备工作。为了提高喷砂效率,每个喷砂嘴供风量不小于 3 ~ 4 m^3/min,风压 0.4 ~ 0.6 MPa 。将经筛选加工过的河砂装满喷砂桶(每立方米河砂约可喷 20 ~ 30 m^2 的钢梁表面)。连接好管路及喷砂机具,检查其性能是否良好、连接是否牢固。高空作业时搭好脚手架。已做好的油漆应加以防护。

a. Preparation. In order to improve the sandblasting efficiency, the air supply volume of each sandblasting nozzle is not less than 3 - 4 m^3/min, and the air pressure is 0.4 - 0.6 MPa. Fill the screened and processed river sand into the sandblasting bucket (per cubic meter river sand for about 20 - 30 m^2 steel girder surface). Connect pipelines and the sandblasting equipment, and check whether the performance is good and the connection is firm. Erect scaffold for aloft work. Finished paint should be protected.

b. 喷砂操作。在风压达到 0.4 MPa 以上时,应先打开喷砂器风阀,再开砂阀(直通旋塞)即可进行喷砂作业。喷砂完毕应先关闭砂阀再关闭风阀以防堵塞。钢梁喷砂顺序一般应自上而下,由一端向另一端推进,以减少干扰。对杆件喷砂时应先喷角落及窄缝处,后喷宽敞部分;先喷边缘后喷中间;先喷铆钉头后喷平面。喷嘴与钢料表面距离以 150 ~ 250 mm、喷射角 45° ~ 80°为宜,移动速度要均匀,使之恰好除去锈蚀和氧化皮而不伤钢板。喷砂嘴以采用 ϕ5 ~ 7 mm 的高氧化铝陶瓷嘴为好。使用新嘴时,喷砂器砂阀应开小一些,随着喷砂工作的不断进行,喷砂嘴口径逐渐磨大,风压也要求高一些,风、砂阀都要开得大一些。一个喷嘴约可清除钢梁旧漆膜及锈蚀的钢梁表面约 30 ~ 60 m^2。如喷砂处所在桥梁上部或离喷砂器较远时,负责调整喷砂器风、操作砂阀的工人与喷砂工人之间要加强联系,固定联络信号,以便及时调整风、砂量。采用双室喷砂器或将两个单室喷砂器串联可以使喷砂工作连续不断,不致因装砂而中断喷砂,可提高工效。喷砂完毕应用压缩空气清除钢梁表面尘埃和积砂,必要时用手工工具进行一次找细,同时检查钢梁有无裂纹。

b. Sandblasting operation. When the wind pressure reaches above 0.4 MPa, first open sandblaster air valve, and then open sandblasting sand valve (straight-through cock) to perform the sandblasting operation. After sandblasting, first close the sand valve, and then close the air valve to prevent clogging. The steel girder should generally be blasted from top to bottom and from one end to the other to reduce interference. When sandblasting rods, first spray corners and narrow seams, and then spacious parts; first the edge, then the middle; first rivet head, and then plane. The distance between the nozzle and the steel surface should be 150 - 250 mm, the spray angle should be 45° - 80°, and the moving speed should be uniform, so that it can just remove rust and scale without damaging steel plates. The sandblasting nozzle is preferably made of high alumina ceramics with a diameter of 5 - 7 mm. When a new nozzle is used, the sand valve of the sandblaster should be opened smaller. With the continuous sandblasting work, the diameter of the sandblasting nozzle is gradually enlarged, and the air pressure is also required to be higher. The air and sand valves should be opened larger. One nozzle can remove about 30 - 60 m^2 of old paint film and corroded steel beam surface. For example, when the sandblasting place is on the upper part of the bridge or far away from the sandblaster, the workers responsible for adjusting the wind of the sandblaster and operating the sand valve and the sandblasting workers should strengthen the contact and fix the contact signal, so as to adjust the wind and sand volume in time. Using a double-chamber sandblaster or connecting two single-chamber sandblasters in series can make the sandblasting work continuous, and the sandblasting will not be interrupted due to sand loading, which can improve work efficiency. After sandblasting, use compressed air to remove the dust and accumulated sand on the surface of the steel beam. If necessary, use hand tools to make a fine search, and check the steel beam for cracks at the same time.

③ 施工注意事项。

③ Construction precautions.

a. 施工人员在喷砂开始前，要穿好工作服，戴好手套，接好防护头罩内输送新鲜空气的管路，喷砂衣要密闭，使衣内砂尘在空气内不超过 2 mg/m^3。

a. Before the sandblasting operation starts, the construction personnel should put on work clothes and gloves, and connect the pipeline for conveying fresh air in the protective hood. The sandblasting clothes should be sealed so that the sand dust inside the clothes does not exceed 2 mg /m^3.

b. 湿喷砂即水喷砂，能消除矽尘对环境的污染和人体的危害。一般在水中加入少量的防锈剂使金属表面钝化，保持短期内不生锈。但效率不及干喷砂，由于极少使用故不详细介绍。

b. Wet sandblasting is water sandblasting, which can eliminate the pollution of silica dust to the environment and the harm to human body. Generally, a small amount of rust inhibitor is added to the water to passivate the metal surface and keep it from rusting in a short period of time. However, the efficiency is not as good as dry sandblasting, and it is not described in detail because it is rarely used.

c. 不准带风修理喷砂设备或更换零件。

c. It is not allowed to repair sandblasting equipment or replace parts with wind.

d. 喷砂时喷嘴不能对人、对车和对船。

d. When sandblasting, the nozzle should not be aimed at people, vehicles and ships.

e. 喷砂胶管应避免弯折过剧，要加强检查，防止管壁因磨损过薄而发生炸裂。

e. The sandblasting hose should avoid excessive bending, and strengthen the inspection to prevent the pipe wall from bursting due to excessive wear.

④ 钢结构表面清理等级要求。

④ Steel structure surface cleaning grade requirements.

a. 电弧喷铝或涂装环氧富锌底漆时，钢表面清理应达到 Sa3 级。

a. When arc spraying aluminum or coating epoxy zinc-rich primer, the cleaning of steel surface should reach Sa3 Grade.

b. 涂装酚醛红丹、醇酸红丹底漆时，钢表面清理应达到 Sa2. 5 级。

b. When coating phenolic red lead and alkyd red lead primer, the cleaning of steel surface should reach Sa2. 5 Grade.

c. 箱形梁内表面涂装环氧沥青底漆时，钢表面清理应达到 Sa2 级。

c. When epoxy asphalt primer is applied on the inner surface of box girder, the steel surface shall be cleaned up to Sa2 Grade.

d. 限高防护架、人行道栏杆、扶手、托架、墩台吊篮、围栏等附属结构及铆钉头、螺栓头或局部维护涂装使用红丹底漆时，钢表面清理应达到 St3 级。

d. When the auxiliary structures such as height-limiting protective frames, sidewalk railings, handrails, brackets, pier hanging baskets, fences, etc., as well as rivet heads, bolt heads or local maintenance and painting use red lead primer, the steel surface cleaning should reach St3 Grade.

3. 钢结构保护涂装

3. Steel structure protection coating

防止钢梁生锈最广泛的方法是在钢结构表面喷涂油漆。油漆涂装一般分为三层，底漆的主要作用是防锈，中间漆和面漆的主要作用是保护和隔离空气、水等。常见的底漆有：红丹防锈漆、云母氧化铁防锈漆（又称云铁防锈漆）、无机富锌防锈漆和有机富锌防锈漆等。常见的面漆有：醇酸树脂磁漆、酚醛树脂磁漆、环氧树脂漆和聚氨酯耐磨漆等。如油漆层次之间附着力不好，应采用中间层漆加以解决。配套漆的目的是使涂料取长补短，解决漆与漆之间互容性、漆与物体之间的附着力和耐久性。

Spraying paint on the steel surface is most widely used to prevent rusting of steel beams. Paint coating is generally divided into three layers. Primer can prevent rust, intermediate paint can improve the adhesion and link strength between primer and topcoat, and topcoat can protect and isolate air and water. Common primers are: red lead primer, micaceous iron oxide primer, inorganic zinc-rich paint and organic zinc-rich paint. Common topcoats are: alkyd resin enamel, phenolic resin enamel, epoxy resin paint and polyurethane paint. If the adhesion between paint layers is poor, the intermediate paint shall be used. The matching paint can make use of each other's strong points, and improve the mutual compatibility between paints, and the adhesion and durability between paint and object.

(1)涂层体系

(1) Coating system

对新钢梁的初始涂装或既有钢梁整孔重新涂装，所采用的涂装体系有：

For the initial coating of new steel beam or the re-coating of the existing steel beam, the coating system adopted includes:

① 钢梁大面积部位涂装体系。

① Coating system for large area of steel beam.

a. 红丹酚醛底漆或红丹醇酸底漆,锌铝醇酸面漆或云铁醇酸面漆。

a. Red lead phenolic primer or red lead alkyd primer, zinc aluminum alkyd topcoat or micaceous iron alkyd topcoat.

b. 环氧富锌底漆或无机富锌底漆,磷化底漆中间层或环氧云铁中间层,锌铝醇酸面漆或云铁醇酸面漆。

b. Epoxy zinc rich or inorganic zinc rich primer, phosphating primer as intermediate paint or epoxy micaceous iron intermediate paint, zinc aluminum alkyd finish or micaceous iron alkyd finish.

c. 不同腐蚀环境下,钢梁热喷锌涂装,在热喷锌后刷涂一道磷化底漆密封锌镀层,再刷一道 C01-7 醇酸清漆。当大气环境呈酸性或碱性、金属易直接遭受化学腐蚀时,需在喷锌镀层上覆盖涂料层,即为锌黄酚醛底漆一道(亦可涂装磷化底漆或环氧云铁底漆中间层,但不得使用红丹底漆)及锌铝醇酸面漆或云铁醇酸面漆两道。

c. In different corrosive environments, first thermally sprayed steel beams with zinc, after that, apply a layer of phosphating primer to seal zinc coating, and then apply another layer of C01-7 alkyd varnish. When metals are subject to chemical corrosion directly in the acidic or alkaline atmospheric environment, it is necessary to cover the sprayed zinc coating with a coating that is, a coat of zinc yellow phenolic primer (it can also apply a phosphating primer or an epoxy micaceous iron oxide primer as the intermediate layer, but mustn't use red lead primer) and two coats of zinc-aluminum alkyd topcoat or mica alkyd topcoat.

② 纵梁、上承板梁、箱梁上盖板顶面采用的涂装体系。

② Coating system used on the top surface of the longitudinal beam, deck plate girder and box girder.

a. 棕黄聚氨酯底漆,银灰聚氨酯面漆。

a. Brown-yellow polyurethane primer, silver-gray polyurethane topcoat.

b. 热喷锌,棕黄聚氨酯底漆,银灰聚氨酯面漆。

b. Thermal spray zinc, brown-yellow polyurethane primer, silver-gray polyurethane topcoat.

c. 铆接梁板层间涂红丹防锈漆一道。栓焊梁连接部位板层间应热喷镀铝镀层或喷涂 78-2 无机富锌漆一道。栓焊梁连接处外露部位,可按钢梁大面积部位涂装体系进行。

c. Apply one coat of red lead primer the inter layers of riveted beams. Thermally spray the connection parts of bolted beams with aluminum coating or 78-2 inorganic zinc-rich paint. Paint the exposed parts of welded beam joints according to the large-area coating system of steel beam.

d. 箱形梁内部涂装低溶剂(溶剂含量在 20 % 以内)环氧沥青厚浆底漆和低溶剂环氧沥青厚浆面漆各一道,每道干膜厚度 125 μm,涂层总厚度不低于 250 μm。

d. Coat the interior of box beams with one layer of low solvent (solvent content is within 20%) high build epoxy asphalt primer and one layer of low solvent high build epoxy asphalt topcoat. Each dry film is 125 μm thick, and the total coating shall not be less than 250 μm thick.

总之,钢梁各部涂装体系可结合实际情况选择。

In short, the coating system of the steel beam member can be selected according to the actual situation.

(2)涂层涂装道数及厚度要求

(2) Coating layers and thickness requirements

漆膜要有一定的厚度才能有一定的保护能力,因此目前油漆施工大多数涂装多层。现在钢梁一般采用喷涂防锈底漆两道和面漆三道,干膜总厚度为 200 ~ 250 μm,即每度约为 40 ~ 50 μm。个别易损部位(如上盖板)还要求增加度数,使总厚度更厚一些。某一种油漆,其干膜厚度与涂刷时为成膜前湿膜厚度之比,称为该油漆的成膜率,一般在 70%。

A certain thickness of paint film has a good protective ability, so most of the current paint construction is coated with multiple layers. At present, steel beams are generally sprayed with two coats of anti-rust primer and three coats of topcoat, and the total dry film thickness is 200 -250 μm, that is, about 40 -50 μm per layer. Individual vulnerable parts (such as the upper cover plate) also require more layers to make the paint film thicker. For a certain kind of paint, the ratio of the dry film thickness after film formation to the wet film thickness before film formation is called the paint film-forming rate, which is generally 70%.

桥梁厂新制钢梁,因制造完毕到工地架设安装通车,相隔时间有的达数年之久,故在杆件出厂以前,除进行彻底除锈涂刷两道防锈底漆和一道面漆外,对铆合杆件节点板束内面,最好在拼铆前,涂红丹底漆一道,以防锈蚀。

The bridge factory's newly-made steel beams take several years from manufacture to erection, installation and put into operation. Therefore, before the rods leave the factory, derust thoroughly and apply two coats of anti-rust primer and one coat of topcoat. For the inner surface of riveted rod node plate bundle, it is best to apply red lead primer before riveting to prevent corrosion.

(3)稀释剂选用

(3) Choice of thinner

油漆的品种不同,所使用的稀释剂也各不相同。一般地,油性漆采用松香水或松节油,醇酸漆采用二甲苯或醇酸稀料,虫胶漆(即洋干漆)采用酒精,硝基漆(即喷漆)采用香蕉水,环氧树脂漆采用丙酮或环氧稀料,聚氨酯桥板漆采用二甲苯及无水环己酮。严禁用煤油、汽油、柴油作为桥梁用漆的稀释剂。

Different types of paints use different thinners. Generally, oil-based paint is used with rosin or turpentine, alkyd paint is used with xylene or alkyd thinner, shellac paint (ie dry paint) is used with alcohol, nitro paint (ie spray paint) is used with lacquer thinner, epoxy paint is used with acetone or epoxy thinner, and polyurethane paint is used with xylene and anhydrous cyclohexanone. It is strictly forbidden to use kerosene, gasoline and diesel as thinners for bridge paint.

稀释剂只在油漆过稠时使用。使用量一般应按油漆厂对该种油漆规定的限度,随气候和施工方法(热喷或冷喷)的不同而不同,具体须视实际情况确定。因为稀释剂仅为满足施工操作需要,所以要尽量少加或不加。除油漆厂规定允许外,对于一般桥梁用漆,掺加的稀释剂宜不超过油漆重量的 2%。

Thinner should only be used if the paint is too thick. Generally, the use amount shall be determined according to the limit specified by the paint factory for this kind of paint, which varies with the climate and construction method (hot spraying or cold spraying), and shall be determined according to the actual situation. Because the thinner is only to meet the needs of construction operation, it should be added as little or no as possible. Unless permitted by the paint factory, the thinner added to the bridge paint generally should not exceed 2% of the paint weight.

(4)涂装施工条件及要求

(4) Coating construction conditions and requirements

钢梁油漆涂装除要满足其技术条件外,还要达到涂装的施工条件和要求。

In addition to meeting its technical conditions, the paint coating of steel beams must also meet the construction conditions and requirements.

a. 环氧类漆不允许在 10 ℃以下施工,无机富锌防锈防滑涂料、酚醛漆、醇酸漆、聚氨酯漆、氟碳面漆不允许在 5 ℃以下施工。夏季最好避免阳光直射施工物件,可在背阴处进行。

a. Epoxy paints are not allowed to be applied below 10 ℃, and inorganic zinc-rich and coatings for anti-rust and anti-skid, phenolic paints, alkyd paints, polyurethane paints, and fluorocarbon topcoats are not allowed to be applied below 5 ℃. In summer, the coating should be constructed in the shade to avoid direct sunlight.

b. 严禁在雨、雾、雪、霜和风沙天气进行涂漆;相对湿度不大于 80% 才能涂装。

b. It is strictly forbidden to paint in rain, fog, snow, frost and sandy day. Only apply the coating when the relative humidity is not more than 80%.

c. 当钢梁除锈完毕后,应在不超过 8 h(湿度较大时 2 ~ 4 h)内,尽快涂头道底漆,并应于当日喷涂完毕。涂漆前应清扫钢梁表面,并最好用干净布蘸松节油或松香水擦拭干净。

c. After derusting, apply the first primer as soon as possible within 8 hours (2 to 4 hours when the humidity is high), and spray on the same day. Clean the steel beam surface before painting with a clean cloth dipped in turpentine or rosin.

d. 底漆充分干燥后,才允许涂次层油漆,其间隔时间视当时施工条件和油漆性能确定。底漆、中间漆最长暴露时间不超过 7 d,两道面漆间隔若超过 7 d 时需用细砂纸打磨涂层表面成细微毛面后,方能涂下一道漆。

d. After the primer is fully dried, apply the sub-layer paint an the interval which is determined by the construction conditions and paint performance at that time. The longest exposure time of primer and intermediate paint is not more than 7 d. If the interval between two topcoats exceeds 7 d, polish the coating surface with fine sandpaper to form a fine rough surface before applying the next paint.

e. 进行下一道涂漆前,应用铲刀将表面上灰尘杂质铲除干净,然后用“00”号砂纸轻轻打磨后再喷,使每层油漆黏结牢固。第一道底漆喷涂后不得露出下面的钢料,上层喷涂后不得露出底层的油漆。

e. Before the next painting, use a shovel to remove the dust and impurities on the surface, and then lightly sand it with “00” sandpaper before spraying, so that each layer of paint is firmly bonded. After the first primer is sprayed, the underlying steel shall not be exposed, and the bottom layer of paint shall not be exposed after the upper layer is sprayed.

f. 为了便于检查所涂油漆的质量,二道面漆也可采用深浅不同的颜色来加以区别。每道应尽量做到喷涂均匀,不得有缺漏、皱纹、流挂,更不应有脱落揭皮的现象。

f. In order to check the paint quality, the second coat can also be distinguished by different shades of color. Sprayed each layer evenly as much as possible without leakage, wrinkles, sagging, and peeling off.

g. 在经受烟熏、落煤灰和蒸汽影响的部位,涂油作业应在较长的列车间隔时间内进行,必要时,应遮挡尚未干燥的油漆。

g. In the parts affected by smoke, coal ash and steam, the oiling operation should be carried out within a long interval between trains, and if necessary, the paint that has not yet dried should be covered.

h. 钢梁油漆完毕应将涂装日期、施工方法、漆膜厚度以及所用油漆品种等标志在显著部位,以观察其耐久性,并恢复钢梁上原有的各种标记。

h. After the steel beam is painted, the date of painting, construction methods, thickness of paint film and the types of used paints should be marked on prominent parts to observe its durability, and the original marks on the steel beam should be restored.

(5)手工涂装与喷射涂漆

(5) Manual painting and spray painting

在合适的施工条件下,钢梁经细致的表面处理后,采用质量优良的油漆材料进行良好的涂装才能得到理想的防护效果,因此,钢梁油漆涂刷必须注重施工质量。

Under suitable construction conditions, after careful surface treatment of steel beams, good coating with high-quality paint materials can obtain the ideal protective effect. Therefore, the painting of steel beams must lay emphasis on construction quality.

① 手工刷涂。

① Manual painting.

手工刷涂的特点是设备简单,操作方便,灵活性大。其缺点为手工劳动,生产效率低,漆膜往往有粗粒及刷痕,对一些快干及涂刷性能差的油漆不适宜手工刷涂。

Manual painting is characterized by simple tools, convenient operation and great flexibility. It also has the disadvantages of manual labor, low production efficiency, and the paint film with coarse grains and brush marks, which is not suitable for the fast drying paints and the paints with poor brushing performance.

漆刷是刷漆施工的主要工具,根据不同的施工对象可以选择不同尺寸不同形状的漆刷。漆刷按形状大致可分为圆形、扁形和歪形三种;按制作材料可分为硬毛刷(以猪鬃制)、软毛刷(用狼毫、羊毛制)两类。

Paint brushes are the main tools for painting construction. According to different objects, paint brushes of different sizes and shapes can be selected. Paint brushes can be roughly divided into three types according to shape: round, flat and crooked; according to the materials, they can be divided into two types: hard brushes (made of pig bristles) and soft brushes (made of wolf hair and wool).

手工刷涂的操作方法:先将油漆均匀地散涂在钢梁表面上(俗称墩油)或刷成S形,然后横刷、竖刷,自上而下、自左而右,先难后易(线脚、角落部位先刷),依次刷匀。漆刷蘸漆不宜过多,蘸漆深度以刷毛的1/3~2/3为宜。刷涂时操作要敏捷,厚薄要均匀合适。但是一般涂刷一次不宜过厚,否则容易发生皱皮现象。油漆施工黏度,要根据温度变化而调节,漆液太稀,易流挂,盖不住底;太稠,不易刷匀,影响干燥。

The operation method of manual painting: first spread paint evenly on the steel beam surface or brush the surface in S shape, and then brush horizontally and vertically, from top to bottom, from left to right, from difficult-to-paint parts to easy-to-paint parts (the lines and corners are brushed first), brush them evenly in turn. The paint brush should not be dipped in too much paint, and the depth of the paint should be 1/3 to 2/3 of the bristles. When brushing, the operation should be agile, and the thickness should be even and appropriate. But in general, one brushing should not be too thick, otherwise wrinkling may easily occur. Adjust the paint viscosity according to the temperature change. Too thin paint is easy to sag and can't cover the bottom, while too thick paint is not easy to brush evenly and will affect drying.

对钢梁的附件也可以用丝头蘸油漆用手搓刷,对栏杆扶手等,在用丝头搓涂后,可用漆刷拉平修整。

The accessories of steel beams can also be rubbed by hand with the wire tip dipped in paint, and railings can be leveled and trimmed by the paint brush after rubbing with the wire tip.

对钢梁杆件之间的狭小间隙部位和相互交叉的隐藏处所,或同一根杆件中由于型钢铆合组拼存在的窄缝处所,因其隐藏,施工困难,要特别注意除锈和油漆质量。该处的涂油工作要根据实际情况,自行制作各种尺寸的小麻刷进行,并防止漏涂或露底。

For the narrow gaps between steel beam members and the hidden places that intersect each other, or the narrow gaps in the same member due to the riveting combination of structure steels, it is difficult to construct due to their hiding properties, and special attention should be paid to the quality of derusting and paints. Oil the place by small hemp brushes of various sizes made according to the actual situation, and prevent missing coating or bottom exposure.

② 喷涂方法和常见机具。

② Spraying method and common equipments.

利用压缩空气在喷枪处产生的负压,将漆流带出并分散为雾状,涂覆于钢梁表面上,这是目前最常用的一种施工方法,它的最大特点是操作比较轻便,工效高(比刷涂可快5~10倍),漆膜平整光滑,适用于不同尺寸的钢梁表面。其缺点是油漆的利用率低,溶剂易挥发,不经济,漆雾大,影响工人健康。

Using the negative pressure generated by the compressed air at the spray gun, the paint flow is sprayed out and dispersed into mist and coated on the steel beam surface. This is the most commonly used construction method at present. It is characterized by easy operation, high efficiency (5 to 10 times faster than brushing), smooth paint film, and suitability for steel beam surfaces of different sizes. However, it has disadvantages of low paint utilization, solvent volatilization, diseconomy, large paint fog, and effect on workers' health.

热喷涂就是将油漆预热到一定温度(根据不同油漆而温度也不同)再喷涂,由于加热升温,降低油漆黏度,减少掺入油漆的稀料,因而能提高油漆质量。

Thermal spraying is to preheat the paint to a certain temperature (the temperature is different according to different paints) and then spray. Due to heating up, the paint viscosity is reduced, and the thinner mixed into paint is reduced, so the painting quality can be improved.

喷漆油漆除供风系统外,主要机具有:

In addition to the air supply system, the main machines for spray painting are as follows:

a. 喷漆枪:由于漆罐储油量小,不适于大面积施工,可以把它除去,改由压力喷漆桶供油。喷漆枪主要分为扁嘴式、对嘴式、压下式等三种。

a. Spray paint gun: due to the small oil storage capacity of the paint tank, it is not suitable for large-scale construction. It can be removed and the oil is supplied by a pressure spray paint bucket. Spray guns can be mainly divided into three types: flat nozzle type, opposite nozzle type, and press-down type.

b. 压力喷漆桶:利用风压将已调好黏度适合的油漆,通过 $\phi 8$ mm 胶管送到喷漆枪上。

b. Pressure spraying bucket: use wind pressure to send the paint with a suitable viscosity to the spray gun through a hose of 8 mm diameter.

c. 油水分离器:能去除压缩空气中的油脂和水分,保证漆膜质量。

c. Oil-water separator: it can remove grease and moisture in the compressed air and ensure the paint film quality.

喷漆前,油漆要搅匀,用筛子过滤去除漆皮和粗粒,根据不同品种的油漆,调整到适合的黏度,空气喷漆压力一般以 0.3 ~ 0.5 MPa 为好。喷枪与钢料表面的距离要适当,以 15 ~ 25 cm 为宜,喷枪与物面应保持正确垂直的角度。喷漆采用横喷或纵喷,每次压叠一半,喷漆速度必须前后均匀一致,不能时快时慢,每喷到两端时必须关风以防端头流挂。喷漆时要特别注意钢梁杆件边角部位及其他隐蔽处所,这些地方最易漏喷或漆膜过薄造成锈蚀产生。

Before spraying, stir the paint evenly, and remove the paint skin and coarse particles by filtering with a sieve. According to different types of paint, adjust to the appropriate viscosity. The air spraying pressure is generally 0.3 - 0.5 MPa. The distance between the spray gun and the steel surface should be appropriate, preferably 15 - 25 cm, and the spray gun and the surface should maintain a correct vertical angle. The spray painting adopts horizontal spraying or vertical spraying, and the layer is half stacked each time. The spraying speed must be uniform before and after, and it can't be fast or slow. When spraying to both ends, the wind must be turned off to prevent the ends from sagging. When painting, pay special attention to the corners of steel beam members and other hidden places, which are most likely to be missed or sprayed thin paint film to cause corrosion.

2.3.4 作业验收

2.3.4 Operation acceptance

1. 混凝土抹面作业验收标准

1. Operation acceptance standards for concrete plastering

抹面压实，无裂纹、空响，砂浆符合规定。

The plaster surface is compacted, without cracks and empty noises, and the mortar meets the requirements.

2. 混凝土裂缝压浆作业验收标准

2. Operation acceptance standards for concrete crack grouting

① 注浆孔位置、深度及灰浆配合比、水灰比符合要求。

① The position and depth of grouting holes, as well as the mortar mix ratio and water-cement ratio meet the requirements.

② 不因钻孔而损坏原圬工，裂纹和空隙内经压水冲洗，并注满浆。

② The original masonry is not damaged due to drilling, and the cracks and voids are flushed with pressurized water and filled with grout.

③ 注浆孔用砂浆填实，无裂纹，淌出灰浆清除干净。

③ The grouting holes are filled with mortar, without cracks, and the drooling mortar is cleaned up.

3. 混凝土修补作业验收标准

3. Operation acceptance standards for concrete repair

① 材料配合比、工艺符合要求。

① The material mix ratio and process meet the requirements.

② 槽宽度误差不超过 ±3 mm，深度不少于 8 mm。

② The groove width error should not exceed ±3 mm, and the depth should not be less than 8 mm.

③ 勾缝平实，凹凸不超过 ±2 mm，与圬工结合牢固，无断道。

③ The joints should be flat, the unevenness should not exceed ±2 mm, and they should be firmly combined with the masonry without breakage.

④ 色泽协调均匀。

④ The color is harmonious and uniform.

4. 钢表面清理作业验收标准

4. Operation acceptance standards for steel surface cleaning

维护涂装底漆时，钢表面清理达到 Sa2.5 级。

When the primer is applied for maintenance, the steel surface shall be cleaned to Sa2.5 Grade.

5. 涂膜粉化清理作业验收标准

5. Operation acceptance standards for coating powder cleaning

涂层表面打磨、污垢清除彻底，不损伤底漆。

Polish the coating surface and remove the dirt thoroughly without damaging the primer.

6. 腻缝作业验收标准
6. Operation acceptance standards for filling seam

作业范围内,凡能积水的缝隙内的旧漆污垢应除净无漏腻,腻子填实压平,无开裂积水。

Within the scope of operation, the old paint and dirt in the gaps that can accumulate water should be removed and filled, and the putty should be compacted and flattened without cracking and water accumulation.

7. 涂装维修作业验收标准
7. Operation acceptance standards for coating maintenance

① 涂装体系、层数、厚度符合规定。

① The coating system, number of coats and thickness meet the regulations.

② 涂层表面平整均匀,新旧涂层衔接平顺,色泽不匀不超过 5%。

② The coating surface is smooth and uniform, the old and new coatings are connected smoothly, and the uneven color does not exceed 5%.

③ 无剥落、裂纹。

③ No peeling or cracking.

④ 无起泡、气孔。

④ No bubbles and pores.

2.4 墩台作业
2.4 Pier and abutment operation

2.4.1 支座及墩台检查
2.4.1 Inspection of bearings and piers

桥梁支座与墩台的日常养护维修和性能检验直接关系到它们的正常使用。检查制度主要为定期检查。各工区建立检查记录簿,按规定认真填写,保证数据准确可靠,为状态分析评定和编制维护工作计划提供依据。为保证检查的精度,应配备必要的检查工具和仪器。

The daily maintenance and performance inspection of bridge bearings and abutments can directly effect their normal use. The inspection system mainly mainly refers to regular inspections. Each working section shall establish an inspection record book, which shall be carefully filled in according to the regulations to ensure the accuracy and reliability of the data, so as to provide a basis for condition analysis and maintenance work plan preparation. To ensure the accuracy of inspection, the necessary inspection tools and instruments should be equipped.

对桥梁支座进行检查,对于结合梁、连续梁支座每半年检查一次,对于简支梁支座每一年至少抽查 30%,3 年全检一次。其中,平板橡胶支座主要检查有无裂纹、不均匀外鼓、钢板外露、剪切变形超限、位置串动等情况,限位装置是否可靠;盆式橡胶支座主要检查有无钢件裂纹、脱焊、锈蚀、聚四氟乙烯板磨损、位移转角超限等情况;支座与梁身、支承垫石间是否密贴。

The bridge bearings shall be inspected. The bearings of combined beams and continuous beams shall be inspected every six months, at least 30% of simply supported beam bearings shall be sampled for inspection every year, and the whole bearings shall be inspected once every three years. Among them, for plate rubber bearings, mainly check whether there are cracks, uneven sags, exposed steel plates, excessive shear deformation, position string movement, etc., and whether limiting devices are reliable; for pot rubber bearings, mainly check whether there are steel cracks, de-soldering, rust, PTFE plate wear, over-limit displacement angle, etc.; whether the bearings are closely attached to the beam body and the supporting pad.

对桥梁墩台进行检查,每半年一次。但对经常被社会车辆撞击的桥墩,每月检查一次。主要检查内容包括:防排水设施是否失效;混凝土保护层中性化是否大于 25 mm;混凝土墩台是否因碱-集料反应导致裂纹产生;是否因意外事故造成墩台混凝土局部溃碎或钢筋变形、折断。

The bridge piers and abutments are inspected every six months. But the bridge piers that are often hit by social vehicles need to be checked once a month. The main inspection contents include: whether waterproof and drainage facilities fail; whether the neutralization thickness of concrete protective layer is greater than 25mm; whether the concrete piers and abutments are cracked due to alkali-aggregate reaction; whether the concrete is partially broken or the steel bar is deformed or broken due to an accident.

对结合梁与连续梁伸缩缝的伸缩量,每年在夏冬季节进行两次的观测记录(梁体做好标记,可结合支座检查一同进行),并对预应力梁封头端进行检查。

Observe and record the expansion and contraction amount of expansion joints on combined beams and continuous beams twice a year in summer and winter (mark beams, and inspect them together with the bearing inspection), and inspect the head ends of prestressed beams.

在秋季应对桥梁设施进行全面检查,据以拟定病害整治措施,安排设备改善计划,确保行车安全。

In autumn, comprehensively inspect bridge facilities, formulate disease treatment measures and arrange equipment improvement plans to ensure driving safety.

2.4.2 支座养护
2.4.2 Maintenance of bearing

各类支座出现表 2-5 中状态时,应及时处理。

For various types of bearings, they shall be handled in time in case of the following conditions in Table 2-5.

表 2-5 桥梁支座病害情况一览表

支座类型	病害情况
板式橡胶支座	① 支座压溃,四周出现明显不规则的凹凸、弯曲或扭曲。 ② 支座剪切变形过大,活载作用时剪切变形≥24°,无活载作用时永久剪切变形≥15°。 ③ 橡胶剥落掉块,导致加劲钢板表面或周边外露长度>100 mm。 ④ 橡胶裂纹宽度≥2 mm,且连续长度达周边长度的 50% 以上。 ⑤ 支座串动大于相应边长的 25% 或有脱空

续表

支座类型	病害情况
盆式橡胶支座	① 盆环开裂或脱焊。 ② 聚四氟乙烯板磨耗严重，外露厚度不足 0.2 mm。 ③ 位移或转角超限，位移量≥10 mm，转角超过设计值的 20%。 ④ 锚栓剪断数量 >25%
钢支座	① 钢部件裂纹深度≥10 mm，主要受力部位焊缝脱焊。 ② 辊轴支座底板变形凹陷≥3 mm。 ③ 销钉剪断或锚栓折断数量 >25%。 ④ 支座位移超限，纵向 >5 mm、横向 >2 mm。 ⑤ 活动支座不活动。 ⑥ 支承垫石开裂、积水、翻浆。 ⑦ 摇轴倾斜、辊轴位移或倾斜超过容许值。 ⑧ 聚四氟乙烯板磨耗严重，外露厚度不足 0.2 mm

Table 2-5　Bridge bearing diseases

Type of bearing	Disease description
Plate rubber bearing	① The bearing is crushed, with obvious irregular bumps, bends, or twists around it. ② The bearing shear deformation is too large, the shear deformation is more than 24° under live loads, and the permanent shear deformation is more than 15° without live loads. ③ The rubber flakes off, and the exposed length of the stiffening steel plate surface or surrounding area is greater than 100 mm. ④ The rubber crack width is more than 2 mm, and the continuous length is more than 50% of the peripheral length. ⑤ The bearing movement due to local bearing is greater than 25% of the corresponding side length or there is a void
Pot rubber bearing	① Through link is cracked or desoldering. ② The PTFE plate is seriously worn, and the exposed thickness is less than 0.2 mm. ③ The displacement or rotation angle exceeds the limit, the displacement is more than 10 mm, and the rotation angle exceeds 20% of the design value. ④ The number of anchor bolts sheared is more than 25% of the total number
Steel bearing	① The crack depth of steel parts is more than 10 mm, and the weld seam of main stress parts is de-welded. ② The deformation of the roller bearing bottom plate is more than 3 mm. ③ The number of pins sheared or anchor bolts broken is more than 25% of the total number. ④ The bearing displacement exceeds the limit, which is more than 5 mm in the longitudinal direction, and more than 2 mm in the transverse direction. ⑤ The active bearing doesn't move. ⑥ The supporting pads are cracked, water accumulated and frost boiling. ⑦ The tilt of the rocker axis, the displacement or the tilt of the roller axis exceeds the allowable value. ⑧ The PTFE plate is seriously worn, and the exposed thickness is less than 0.2 mm

1. 支座保养

1. Maintenance of bearings

① 用扫帚、钢丝刷、铲刀、破布清除各部分灰尘和污垢，卸开防尘罩。

① Clean up dust and dirt from various parts with brooms, steel wire brushes, blades and rags, and remove the dust cover.

② 清除上下摆污垢和铁锈,涂刷防锈漆。

② Remove dirt and rust from the upper and lower hem, and apply anti-rust paint.

③ 清洁滚动面,掏出原有黄油,重新压填黄油或擦石墨。黄油表面封贴纸条或塑料薄膜。

③ Clean the rolling surface, take out the original butter, re-press the butter or wipe the graphite. Sealing paper strip or plastic film on the butter surface.

④ 装好防尘罩,并将缝隙封闭,以防灰尘浸入。

④ Install the dust cover and close the gap to prevent dust from entering.

2. 支座除锈

2. Derusting of bearings

支座除锈作业,是对锈蚀的支座用打磨机除锈并施以油漆涂装的一种作业。对于每平方米的支座钢结构表面需要环氧富锌底漆 1.5 kg 和氯化橡胶面漆 1.5 kg。所需工具主要有打磨机和空压机。

The bearing derusting is to remove the rust off bearings with a grinder and apply paints on them. For each square meter of bearing steel structure surface, 1.5 kg of epoxy zinc-rich primer and 1.5 kg of chlorinated rubber topcoat are required. The tools required are mainly grinders and air compressors.

(1)操作程序

(1) Operation procedure

① 打磨机除锈,全出白。

① Remove rust by grinder until there is no rust, paint skin and dirt on bearings and the original color of metal is exposed.

② 底漆分别两度,待干。

② Apply two coats of primer, and leave it to dry.

③ 面漆分别两度,待干。

③ Apply two coats of topcoat, and leave it to dry.

(2)质量控制

(2) Quality control

① 整体除锈要全出白,局部除锈可保留底漆,现场根据具体情况确定。

① After the overall rust removal, there is no rust, paint skin and dirt on bearings and the original color of metal. The local rust removal can retain the primer, which is determined according to the specific situation on site.

② 除锈应达到 Sa2.5 级除锈标准,即钢材表面无可见的油脂、污垢、氧化皮、铁锈和油漆涂层等附着物,仅残留点状或条纹状的轻微色斑。工作表面粗糙度可达 40 ~ 60 μm。

② The rust removal should reach the Sa2.5 Grade, that is, Rust removal surface should be free of visible grease, dirt, oxide scale, rust, paint coating, and impurities, and the residue traces only show slight spots or streaks. The working surface roughness can reach 40 ~ 60 μm.

③ 钢结构表面要求在除锈后 4 h 内必须干燥,并立即刷底漆,避免形成二次生锈。

③ The surface of steel structure shall be dry within 4 h after derusting, and apply primer immediately to avoid rusting again.

④ 涂刷厚度符合设计要求,不小于 70 μm。涂刷牢固,无剥落、皱纹、气泡、针孔等缺陷。

④ The brushing thickness shall meet the design requirements and shall not be less than 70 μm. The coating shall be firm without peeling, wrinkles, bubbles, pinholes and other defects.

⑤ 底漆干燥时间:25 ℃表干 0.5 ~1 h,实干 24 h,完全固化 7 天。

⑤ Drying time of primer: at 25 ℃, surface dry for 0.5 -1 h, thorough dry for 24 h, and fully cured for 7 days.

⑥ 底漆涂装间隔:5 ℃最短 48 h,最长 7 天。20 ℃最短 24 h,最长 3 天。

⑥ Coating interval of primer: at 5 ℃, the shortest is 48 h and the longest is 7 days. At 20 ℃, the shortest is 24 h and the longest is 3 days.

⑦ 面漆干燥时间:25 ℃表干 2 h,实干 8 h,完全固化 7 天。

⑦ Drying time of topcoat: at 25 ℃, surface dry for 2 h, thorough dry for 8 h, and fully cured for 7 days.

⑧ 面漆涂装间隔:0 ℃最短 24 h,最长不限。20 ℃最短 8 h,最长不限。30 ℃最短 6 h,最长不限。

⑧ Coating interval of topcoat : at 0 ℃, the shortest is 24 h and the longest is unlimited. At 20 ℃, the shortest is 8 h and the longest is unlimited. At 30 ℃, the shortest is 6 h and the longest is unlimited.

3. 支座的整修

3. Repair of bearings

(1)支座上锚栓折断、弯曲、锈死

(1) The anchor bolt on the bearing is broken, bent or rusted

支座上摆的四根锚栓,在梁底镶角板间被剪断时,先将支座上摆移正,然后将上摆与镶角板两侧焊接,也可用化学结构胶将上摆与镶角板粘接。

When the four anchor bolts on the upper swing of the bearing are cut between the gusseted plates at the bottom of the beam, first move the upper swing of the bearing upright, then weld the upper swing to both sides of the gusseted plate, the upper swing can also be bonded to the gusseted plates with a chemical structural adhesive.

(2)下锚栓折断、弯曲、锈死

(2) The lower anchor bolt is broken, bent and rusted

① 备好新锚栓及螺帽垫圈等。

① Prepare new anchor bolts and nut washers, etc.

② 开凿出锚栓孔,在支座旁斜向凿孔,侧面取出旧锚栓。

② Drill out the anchor bolt hole, drill the hole obliquely beside the bearing, and take out the old anchor bolt from the side.

③ 清除锚栓孔内碎渣、粉末;冲洗干净,掏净积水。

③ Remove slag and powder in the anchor bolt hole. Wash the hole and clean up the ponding.

④ 插入新锚栓:从侧面将锚栓插入座板锚栓孔内。

④ Insert the new anchor bolt: Insert the anchor bolt into the anchor bolt hole of the seat plate from the side.

⑤ 填入部分砂浆，初步捣实，调整位置和高度。边填边捣，顶部压平抹光，做好排水。

⑤ Fill in part of the mortar, preliminarily compact it, and adjust the position and height. Pound while filling, flatten and smooth the top, and drain well.

⑥ 用湿草袋等覆盖，及时浇水，养生不少于 7 天。

⑥ Cover with wet grass bags, water in time, and maintain health for not less than 7 days.

⑦ 砂浆凝固后方准进行螺栓涂油并拧紧螺帽，盖好防尘罩。

⑦ After the mortar is solidified, oil the bolts, tighten the nuts, and cover the dust cover.

(3) 支座悬空、支承垫石损裂

(3) The bearing is suspension of the bearing, damage and cracking of the supporting pad

① 预凿部分混凝土。

① Pre-chisel part of the concrete.

② 固定支座，准备锚栓。

② Fix the bearing and prepare the anchor bolt.

③ 起梁。

③ Lift the beam.

④ 凿除混凝土。

④ Chisel the concrete.

⑤ 清理、支模。

⑤ Clean off and mold support.

⑥ 拌制干硬砂浆。

⑥ Mix dry hard mortar.

⑦ 分层捣垫。

⑦ Tamp layer by layer.

⑧ 落梁。

⑧ Drop the beam.

(4) 支座沉陷、积水、翻浆

(4) Subsidence of the bearing, water accumulation, and pulping

支座底板四周细凿垫石做 3% 流水坡；墩台面也凿成大于 3% 的坡，利于排水。

Finely chisel cushion stones around the base plate of the bearing to make a 3% flowing water slope; the pier table is also chiseled into a slope of more than 3%, which is conducive to drainage.

(5) 活动支座不活动

(5) The movable bearing is not movable

对平板、弧形支座顶起梁身，将穿销涂黄油除锈，并清污；对摇轴和滚轴找出原因，必要时更换。

Jack up the beam on the flat bearing or rocker bearing, apply grease to remove rust and dirt on the threaded pins. Identify the cause of the rocker and roller shafts, and replace them if necessary.

2.4.3　运营线路桥梁支座更换

2.4.3　Replacement of bridge bearings on operating lines

1. 搭设支架和施工平台

1. Set up the support and the construction platform

① 桥台支座更换利用桥台作为施工平台，对空间不够部位采用支架措施，以确保施工的安全实施。

① Use the abutment as the construction platform to replace the abutment bearing, and adopt bracket measures for the parts with insufficient space to ensure the safe implementation of the construction.

② 对于桥墩支座的更换，采用特制钢挂架固定于墩身或盖梁上作为施工平台。

② For the replacement of the pier bearing, a special steel hanger is used to fix the pier body or the cover beam as a construction platform.

2. 台帽、盖梁顶面清理

2. Clean the top surface of the abutment cap and bent cap

① 清理台帽或盖梁顶面沉积的土石块及混凝土块，必要时可采用钢钎对混凝土垃圾进行清理。

① Clean up the soil stones and concrete blocks deposited on the top surface of the abutment cap or bent cap, and use steel fiber to clean up the concrete waste if necessary.

② 用钢丝刷对台帽或盖梁顶面进行清洁，保证支座更换时作业面干净整洁。

② Use a wire brush to clean the top surface of the abutment cap or bent cap to ensure that the working surface is clean and tidy when the bearing is replaced.

③ 清理伸缩缝内沉积的垃圾和杂物，以防止顶升内梁体间互相挤压。

③ Clean up the rubbish and sundries deposited in the expansion joint to prevent the inner beams from being squeezed against each other.

3. 支座调查与复检

3. Investigation and re-inspection of bearing

① 对要更换的支座部位进行确认和检查，现场记录支座位置、编号、病害情况，并拍照记录，照片应拍摄完整的施工工序即原状、更换过程及更换完成情况，妥善保存检查记录，作为交工文件之一。

① Confirm and inspect the part of the bearing to be replaced, record the location, serial number, and disease condition of the bearing on site, and take photos to record. The photos should be taken of the complete construction process, that is, the original state, the replacement process and the completion of the replacement, and the inspection records should be properly kept as one of the delivery documents.

② 复核原支座型号与设计院提供的型号是否一致，并根据支座的设计承载力确定顶升重量及千斤顶的型号和数量。

② Check whether the original bearing model is consistent with the model provided by the design institute, and determine the jacking weight and the type and quantity of jacks according to the design bearing capacity of the bearing.

③ 测量梁底高程,并根据设计图纸提供的梁底高程进行复核,并将复核情况详细记录并妥善保存,作为交工文件之一。

③ Measure the beam bottom elevation, and review it according to the beam bottom elevation provided by the design drawings, and record the review in detail and keep it properly as one of the delivery documents.

④ 根据测量记录确定支座垫石顶面高程的调整高度。对于需要将普通支座更换为四氟滑板支座的情况,应根据要更换的四氟滑板支座的型号、高度确定支座垫石改造后的顶面高程,以保证支座更换后桥面高程符合设计要求。

④ Determine the adjustment height of the top elevation of the bearing cushion stone according to the measurement record. For the case where the ordinary bearing needs to be replaced with a PTFE sliding plate bearing, the top surface elevation after the transformation of the bearing cushion should be determined according to the model and height of the PTFE sliding plate bearing to be replaced, so as to ensure that the bridge deck elevation meets the design requirements after the bearing is replaced.

4. 千斤顶、百分表安放与设置

4. Placement and setting of jack and dial indicator

① 千斤顶数量应与每个桥台下的支座数量相同。

① The number of jacks should be the same as the number of bearings under each abutment.

② 布设百分表:为精确测量顶升高度并在梁体顶升过程中控制梁体姿态,需在梁台两侧布设百分表,顶升过程中应有专人负责记录百分表读数。

② Layout dial indicator: in order to accurately measure the jacking height and control the beam posture during the lifting process of the beam body, dial indicators should be arranged on both sides of the beam platform, and a special person should be responsible for recording the dial indicators during the jacking process.

5. 顶升系统调试

5. Debugging of jacking system

① 液压系统检查。

① Hydraulic system inspection.

② 控制系统检查。

② Control system inspection.

③ 初值设定与读取。

③ Initial value setting and reading.

6. 试顶

6. Test of pushing in jack

① 试顶前检查。

① Inspection before the test of pushing in jack.

a. 千斤顶安装是否垂直牢固。

a. Whether the jack is installed vertically and firmly.

b. 影响顶升的设施是否已全部拆除。

b. Whether all the facilities affecting jacking have been dismantled.

c. 顶升部分结构与其他结构的连接是否已全部去除。

c. Whether the connection between the jacked part of the structure and other structures has been completely removed.

② 顶升系统启动后现场各组人员各就各位，密切观察桥梁是否有异常状况出现，设备、仪表是否正常工作，显示读数是否在合理范围内。

② After the jacking system is started, each group of personnel on the site shall take their place, and closely observe whether there is any abnormal condition on the bridge, whether the equipment and instruments are working normally, and whether the display reading is within a reasonable range.

③ 控制顶升速度不超过 1 mm/min，最大顶升高度不超过 5 mm。

③ Control the jacking speed not to exceed 1 mm/min, and the maximum jacking height not to exceed 5 mm.

④ 顶升就位后，持荷 10 min 观察梁体及设备状况。有异常情况，应立即回油、落梁，问题解决后再进行试顶，直至梁体受力及设备运行正常。

④ After the jacking is in place, hold the load for 10 minutes to observe the condition of the beam and equipment. If there is any abnormal situation, the oil should be returned immediately, the beam should be dropped, and the roof should be tested after the problem is solved until the beam body is stressed and the equipment operates normally.

⑤ 顶升就位后，根据控制系统显示的顶升重量复核支座型号及各支座承受的压力，如有异常，则应考虑调整支座型号。

⑤ After the jacking is in place, check the bearing model and the pressure on each bearing according to the jacking weight displayed by the control system. If there is any abnormality, consider adjusting the bearing model.

⑥ 试顶正常后，应平稳落梁。

⑥ After the test is normal, the beam should be lowered steadily.

7. 梁体同步顶升

7. Lift beam synchronously

① 顶升过程中以每顶升 2 mm 为一步，分级顶升，各顶高差严格控制在 0.5 mm 范围内，全程采用位移传感器监测梁体顶升位移情况。实时监测整个千斤顶间位移传感器升量高差，若高差超过控制值时，必须进行适时调整后才进入下一个顶升周期，达到同步顶升的目的。

① During the jacking, every 2 mm is taken as a step, and the jacking is carried out in stages. The height difference of each jack is strictly controlled within the range of 0.5 mm. The displacement sensor is used to monitor the lifting displacement of the beam body throughout the whole process. The jacking height difference of displacement sensors between jacks is monitored in real time. If the height difference exceeds the control value, it must be adjusted in time before entering the next lifting cycle to achieve the purpose of synchronous lifting.

② 箱梁两侧布设百分表监测箱梁转动的情况，同时也作为位移传感器的对比验证数据，箱梁每顶升一级百分表读数一次。观测人员随时根据监测值反馈至控制室，指导操作人员进行操作。

② A dial indicator is arranged on both sides of the box girder to monitor the rotation of the box girder, and it is also used as the comparison and verification data of the displacement sensor. The dial indicator reads once every time the box girder is lifted. The observers can feed back to the control room at any time according to the monitoring value, and guide the operators to operate.

③ 顶升时梁每升高 5 ~6 mm，临时支撑加垫一块钢板。

③ When the beam is lifted by 5 - 6 mm, a steel plate shall be added to the temporary bearing.

④ 同步顶升高度为可拆除既有支座和安装新支座所需的工作空间，约为 10 ~15 mm。

④ The height of synchronous jacking is the working space required to remove the existing bearing and install the new bearing, which is about 10 - 15 mm.

⑤ 顶升到位后将梁体由千斤顶转落至临时支撑上。

⑤ After the jack is in place, turn the beam body from the jack to the temporary bearing.

8. 支座更换

8. Replacement of bearing

① 用铁钩或人工取出旧支座，如旧支座已与垫石黏结而较难取出，可用钢钎、铁锤敲击松动后取出。取出旧支座前应拍照记录其缺陷状况。

① Take out the old bearing with an iron hook or manually. If the old bearing has been bonded with the cushion stone and it is difficult to take it out, it can be taken out by tapping it with steel fiber and a hammer to loosen it. Before taking out the old bearing, take pictures to record its defect status.

② 用人工配合钢丝刷清洁支座垫石表面，如有支座下钢板，则应打磨去除铁锈。

② Clean the surface of the cushion stone of the bearing by hand with a wire brush. If there is a steel plate under the bearing, it should be polished to remove the rust.

③ 测量垫石顶面高程，如顶不平整，则用环氧砂浆抹平。垫石顶面如需加高，则应采用环氧砂浆加高至设计高程并抹平；垫石顶面如需降低，则应钢钎凿除部分混凝土至设计高程并用环氧砂浆抹平。支座垫石顶面高程允许偏差不超过 ±2 mm，顶面四角高差不超过 1 mm，轴线偏位不超过 5 mm。

③ Measure the elevation of the top surface of the pad, if the top is uneven, smooth it with epoxy mortar. If the top surface of the cushion stone needs to be increased, epoxy mortar should be used to raise it to the design elevation and smooth; if the top surface of the cushion stone needs to be lowered, part of the concrete should be removed by steel fiber to the design elevation and smoothed with epoxy mortar. The allowable deviation of the top surface elevation of the bearing cushion stone shall not exceed ±2 mm, the height difference of the four corners of the top surface shall not exceed 1 mm, and the axis deviation shall not exceed 5 mm.

④ 在支承垫石上根据设计图纸标出支座位置中心线，同时在橡胶支座上也标出十字交叉中心线，将橡胶支座安放在垫石上，使支座的中心线与墩台的设计位置中心线重合，支座就位准确。

④ Mark the center line of the bearing position on the supporting pad according to the design drawings, and at the same time mark the cross center line on the rubber bearing, and place the rubber bearing on the pad so that the center line of the bearing is in line with the pier. The center line of the design position coincides, and the bearing is in place accurately.

⑤ 所有支座更换完毕后，再对安装的新支座进行全面检查，确保各项指标满足设计及规范要求。

⑤ After all the bearings are replaced, conduct a comprehensive inspection of the installed new bearings to ensure that all indicators meet the design and specification requirements.

9. 落梁

9. Lower the beam

① 落梁前在梁体两侧的桥台或桥墩挡块与梁体间加塞木板，防止落梁时梁体发生水平位移。

① Before lower the beam, add wooden boards between the abutments or pier blocks on both sides of the beam body and the beam body to prevent the horizontal displacement of the beam body when the beam is dropped.

② 开启同步顶升系统，平稳降落梁体。

② Turn on the synchronous jacking system and lower the beam stably.

③ 梁体就位后检查支座上下钢板与垫石、梁底之间的密贴情况，应尽量保证支座上下面全部密贴。如果支座出现偏心受压、不均匀支承或脱空的现象，则应重新顶升梁体，并在支座下钢板下加设抄垫钢板进行微调，直至支座上下面全部密贴。

③ After the beam body is in place, check the close adhesion between the upper and lower steel plates of the bearing, the cushion stone, and the bottom of the beam, and try to ensure that all the upper and lower parts of the bearing are closely adhered. If the bearing is eccentrically compressed, unevenly supported or empty, the beam should be lifted again, and a pad steel plate should be added under the steel plate under the bearing for fine-tuning until all the top and bottom of the bearing are adhered tightly.

④ 支座检查合格后拆除千斤顶、临时支承钢板等顶升设备。

④ After the bearing has passed the inspection, remove the jacks, temporary support steel plates and other lifting equipment.

⑤ 取出梁体与挡板间木板，清理施工废物及垃圾。

⑤ Take out the wooden board between the beam body and the baffle, and clean up the construction waste and garbage.

2.4.4 墩台裂缝修补

2.4.4 Crack repair of pie and abutment

因混凝土内部水化热、外部气温温差、不均匀沉降、局部应力等原因,常见裂缝包括:桥墩的竖向裂纹、墩台的横向裂纹、桥台的竖向裂缝和墩台局部表面网状裂纹或局部裂纹。裂缝的存在可能不同程度降低混凝土的结构承载力或耐久性,因此,应查明分析其成因,掌握其发展规律,采取有效控制措施对既有裂缝进行处理。

Due to the internal hydration heat of concrete, external air temperature difference, uneven settlement, local stress and other reasons, common cracks include: vertical cracks of bridge piers, transverse cracks of pier abutments, vertical cracks of bridge abutments and local surface network cracks of pier abutments or local cracks. The existence of cracks may reduce the structural bearing capacity or durability of concrete to varying degrees. Therefore, its causes should be identified and analyzed, its development law should be mastered, and effective control measures should be taken to deal with existing cracks.

1. 常见整治方法

1. Common treatment methods

各种常见整治方法的具体作业要点见表2-6。

The specific operation points of various common remediation methods see Table 2-6.

表2-6 常见整治方法的具体作业要点

整治方法	作业要点
填缝	用1:2.5或1:3水泥砂浆填入砖石结构裂缝。填补对结构的美观和耐久性起作用,但并不增强结构的强度
表面涂抹	用水泥砂浆、水泥浆或环氧砂浆等涂料,涂在裂缝部位混凝土表面进行修补
表面粘贴修补	用黏结剂将玻璃布或钢板等材料粘贴在裂缝部位的混凝土表面封闭裂缝
凿槽修补法	沿混凝土裂缝做一条深槽,然后在槽内嵌补环氧砂浆、沥青等化学补强剂进行修补
表面喷浆	在凿毛处理的裂缝表面,喷射一层密实且强度高的水泥砂浆保护层来封闭裂缝。可分为无筋素喷浆或挂网喷浆等
围箍加固法	对墩身竖向开裂,如果是基础不均匀沉降所引起,且沉降还未停止,应先加固地基,再用泥浆或砂浆灌缝封闭,然后采用箍筋以控制裂缝的开展。箍筋可以是扁钢或者其他钢材制品

Table 2-6 Specific work points of common remediation methods

Remediation method	Operation points
Caulk	Fill cracks in masonry structures with 1:2.5 or 1:3 cement mortar. Padding contributes to the aesthetics and durability of the structure, but does not enhance the strength of the structure
Surface smear	Use cement mortar, cement paste or epoxy mortar and other coatings to coat the concrete surface of the cracks for repair
Surface paste repair	Use adhesive to stick glass cloth or steel plate and other materials on the concrete surface of the cracked part to seal the crack
Gouge repair	A deep groove is made along the concrete crack, and then chemical reinforcing agents such as epoxy mortar and asphalt are embedded in the groove for repair

continued

Remediation method	Operation points
Surface shotcrete	On the surface of the chiseled crack, spray a layer of dense and high-strength cement mortar protective layer to seal the crack. It can be divided into non-gluten shotcrete or hanging net shotcrete
Hoop reinforcement	For vertical cracking of the pier body, if it is caused by uneven settlement of the foundation and the settlement has not stopped, the foundation should be reinforced first, and then the joint should be sealed with mud or mortar, and then stirrups should be used to control the development of the crack. Stirrups can be flat steel or other steel products

2. 低压注浆法

2. Low pressure grouting method

对于墩台表面宽度为 2 ~ 5 mm 的裂缝,常采用“低压注浆法”修补。每米裂缝需要注浆基座 4 个、SDW 环氧封闭胶 1 kg、DP40 环氧 1 kg。所需工具主要是自动注浆器。

For cracks with a surface width of 2 to 5 mm, the “low pressure grouting method” is often used to repair them. Each meter crack requires four grouting bases, 1 kg SDW epoxy sealant, and 1 kg DP40 epoxy. The tools required are mainly automatic grouts.

(1)操作程序

(1) Operation procedure

① 表面处理。

① Surface treatment.

a. 用钢丝刷和砂轮清理裂缝两侧各 3 cm 的表面。

a. Use a wire brush and a grinding wheel to clean the surface within 3 cm on both sides of the crack.

b. 用丙酮清除表面油污,松动混凝土应用钢钎凿除,浮尘应用略湿的抹布清除,确保裂缝清洁。

b. Use acetone to remove the oil stain on the surface area, remove the loose concrete with a steel fiber, and remove the floating dust with a slightly damp rag to ensure that the cracks are clean.

c. 确定混凝土裂缝上注浆点位置,其间距宜为 300 mm。

c. Determine the position of the grouting point on the concrete crack, and the distance should be 300 mm.

② 安装注浆基座。

② Installation of grouting base.

a. 用两把干净并干燥的抹刀按 3:1 的比例分别取环氧封闭胶 A、B 组分。

a. Use two clean and dry spatulas to take components A and B of the epoxy sealant in a ratio of 3:1.

b. 用抹刀将托灰板上的环氧封闭胶 A、B 组分搅拌均匀。

b. Stir the epoxy sealant A and B components on the ash board evenly with a spatula.

c. 将胶涂刮在注浆基座底部,胶体厚度不少于 2 mm,然后将注入孔对准裂缝,稍加用力按放基座使其粘住,用手固定基座再用胶包覆基座四周,至少 1 cm。

c. Scrape the glue on the bottom of the grouting base, the thickness of the glue is not less than 2 mm, then align the injection hole with the crack, press the base with a little force to make it stick, fix the base by hand and then wrap it with glue around the base, at least 1 cm.

③ 裂缝密封。

③ Crack sealing.

沿裂缝走向 6 cm 范围内用抹刀刮抹环氧黏结剂,厚度约 2 mm,尽量一次完成,对缺损的混凝土应填实。

Scrape the epoxy adhesive with a spatula within 6 cm along the direction of the crack, with a thickness of about 2 mm, try to complete it at one time, and fill in the defective concrete.

④ 注浆。

④ Grouting.

a. 将环氧浆液 A、B 按 100∶30 的比例混合均匀,拉动注浆器把手,将混合物吸入注浆器内,固定把手,安装至基座上,放开把手,利用压簧的压力使浆液慢慢渗入裂缝中。

a. Mix components A and B of epoxy slurry evenly in a ratio of 100∶30, pull the handle of the grouting machine, suck the mixture into the grouting machine, fix the handle, install it on the base, release the handle. Using the pressure of the compression spring, the slurry slowly penetrates into the crack.

b. 注浆顺序:由低到高,一侧向另一侧逐渐靠近。尽量做到后一个基座冒浆时再安装注浆器,对进浆量大的基座应及时补充浆液。

b. Grouting sequence: from low to high, gradually approaching from one side to the other. Try to install the grouting device when the latter base is grouted, and replenish the grout in time for the base with a large amount of grouting.

⑤ 固化判断和表面修饰。

⑤ Solidification judgment and surface modification.

a. 固化时间与气温有很大关系,具体时间可通过拉动注浆器把手来判断,必须在确定固化的情况下才能拆除注浆器。

a. The curing time has a lot to do with the air temperature. The specific time can be judged by pulling the handle of the grouting device. The grouting device only be removed after the curing is confirmed.

b. 固化后拆除注浆器,敲除基座,必要时用砂轮打磨封胶,使施工面光洁平整。

b. After curing, remove the grouting device, knock out the base, and polish the sealant with a grinding wheel if necessary to make the construction surface smooth.

(2)质量控制

(2) Quality control

① 清理裂缝表面油污应用丙酮,松动混凝土应用钢钎除去,浮尘应用略湿的抹布清除。

① When cleaning the crack surface, oil should be removed with acetone, loose concrete should be removed with steel fiber, and dust should be removed with a slightly damp rag.

② 选择注浆点时原则上要求相邻两个注浆点的间距不超过裂缝本身的深度。

② When selecting grouting points, in principle, the distance between two adjacent grouting points should not exceed the depth of the crack itself.

③ 在封闭胶固化过程中应防止其接触水。

③ During the curing process of the sealant, it should be prevented from contacting water.

④ 注浆须在封胶 12 h(20 ℃)后进行,随天气的气温升降可增减注浆时间,但一定要达到封闭胶固化。

④ The grouting must be carried out after sealing for 12 h (20 ℃). The grouting time can be increased or decreased with the temperature rise and fall of the weather, but the sealing glue must be cured.

⑤ 注浆顺序应由低到高,由一侧向另一侧逐渐靠近。尽量做到后一个基座冒浆时再安装注浆器,对进浆量大的基座应及时补充浆液。

⑤ The grouting sequence should be from low to high, gradually approaching from one side to the other. Try to install the grouting device when the latter base is grouted, and replenish the grout in time for the base with a large amount of grouting.

2.4.5 作业验收
2.4.5 Operation acceptance

各项墩台作业的验收标准见表 2-7。

The acceptance standards for various pier operations see Table 2-7.

表 2-7 墩台作业验收标准

项目	验收标准
支座整平修正作业	① 各部分清洁,无灰渣,无锈蚀,活动端涂固体油脂或擦石墨涂擦均匀,无缺漏。 ② 支座基面平整密实,各部分相互密贴。 ③ 锚栓无松动、缺少、锈蚀。 ④ 排水良好,无翻浆、流锈
捣垫砂浆作业	① 原表面凿毛洗净。水灰比、砂浆配合比符合规定,拌和均匀,捣固密实,周围抹面平整,无裂纹空响。 ② 与座板间缝隙小于 0.5 mm,深度小于 30 mm。 ③ 排水良好
混凝土抹面作业	① 抹面颜色一致。 ② 不起砂不起泡,各层砂浆结合牢固。 ③ 表面平整、光滑、无裂纹、无空声
混凝土裂缝压浆作业	① 注浆孔位置、深度及灰浆配合比、水灰比符合要求。 ② 不因钻孔而损坏原圬工,裂纹和空隙内经压水冲洗,并注满浆。 ③ 注浆孔用砂浆填实,无裂纹,淌出灰浆清除干净
混凝土修补作业	① 材料配合比、工艺符合要求。 ② 槽宽度误差不超过 ±3 mm,深度不少于 8 mm。 ③ 勾缝平实,凹凸不超过 ±2 mm,与圬工结合牢固,无断道。 ④ 色泽协调均匀

Table 2-7 Acceptance standards for pier and abutment operations

Items	Acceptance standards
Bearing leveling and correction	① All parts are clean, no ash, no rust, the movable end is coated with solid grease or graphite is evenly coated, and there is no leakage. ② The bearing base is flat and compact, and each part is closely attached to each other. ③ Anchor bolts are not loose, missing or corroded. ④ Good drainage, no pulping and rust
Mortar tamping	① The original surface is chiseled and washed. The water-cement ratio and the mortar mix ratio are in compliance with the regulations, the mixing is uniform, the tamping is dense, the surrounding surface is smooth, and there is no crack and empty sound. ② The gap with the seat plate is less than 0. 5 mm, and the depth is less than 30 mm. ③ Good drainage
Concrete plastering	① The color of the plaster is consistent. ② No sand or bubbles, and the mortar of each layer is firmly bonded. ③ The surface is flat and smooth without cracks or hollow sounds
Concrete crack grouting	① The position and depth of the grouting hole, the mortar mix ratio and the water-cement ratio meet the requirements. ② No damage due to drilling, the cracks and voids are flushed with pressurized water and filled with grout. ③ The grouting hole is filled with mortar, and there is no crack, and the dripping mortar is cleaned up
Concrete repair	①The material mix ratio and process meet the requirements. ② The groove width error should not exceed ±3 mm, and the depth should not be less than 8 mm. ③ The joints are flat, the unevenness does not exceed ±2 mm, and the joint with the work is firm, without breakage. ④ The color is harmonious and even

2.5 桥梁维护验收及质量评定

2.5 Acceptance and quality assessment of bridge maintenance

2.5.1 桥梁维护管理

2.5.1 Bridge maintenance management

1. 维护组织

1. Maintenance organization

桥梁设施维护工作实行综合维修和保养相结合的方式,以保证设施状态完好,确保行车安全。

The maintenance of bridge facilities shall be implemented by comprehensive maintenance and comprehensive maintenance to keep facilities in good condition and increase traffic safety.

公司应根据实际情况确定综合维修和保养的周期,编制年度、分月计划,经上级部门批准后实施;各车间根据规定的检查、保养、维修周期和管辖的桥涵建筑物实际状态,编制月度保养、检查、维修计划,经公司批准后下达给相应工区实施。

The company should determine the comprehensive maintenance cycle according to the actual situation, draw up an annual and monthly plan, and implement it after approval by the superior department. Each workshop prepares the plans for monthly maintenance, inspection and repair according to the prescribed cycle and the actual state of bridges and culverts under its jurisdiction, and sends them to the corresponding work area for implementation after being approved by the company.

2. 综合维修

2. Comprehensive maintenance

桥梁建筑物的综合维修应以整座设施进行,通过对桥梁设施适时预防性的修理和病害整治,恢复各部件的功能,保持整座设施质量均衡完好。

The comprehensive maintenance of bridge should be carried out on the entire bridge and includes all the items. Through timely preventive repairs and disease renovation, restore bridge facilities back to their original standards and preserve their operating condition.

按照不同设备类型确定桥梁建筑物综合维修周期:钢梁桥(含混合桥钢梁、钢拱)3 年,混凝土桥及救援疏散通道 5 年,涵洞视设备状态而定,一般 5 ~ 8 年。

The preventative comprehensive maintenance cycle of bridges based on different types is: 3 years for steel beam bridges (including steel girders of hybrid bridges and steel arches), 5 years for concrete bridges and rescue evacuation channels, and usually 5 - 8 years for culverts.

综合维修主要工作范围如下:

Main contents of comprehensive maintenance are as follows:

① 梁部:结合梁桥、拱桥钢结构局部维护性涂装、死角防锈、更换失效螺栓,进入孔盖板更换;混凝土梁裂纹露筋修补、修理局部失效防水层、排水系统局部整修、梁端伸缩缝整修。

① Beam: coating of steel structure, rust proof of dead corners, replacement of failed bolts, and replacement of manhole cover plate; Repair of cracks and exposed reinforcement of concrete beam, repair of invalid waterproof layer, renovation of drainage system, and renovation of expansion joints at beam end.

② 支座:整平、调正、涂油和捣垫砂浆,处理折断锚栓,支座钢质部分除锈涂漆。

② Bearing: leveling, adjusting, oiling and padding mortar, replacement of broken anchor bolts, and rust removal and painting of the steel part of bearings.

③ 墩台基础:病害墩台整治,裂纹缺损修补,顶面排水处理,基础防护整修等。

③ Pier and abutment: treatment of damaged piers and abutments, mending of cracks and defects, dredging of drainage on the top surface, renovation of protective ancillary facilities , etc.

④ 涵洞:裂纹整治、砌体勾缝、抹面、小量喷浆和压浆,排水设备修理和部分增设。淤积清理疏通,进出口铺砌整修等。

④ Culvert: crack treatment, masonry pointing, plastering, small amount of spraying and grouting, repair of drainage facilities and partial addition. The siltation shall be cleared and dredged, and the inlet and outlet shall be paved and repaired.

⑤ 声屏障、装饰板的更换。

⑤ Replacement of sound barriers and decorative panels.

⑥ 附属设备。

⑥ Ancillary facilities.

a. 各种防护设备的砌体勾缝修补,各类栏杆设备整修加固、更换。

a. Masonry pointing and repairing of various protective facilities, renovation and replacement of various railings.

b. 防撞墙、作业通道、安全检查设备、抗震设施局部整修。

b. Partial renovation of anti-collision walls, working passages, safety inspection equipment, and seismic facilities.

c. 各种桥梁标志的增设、修理和更换。

c. Addition, repair and replacement of various bridge signs.

d. 桥梁限高防护架整治修复。

d. Renovation of height warning gantry.

3. 保养

3. Preventative maintenance

通过对桥梁设施的保养,及时发现和消灭超限处所和临近超限处所,保持桥梁设施状态完好,确保行车安全平稳。

Preventative maintenance, which means regularly checking bridge facilities for small problems and fixing them before failure can occur, can reduce unexpected downtime, keep them in a well-balanced state and ensure safe and stable driving.

保养工作根据当月检查情况逐月编制,按 6 个月为一个周期安排处理。在做好适时保养的同时,还应加强预防性的周期保养,使设施质量经常控制在保养维修合格状态。

The maintenance plan is prepared month by month according to the inspection of current month, and arranged in a cycle of 6 months. In addition to timely maintenance, preventive periodic maintenance should also be strengthened, so that the quality of facilities is often controlled in a qualified state.

主要保养工作范围如下:

Main contents of preventative maintenance are as follows:

① 桥面各部位过水孔疏通。

① Dredging discharge holes on the deck.

② 伸缩缝清理。

② Cleaning expansion joint.

③ 声屏障构件防腐、加固。

③ Anti-corrosion and reinforcement of sound barrier components.

④ 装饰板加固。

④ Reinforcement of decorative panels.

⑤ 各种连接铁件、螺栓涂油。

⑤ Oiling all kinds of iron connecting parts and bolts.

⑥ 钢梁清扫和补充，拧紧少量高强度螺栓，少量油漆涂装。

⑥ Cleaning and replenishing of steel beams, tightening a small amount of high-strength bolts, and painting a small amount of paint.

⑦ 各种标志的刷新和补充。

⑦ Refurbishing and addition of various signs.

⑧ 修补圬工梁、墩台及护坡勾缝，清除梁端石渣，疏通泄水管。

⑧ Repairing masonry beams, piers and slope protection joints, removing the stone ballast at the beam ends, and dredging the drainage pipes.

⑨ 涵洞少量清淤。

⑨ Dredging culverts.

⑩ 及时消除可能危及行车安全的任何病害。

⑩ Eliminating any disease that may endanger driving safety in time.

2.5.2　综合维修验收

2.5.2　Acceptance of comprehensive maintenance

桥梁综合维修作业质量的验收，要严格执行分级把关，控制质量的原则。

For the quality acceptance of bridge comprehensive maintenance, grading check and quality control shall be implemented.

作业过程中，应在作业中及收工前进行质量验收，发现不符合标准的项目应及时返修达标。应对钢梁涂装、圬工维修等隐蔽工程项目认真检查把关，做到每项作业勤检细修一次达标，每次检查的情况都应记在日计划完成表或施工日志上。

The quality inspection should be carried out during the operation and before the end of work, and the item that doesn't meet the standard should be repaired in time. Concealed engineering such as steel beam painting and masonry repairing should be carefully checked, and each operation shall reach the standard once through frequent inspection and careful repair. Each inspection should be recorded in the maintenance log.

每座设施综合维修作业全部完成后，应按《桥梁设施综合维修作业验收标准》（见表 2-8）的有关规定，进行综合维修作业质量验收评定，并填写“桥梁综合维修验收单”。综合维修作业质量评定分为优良、合格、不合格三个等级，扣分在 15 分之内即评为“优良”，扣分在 15 至 40 分之内为“合格”，否则为“不合格”。若出现不合格处所，经返修复验合格，只能评为“合格”。综合维修作业应严格按照作业标准进行，实行质量控制，保证达到规定的质量要求。

After all comprehensive maintenance operations for each facility, the maintenance quality shall be assessed according to the relevant provisions of acceptance standards for comprehensive maintenance of bridge facilities (see Table 2-8), and comprehensive bridge maintenance acceptance sheet shall be filled out. The maintenance quality is divided into three grades: excellent, qualified, and unqualified. The comprehensive deduction within 15 points is rated as "excellent", and the deduction within 15 to 40 points is "qualified", otherwise it is "unqualified". If there is any unqualified item, it can only be rated as "qualified" after re-repair and re-inspection. In order to meet the specified quality requirements, comprehensive maintenance should be carried out strictly in accordance with the operating standards.

表 2-8　桥梁设施综合维修作业验收标准

分　类	工作项目	验收标准	扣　分
桥面	螺栓	螺杆、螺帽及垫圈除锈彻底,沾油厚度适宜或经镀锌处理	5
		螺栓拧紧无松动	5
		垫圈符合标准无缺少	5
	防水层	垫层抹平无坑洼,与原圬工联牢	5
		防水层平顺密实,与边墙及泄水孔衔接严密,无渗漏现象	5
		保护层厚度不小于 30 mm, 坡度不小于 3%, 压实抹平, 无裂损和空响	5
	防撞墙	无露筋掉块、裂纹	5
	伸缩缝	缝内尘土清除干净,填塞密实,表面平整,无漏水断裂或挤出	5
钢结构	钢表面清理	维护涂装底漆时,钢表面清理达到 Sa2.5 级	5
	涂膜粉化清理	涂层表面打磨、污垢清除彻底,不损伤底漆	5
	腻缝	作业范围内,除净凡能积水的缝隙内的旧漆污垢,腻子填实压平,无漏腻,无开裂积水	5
	涂装涂层	涂装体系、层数、厚度符合规定	5
		涂层表面平整均匀,新旧涂层衔接平顺,色泽不匀不超过 5%	5
		无剥落、裂纹	5
		无起泡、气孔	5
圬工梁拱及墩台	抹面	抹面压实,无裂纹、空响,砂浆符合规定	5
	压浆	注浆孔位置、深度及灰浆配合比、水灰比符合要求	5
		不因钻孔而损坏原圬工,裂纹和空隙内经压水冲洗,并注满浆	5
		注浆孔用砂浆填实,无裂纹,淌出灰浆清除干净	5
	修补	材料配合比、工艺符合要求	5
		槽宽度误差不超过 ±3 mm,深度不少于 8 mm	5
		勾缝平实,凹凸不超过 ±2 mm,与圬工结合牢固,无断道	5
		色泽协调均匀	5

续表

分　类	工作项目	验收标准	扣　分
圬工梁拱及墩台	维修更换泄水管	管内畅通,无杂物堵塞	5
		外露部分无损坏	5
		排水不污染梁体	5
支座	支座调平	各部分清洁,无灰渣,无锈蚀,活动端涂固体油脂或擦石墨涂擦均匀,无缺漏	5
		支座位置平整密实,各部分相互密贴	5
		锚栓无松动、缺少、锈蚀	5
		排水良好,无翻浆、流锈	5
	捣垫砂浆	原圬工面凿毛洗净。水灰比、砂浆配合比符合规定,拌合均匀,捣固密实,周围抹面平整,无裂纹空响	5
		与座板间缝隙小于0.5 mm,深度小于30 mm	5
		排水良好	5
涵洞	整修涵洞	清除淤泥、排水通畅;伸缩缝无漏水、漏土(备注:混凝土部分标准参照圬工梁拱及墩台)	5
附属设施	更换声屏障	声屏障材料质量符合规定	5
		固定螺栓紧固,位置正确,封头平整无蜂窝麻面	5
		屏体与立柱及屏体间的缝隙必须密实	5
	更换装饰板	装饰板质量符合要求	5
		与固定组件联结牢固,无松动脱落	5
	维修栏杆	栏杆构件无缺少、裂损、锈蚀	5
		栏杆平直、联结牢固、无扭曲	5
	维修增设桥梁标志、限高防撞架	桥梁标志尺寸字样准确、标志清晰	5
		限高防撞架无损坏、锈蚀	10

Table 2-8　Acceptance standards for comprehensive maintenance of bridge facilities

Classification	Item	Acceptance standard	Deduction (/position)
Bridge deck	Bolts	Screws, nuts and gaskets are thoroughly rusted, and the thickness of oil is suitable or galvanized	5
		Bolts are tightened without looseness	5
		Gaskets meet the standard without missing	5
	Waterproof layer	Cushion is smoothed without potholes, and it is bonded with original masonry	5
		Waterproof layer shall be plat, tightly connected with side walls and drain holes, without leakage	5
		The thickness of protective layer is not less than 30 mm, the slope is not less than 3%, The protective layer should be compacted and leveled without crack and empty sounds	5

continued

Classification	Item	Acceptance standard	Deduction (/position)
Bridge deck	Crash wall	No exposed ribs, blocks, cracks	5
	Expansion joint	The dust in the joints is cleaned, the packing is dense, the surface is smooth, and there is no leakage, breakage or extrusion	5
Steel structure	Steel surface cleaning	When painting the primer, the steel surface shall be cleaned to Sa2. 5 Grade	5
	Coating powder cleaning	The coating surface is polished and the dirt is thoroughly removed without damaging the primer	5
	Joint filling with putty	Within the operation scope, the old paint and dirt in the gaps that can accumulate water should be removed, and the putty should be filled and flattened without missing, cracking and water accumulation	5
	Paint coating	The coating system, layer number and thickness meets the regulations	5
		The coating surface shall be flat and the connection between the new and old coatings is smooth Uneven color shall not exceed 5%.	5
		No peeling and cracking	5
		No blistering and air hole	5
Masonry beams, arches and piers	Plastering	The plastering surface is compacted, without cracks and empty sounds, and the mortar meets the requirements	5
	Grouting	The position and depth of grouting holes, the mortar mix ratio and the water-cement ratio meets the requirements	5
		The original masonry is not damaged due to drilling, and the cracks and voids are flushed with pressurized water and filled with grout	5
		Grouting holes are filled with mortar without cracks, and the dripping mortar is cleaned up	5
	Patching	The material mix ratio and process meet the requirements	5
		The error of groove width shall not exceed ± 3 mm, and the depth shall not be less than 8 mm	5
		The pointing shall be flat, the concave convex shall not exceed ±2 mm, and it shall be firmly combined with th. e masonry without breaking	5
		The color is coordinated and uniform	5
	Repairing and replacing drain pipes	The drain pipes is unobstructed and no debris is blocked	5
		The exposed parts are not damaged	5
		Drainage does not pollute beams	5
Bearings	Bearing leveling correction	All parts are cleaned without ash and rust, the movable ends are coated with solid grease or graphite evenly without missing	5

continued

Classification	Item	Acceptance standard	Deduction (/position)
Bearings	Bearing leveling correction	The bottom of bearings is flat and compact, and each part is closely attached	5
		The anchor bolts are not loose, missing or corroded	5
		Good drainage without mud boiling and rust flowing	5
	Tamping and plastering mortar	The original masonry surface is chiseled and cleaned. The water-cement ratio and the mortar mix ratio are in compliance with the regulations, the mixing is uniform, the tamping is compact, the surrounding surface is smooth without cracks and empty sounds	5
		The gap between bearing and base plate is less than 0. 5 mm, and the depth is less than 30 mm	5
		Good drainage	5
Culverts	Repairing culverts	Sludge removal and smooth drainage; no water and soil leakage in the expansion joints (Note: the concrete standard shall refer to masonry beam arch and pier abutment)	5
Auxiliary facilities	Replacing sound barriers	Sound barrier material meets the requirements	5
		Fixing bolts are fastened on the correct position, and the head is flat without honeycomb pitting	5
		The gaps between screen and column and between screens must be tight	5
	Replacing decorative panels	Decorative panels meet the requirements	5
		Decorative panels are firmly connected with fixing components, and there is no looseness and falling off	5
	Repairing railings	There are no missing, cracked or corroded railing components	5
		Railings are straight, firmly connected, and free from twisting	5
	Maintenance and addition of bridge signs and height warning gantries	The size and words of bridge signs are accurate and clear	5
		There is no damage or rust on height warning gantries	10

每月的综合维修作业全部结束后,维修部门应对设施进行整体验收,公司进行抽验。

When the monthly comprehensive maintenance operations are all completed, the maintenance department shall conduct an overall acceptance of facilities, and the company shall conduct random inspections.

2.5.3 保养验收

2.5.3 Acceptance of preventive maintenance

桥梁维修作业质量的验收,要严格执行工区自验,生产维护部门、公司联合验收制,分级把关,控制质量。

The quality acceptance of bridge maintenance operation should strictly carry out self-inspection of work area, joint acceptance of maintenance department and company, grading check and quality control.

每座桥梁设施的保养质量评定,均应填写《桥梁保养质量评定记录表》,以备抽查。桥梁设施的保养质量是按照《桥梁设施保养质量评分标准》(见表 2-9)的规定,根据扣分的情况来评定保养质量的优劣。每座设备扣分的总和除以该设备的维修长度(取整数)即为该设备的保养质量平均分。保养质量每米平均分在 5 分及以下且无单项质量扣 10 分者为合格,否则为不合格。

For the quality assessment of each bridge maintenance, the "Bridge maintenance quality assessment record form" shall be filled out for random inspection. According to the provisions of "Scoring standard for bridge maintenance quality" (shown in Table 2-9), and the maintenance quality are evaluated according to the score deduction. The average score of maintenance quality is the sum of points deducted for each bridge divided by the maintenance length (rounded). The maintenance quality is qualified if the average score per meter is 5 points or less and there is no single item with 10 points deducted, otherwise it is unqualified.

表 2-9 桥梁设施保养质量评分标准

分类	项目	失格标准	扣分
桥面	铺装层	桥面找平层表面有纵横裂缝、剥落	5
		桥面防水层失效面积大于 10 m^2	5
		泄水孔堵塞、周围渗水	5
	声屏障	声屏障螺栓或立柱锈蚀超过 10%	5
		螺栓缺少、松动	5
		屏体表面或玻璃破损	5
	装饰板	装饰板连接松动	5
		装饰板锈蚀面积大于 10 m^2	5
	栏杆	栏杆锈蚀、损坏严重	5
梁拱及墩台	表面	表面掉块露筋	5
	梁端	缝内有石渣、杂物,影响梁体伸缩	5
	泄水管	泄水管堵塞、损坏或缺失	5
钢梁	梁体	梁体有灰渣、尘土堆积	5
	螺栓	高强度螺栓松动、缺失	5
	涂层	局部锈蚀大于 25 cm^2	5
	腻缝	腻缝开裂、脱落、锈蚀	5
支座	支座	支座钢件锈蚀	5
		上下各部分不密贴	10
		支座不洁,活动部分摩擦附有灰尘或污物	5
	螺栓	螺栓或螺帽缺少、松动、折断	5
	排水	支座积水、翻浆、流锈	5

续表

分类	项目	失格标准	扣分
涵洞	排洪	涵内淤积，影响排洪	10
	管节	接缝脱落	5
		漏土	10
	表面	剥落掉块致使露筋	5
其他	抗震设施	失修损坏	5
	防撞设施	涂装失效	5
		被撞损坏	10
	检查设施	涂装失效	5
		失修损坏	5
	各类标志	各类标志缺少、破坏、不清晰	5

Table 2-9　Scoring standards for bridge facilities maintenance quality

Classification	Item	Unqualified criteria	Deduction (/position)
Bridge deck	Pavement layer	There are vertical and horizontal cracks on the surface of leveling layer, and leveling layer peels off	5
		The failure area of waterproof layer is greater than 10 m^2	5
		Scupper is blocked and the surrounding water seeps	5
	Sound barrie	The corroded sound barrier bolts or columns exceed 10% of the total	5
		Bolts are missing or loose	5
		The screen surface or glass is damaged	5
	Decorative panel	The connection of decorative panels is loose	5
		The corroded the decorative panel is greater than 10 m^2	5
	Railing	Railings are corroded and seriously damaged	5
Beam, arch and pier, abutment	Surface	Concrete blocks falling from the surface and reinforcement exposure	5
	Beam end	There are stone ballast and debris in the joints, which affect the expansion and contraction of beam	5
	Drain pipe	The drain pipe is blocked, damaged or missing	5
Steel beams	Beam	Ash and dust mounding on the beam	5
	Bolts	High-strength bolts become loose or missing	5
	Coating	Local corrosion is greater than 25 cm^2	5
	Welding seam	Cracking, falling off and rusting of welding seam	5
Bearing	Bearing	Corrosion of steel part	5
		The upper and lower parts are not closely attached	10
		The bearing is unclean, and the friction pair is rubbed with dust or dirt	5
	Bolts	Bolts or nuts are missing, loose, or broken	5
	Drainage	Water ponding, mud boiling, and rust flowing on the bearing	5

continued

Classification	Item	Unqualified criteria	Deduction (/position)
Culvert	Flood discharge	Sedimentation in the culvert, affecting flood discharge	10
	Pipe	Seams falling off	5
		Soil leakage	10
	Surface	Concrete blocks falling from the surface and reinforcement exposure	5
Others	Seismic facilities	Damaged in a bad state of repair	5
	Anti-collision facilities	Coating failure	5
		Damaged by crash	10
	Checking facilities	Coating failure	5
		Damaged in a bad state of repair	5
	Signs	Signs are missing, damaged or unclear	5

2.5.4 桥梁质量评定

2.5.4 Quality assessment of bridge

对于桥梁的质量评定,采用“只要达到任意一条失格标准,即判为质量不合格”的方法。具体的标准见表2-10。

For the quality assessment of bridges, as long as any one of the disqualification standards is met, the quality is judged to be unqualified. The specific standards see Table 2-10.

表2-10 桥梁评定标准

分类	项目	失格标准
圬工梁、拱	裂纹	预应力混凝土梁、钢筋混凝土梁、拱裂纹超过限值且未处理
	承载能力不足	检定承载系数 $K<1$
	梁拱漏水	结构内部漏水未处理
	梁不能自由伸缩	相邻两孔圬工梁端之间顶死,使梁不能自由伸缩
钢结构	保护涂装失效	整孔钢梁涂装失效达50%及以上;钢梁上盖板锈蚀达50%及以上
	焊缝裂纹	因受力而有发展的焊缝裂纹未处理或加固
	承载能力不足	检定承载系数 $K<1$
	梁不能自由伸缩	相邻两孔钢梁梁端之间顶死,使梁不能自由伸缩
支座	未按规定安装	应安装支座而未安装支座;支座类型或活动、固定支座安装不合规定
	橡胶支座不良	板式橡胶支座达到以下状态: ① 支座压溃,周围出现明显不规则的凹凸、弯曲或扭曲; ② 支座剪切变形过大,活载作用时剪切变形≥24°,无活载作用时永久剪切变形≥15°; ③ 橡胶剥落掉块,导致加劲钢板表面或周围外露长度>100 mm; ④ 橡胶裂纹宽度≥2 mm,且连续长度达周边长度的50%以上; ⑤ 支座串动大于相应边长的25%

续表

分　类	项　目	失格标准
支座	橡胶支座不良	盆式橡胶支座达到以下状态： ① 盆环开裂或脱焊； ② 聚四氟乙烯板磨耗严重，外露厚度不足 0.5 mm； ③ 位移或转角超限，位移量≥10 mm，转角超过设计值的 20%； ④ 锚栓剪断数量超过 25%
墩台	严重腐蚀及松动断裂	混凝土及钢筋混凝土严重腐蚀未处理
	裂损与不稳定	混凝土及钢筋混凝土裂纹超过限值未处理； 墩台出现下沉，倾斜，滑动、冻害等现象
涵洞	变形损坏	涵身严重变形、断裂冻害影响排水或造成路基下沉
	基底掏空	洞身基底冒水、潜流造成基底掏空
	孔径不足	涵洞孔径不足及净空不能安全通过规定洪水泥石流，淤积严重影响排洪而未整治
附属设施	未按规定安装栏杆	应设未设
	抗震设施缺少、失效	无抗震设施或抗震设施失效

Table 2-10　Evaluation standards of bridge

Classification	Item	Unqualified criteria
Masonry beam or arch	Crack	Cracks of prestressed concrete beams, reinforced concrete beam or arch exceed limits and are not treated
	Insufficient carrying capacity	Verified bearing coefficient $K<1$
	Leakage of beam or arch	Untreated water leakage through the interior of structure
	Beams cannot expand and contract freely	Both two ends of adjacent masonry beams are stuck, so that the beams cannot expand and contract freely
Steel structure	Failure of protective coating	The coating failure of the whole-hole steel beam is 50% or more. The corrosion of cover plates on the steel beam reaches 50% or more
	Weld cracks	Weld cracks that have developed due to stress are not treated or reinforced
	Insufficient carrying capacity	Verified bearing coefficient $K<1$
	Beams cannot expand and contract freely	Both two ends of adjacent masonry beams are stuck, so that the beams cannot expand and contract freely
Bearing	Not installed as specified	The bearing should be installed but not installed. The type of bearings or the installation of movable and fixed bearings is not in compliance with regulations
	Unqualified rubber bearing	The plate rubber bearing reaches the following states: ① The bearing is crushed, and there are obvious irregular bumps, bends or twists around it. ② The shear deformation of the bearing is too large, the shear deformation is more than 24° under live loads, and the permanent shear deformation is more than 15° without live loads. ③ The rubber flakes off, and the exposed length of the stiffening steel plate surface or surrounding area is greater than 100 mm.

continued

Classification	Item	Unqualified criteria
Bearing	Unqualified rubber bearing	④ The rubber crack width is more than 2 mm, and the continuous length is more than 50% of the peripheral length. ⑤ The bearing dislocation is greater than 25% of the corresponding side length. The pot rubber bearing reaches the following states: ① The pot ring is cracking or welding off; ② The PTFE plate is seriously worn, and the exposed thickness is less than 0. 5 mm; ③ The displacement or rotation angle exceeds the limit, the displacement is more than 10 mm, and the rotation angle exceeds 20% of the design value; ④ The number of sheared anchor bolts exceeds 25% of the total
Pier or abutment	Serious corrosion and loosening or rupturing	Concrete and reinforced concrete are severely corroded and untreated
	Cracks and instability	Concrete and reinforced concrete cracks exceeding the limit are not treated. Subsidence, inclination, sliding, freezing, etc. occurs on the piers or abutments
Culvert	Deformation	The culvert is seriously deformed, fractured and frozen, affecting drainage or causing subgrade . subsidence
	Cavity under the basement.	Due to water and undercurrent under the basement, the cavity develops and hasn't been . treated
	Insufficient aperture	The diameter and gauge of culvert cannot safely pass the prescribed floods and mud-rock flow, and the siltation seriously affects the flood discharge and has not been restored
Ancillary facilities	Fail to install railings as required	Railings should be set but not set
	Lack or failure of seismic facilities	No seismic facilities or failure of seismic facilities

课 后 练 习
Exercises

1. 桥梁支座病害有哪些?

1. What diseases will happen to bridge bearings?

2. 桥面专项检查包括哪些内容?

2. What does the special inspection of bridge deck include?

3. 伸缩缝日常检查的主要工作内容包括哪些?

3. What are the main work contents of daily inspection of expansion joints?

4. 如何进行桥面排水设施养护?

4. How to maintain the drainage facilities of bridge deck ?

5. 简述栏杆涂油的作业程序。

5. Briefly describe the operation procedure of handrail oiling.

6. 简述钢梁油漆涂装的施工条件及要求。

6. Briefly describe the construction conditions and requirements of steel beam painting.

7. 什么情况下需要支座整修?

7. When is the bearing repair required?

8. 简述墩台裂缝修补"低压注浆法"的操作流程。

8. Briefly describe the operation procedure of "low pressure grouting method" for pier and abutment crack repair.

9. 简述混凝土修补作业的验收标准。

9. Briefly describe the acceptance standards of concrete repair operation.

第3章 隧道作业

Chapter 3 Tunnel Operations

学习目标(Learning Objectives)

1. 能力目标

1. Capability objectives

(1)能够对隧道设施常见病害的成因进行分析。

(1) Be able to analyze the causes of common diseases of tunnel facilities.

(2)能够进行隧道维修作业,并达到验收标准。

(2) Be able to carry out tunnel maintenance and meet the acceptance standards.

2. 知识目标

2. Knowledge objectives

(1)掌握隧道设施常见病害及成因。

(1) Master the common diseases and causes of tunnel facilities.

(2)掌握隧道维修作业操作流程及验收标准。

(2) Master the process and acceptance standards of tunnel maintenance operations.

(3)熟悉隧道维修养护管理的工作内容。

(3) Be familiar with the work contents of tunnel maintenance management.

3. 素质目标

3. Quality objectives

(1)具有发现问题、解决问题的能力以及创新实践能力。

(1) Have the ability to find and solve problems as well as the ability to innovate and practice.

(2)遵守劳动纪律,具备质量意识、安全意识、团队精神和工匠精神。

(2) Abide by labor discipline and have quality awareness, safety awareness, team spirit and craftsmanship spirit.

(3)具有统领全局的大局观和可持续发展的理念。

(3) Have the great vision of commanding the overall situation and the concept of sustainable development.

3.1 隧道常见病害
3.1 Common diseases of tunnel

3.1.1 渗漏水
3.1.1 Water leakage

隧道渗漏水病害是指在隧道运营过程中遇到水的干扰和危害，是最常见的隧道病害。渗漏水病害包含衬砌的漏水和涌水、衬砌周围积水、潜流冲刷。渗漏水对隧道稳定、洞内设施、行车安全、地面建筑和隧道周围水环境产生诸多不良影响。严重时，渗漏水病害损伤内部结构及附属设施，缩短使用寿命，甚至危害到隧道及地下工程的运营安全。

Tunnel water leakage disease refers to the interference and harm of water in tunnel operation, which is the most common tunnel disease. Water leakage diseases include water leakage and gushing of lining, ponding around lining and undercurrent scouring. The water leakage has many adverse effects on tunnel stability, facilities in the tunnel, traffic safety, ground buildings and water environment around the tunnel. In serious cases, it damages the internal structure and ancillary facilities, shorten service life, even endangers the operation safety of tunnel and underground works.

1. 渗漏水种类
1. Types of water leakage

根据水量、水压的大小不同，隧道衬砌的渗漏水现象一般表现为渗、滴、淌、涌。

According to the different volume and pressure of water, the leakage of tunnel lining is generally divided into seepage, dripping, flowing and gushing.

"渗"是指地下水从衬砌外向内润湿，使衬砌内出现面积大小不等的渗润，但水仍附着在衬砌的内表面；衬砌表面呈湿润状态，并像冒汗一样出现水珠。

Seepage refers to that the groundwater is wetted from the outside to the inside of the lining with infiltration of different sizes on the lining, but the water is still attached to the inner surface of lining. The lining surface is wet and water drops appear like sweating.

"滴"是指水滴间断地脱离衬砌落入隧底，有时连续出水，也称作滴水成线；拱部漏水成为水滴，不断下滴。

Dripping means that water drops break away from the lining intermittently and fall into the bottom of tunnel, sometimes continuously drip into a line. Water leaks from the arch and drops continuously.

"淌"是指漏水连续顺衬砌内侧墙流淌而下，漏水呈明显水流从裂隙中流出或拱部滴水成线。

Flowing refers to the continuous flow of water along the inner wall of lining. Water flows out of cracks obviously, or water from the arch drips into a line.

"涌"是指有一定压头的水从衬砌裂隙中喷出。

Gushing means that water under pressure comes out of cracks.

以上四种漏水现象，其出露部位与水量不同，对隧道产生的危害也不同。

For the above four types of water leakage, different exposure positions and water quantities will cause different hazards to the tunnel.

2. 隧道衬砌周围积水

2. Ponding around tunnel lining

运营隧道中地表水或地下水向隧道周围渗流汇集，如果不能迅速排走将会引起以下病害：

The surface water or groundwater in running tunnel flows and collects around the tunnel. If it cannot be discharged quickly, the following diseases will be caused.

① 水压较大时会导致衬砌破裂。

① High water pressure will lead to lining rupture.

② 使原完好的围岩及围岩的结构面软弱夹层因浸水而软化或泥化，失去承载力，对衬砌压力增大而导致衬砌破裂。

② Due to immersion, the original intact surrounding rock and the weak interlayer between structure planes will soften or muddy, lose the bearing capacity, increase the pressure on the lining and cause the lining rupture.

③ 使膨胀性围岩体积膨胀，导致衬砌破坏。

③ Make swelling rock expand and result in lining damage.

④ 在寒冷地区发生冰胀和冻胀，快速导致衬砌破坏。

④ Ice heaving and frost heaving of surrounding rock in cold areas causes lining damage.

3. 潜流冲刷

3. Undercurrent scouring

潜流冲刷主要是指由于地下水渗流和流动而产生的冲刷和溶蚀作用，其危害有：

Undercurrent scouring mainly refers to the scouring and corrosion caused by groundwater seepage and flow, and its hazards include:

① 衬砌基础下沉，衬砌开裂或者仰拱、整体道床下沉开裂。

① The lining foundation sinks and the lining cracks, or the inverted arch and monolithic track bed sinks and cracks.

② 围岩滑移错动导致衬砌变形开裂。

② The slip and dislocation of surrounding rock leads to the deformation and cracking of lining.

③ 对超挖回填不密实或未全部回填者，引起围岩坍塌，导致衬砌破坏。

③ If the over excavation backfilling is uncompacted or not fully backfilled, the surrounding rock will collapse and the lining will be damaged.

④ 侵蚀性水对衬砌的侵蚀。

④ Corrosive water will erode the lining.

4. 渗漏水的成因

4. Causes of water leakage

① 除地下水丰富外，主要是由隧道设计与施工不当造成的。如对衬砌周围地下水的

水源、水量、水质调查分析不足,对防排水考虑不周,对结构防蚀、耐冻、抗渗也未做专项设计。

① In addition to abundant groundwater, it is mainly caused by improper tunnel design and construction. For example, the investigation and analysis of source, quantity and quality of groundwater around the lining is insufficient, the waterproof and drainage are not comprehensively considered, and the special design of corrosion prevention, frost resistance and anti-permeability is not made.

② 隧道穿过含水的地层。如穿过砂类土或漂卵石类土含水地层;断层带节理及裂隙发育,含裂隙水的岩层;石灰岩、白云岩等可溶性岩层,有充水的溶洞或暗河等与隧道相连通时;浅埋隧道地段,地表水沿覆盖层的裂隙渗到隧道内。

② The tunnel passes through water bearing stratum, such as sandy soil or floating pebble soil water bearing stratum, the rock stratum with fissure water in the fault zone of developed joints and fissures, limestone, dolomite and other soluble rock with water filled karst caves or underground rivers linking the tunnel, the shallow tunnel section where surface water seeps into the tunnel along the cracks of the overburden.

③ 隧道衬砌综合治水设施不完善或年久失效。如原建隧道衬砌防排水设备不全,隧道衬砌背后存在积水或承压水;混凝土衬砌施工质量差,孔隙裂缝多,自身防水能力差;防水层(内贴式、外贴式或中间夹层)施工质量不良,或材质耐久性差;施工缝、伸缩缝、沉降缝等接缝处理不当,或未做好防水处理;衬砌变形、腐蚀后产生的裂缝渗漏水;既有排水设备,如衬砌背后的暗沟、盲沟、无衬砌的辅助坑道、排水孔等年久失修阻塞。

③ The comprehensive water control facilities of tunnel lining are imperfect or have failed for a long time. Due to the incomplete waterproof and drainage equipment of original tunnel lining , there is ponding or confined water behind the tunnel lining. Poor construction quality of concrete lining causes many pores and cracks, so that its own waterproof capacity is poor. The construction quality of waterproof layer (internal, external, or interlayer) is bad, or the material durability is poor. Construction joints, expansion joints, settlement joints and other joints are not well dealt with, or no waterproof measures are taken. Cracks and water leakage is caused by lining deformation and corrosion. Existing drainage equipment, such as sewers and ditches behind the lining, unlined auxiliary tunnels, drainage holes, etc., have been out of repair for a long time and blocked.

3.1.2 衬砌裂损
3.1.2 Lining damage

隧道衬砌是为了防止围岩变形或坍塌,沿隧道洞身周边用钢筋混凝土等材料修建的承受地层压力的永久性支护结构。由于形变压力、松动压力、地层沿隧道纵向分布的不均匀作用、温度和收缩应力作用、围岩膨胀性或冻胀性压力作用、腐蚀性介质作用、施工人为因素、运营车辆的循环荷载作用等,隧道衬砌结构物产生裂缝和变形,影响隧道的正常使用,统称为隧道衬砌裂损病害。衬砌裂损是隧道病害的主要形式,其类型主要有衬砌变形、衬砌移动、衬砌开裂、衬砌缺陷四种。

Tunnel lining is a permanent support structure built along the tunnel with reinforced concrete and other materials to bear the stratum pressure in order to prevent the deformation or collapse of surrounding rock. Due to deformation pressure, loosening pressure, uneven distribution of stratum along the tunnel, temperature and shrinkage stress, swelling or frost heaving pressure of surrounding rock, corrosive medium, human factors in construction, cyclic load of operating vehicles, etc., cracks and deformation occur in the lining, which affects the normal use of tunnel. Lining damage is one of the common diseases of tunnels, and it includes four types of lining deformation, lining movement, lining cracking and lining defects.

1. 衬砌变形

1. Lining deformation

衬砌变形主要是指衬砌发生收敛变形，造成隧道净空减小，或侵占预留的加固空间，包括断面变形、错台错缝、边墙下沉等。衬砌断面变形是指衬砌由于受力而引起拱轴形状的改变。错台错缝一般发生在隧道起拱线或施工缝处，其产生的主要原因是隧道起拱线或施工缝处较为薄弱，受剪切应力作用而出现错台错缝。通常，边墙下沉伴随着隧道底板隆起，继而造成隧底上抬和整体下沉，使隧道衬砌发生变形和破坏。

Lining deformation mainly refers to the convergence deformation of lining, which results in the reduction of tunnel clearance or occupies the reserved reinforcement space. It includes section deformation, segment dislocation, side wall subsidence, etc. The deformation of lining section refers to the change of arch axis shape caused by the stress. Under the shear, segment dislocation generally occurs at the camber line or construction joint which is relatively weak. The subsidence of side wall is usually accompanied by the deformation of tunnel floor. Usually, the subsidence of the side wall is accompanied by the tunnel floor heave, which will lead to the uplift of tunnel floor and the integral subsidence, and result in the deformation and destruction of tunnel lining.

2. 衬砌移动

2. Lining movement

衬砌移动是指衬砌的整体或其中一部分出现转动（倾斜）、平移和下沉（或上抬）等变化，也有纵向与横向移动之分。对于大多数发生裂损的衬砌，往往是纵向与横向移动同时出现。

Lining movement refers to the rotation (inclination), translation, sinking (or lifting) and other changes of the whole or part of the lining. It can also be divided into longitudinal movement and transverse movement. For most of the linings with cracks, longitudinal movement and transverse movement often occurs at the same time.

3. 衬砌开裂

3. Lining cracking

衬砌开裂是指衬砌表面出现裂纹、裂缝或贯通衬砌全部厚度的裂纹，包括张裂、压溃和错台：①张裂。张裂是弯曲受拉和偏心受拉引起的裂损。②压溃。压溃是弯曲或偏心受压引起的衬砌裂损。③错台。错台是由剪切应力引起的裂缝。

Lining cracking refers to cracks on the lining surface or through the whole thickness of the lining, including tension cracking, crushing and segment dislocation: ①Tension cracking, which is caused by bending tension and eccentric tension. ②Crushing, which is caused by bending or eccentric compression. ③Segment dislocation, which is caused by shear force.

隧道衬砌裂缝根据裂缝走向及其和隧道长度方向的相互关系，分为纵向裂缝、环向裂缝和斜向裂缝三种，如图 3-1 所示。环向裂缝，一般对于衬砌结构正常承载影响不大。拱部和边墙的纵向和斜向裂缝，破坏结构的整体性，危害较大。

Tunnel lining cracks are divided into longitudinal cracks, circumferential cracks and oblique cracks according to the crack direction and its relationship with the tunnel lengthwise, as shown in Figure 3-1. Circumferential cracks generally have little effect on the normal bearing capacity of lining structures. Longitudinal and oblique cracks in the arch and side walls will destroy the integrity of structure and have potential hazards.

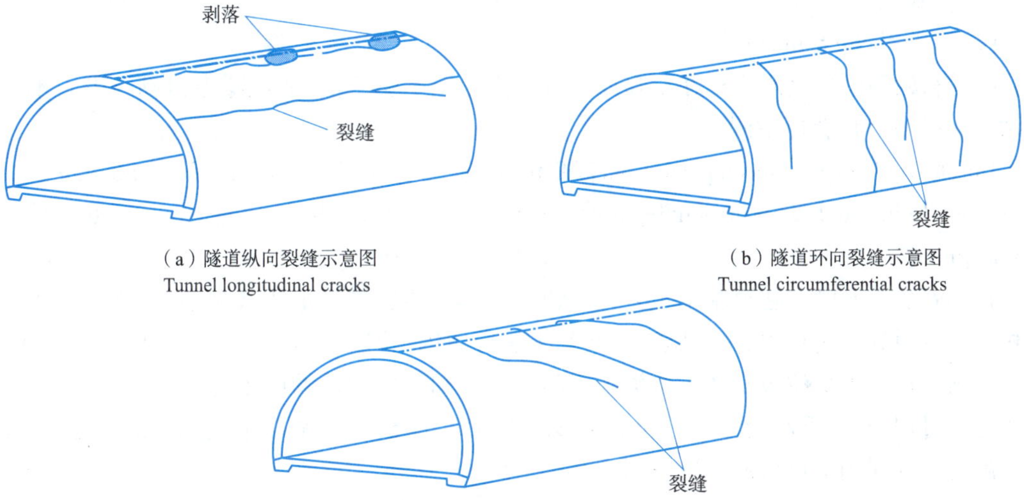

（a）隧道纵向裂缝示意图
Tunnel longitudinal cracks

（b）隧道环向裂缝示意图
Tunnel circumferential cracks

（c）隧道斜向裂缝示意图
Tunnel oblique cracks

图 3-1 隧道衬砌裂缝示意图

Figure 3-1 Schematic diagram of tunnel lining cracks

剥落：spalling　　裂缝：cracks

4. 衬砌缺陷

4. Lining defects

隧道可能存在的衬砌厚度不足、衬砌背后严重空洞、衬砌背后回填不密实等缺陷。这些缺陷在外界各种因素的影响下继续发展，就会进一步引起隧道发生开裂、变形等各种形式的破坏，使得衬砌结构的稳定性和可靠性受到影响。

The tunnel may have defects such as insufficient lining thickness, serious cavities behind the lining, and uncompacted backfill behind the lining. If these defects continue to develop under the influence of various external factors, they will further cause cracking, deformation and other forms of damage to the tunnel, and even affect the stability and reliability of lining structure.

（1）衬砌厚度不足

(1) Insufficient lining thickness

隧道建设过程中，如果施工单位偷工减料或未按照设计图纸进行施工，使建成隧道衬砌厚度未达到设计要求厚度，导致衬砌结构承载力无法达到设计值，直接危害到结构的安全性。值得指出的是，早期隧道衬砌拱顶常因施工工艺等问题无法达到设计的厚度。

In the tunnel construction, if some construction units cheat in work and cut down on materials or do not construct according to the design paper. The lining thickness did not meet the design requirements. The lining bearing capacity cannot reach the design value. The safety of lining structure is threatened. It should be pointed out that the arch crown of early tunnel lining could not reach the designed thickness due to construction technology and other problems.

（2）衬砌背后空洞

(2) Cavity behind lining

隧道衬砌与围岩之间常存在空隙或两者之间回填不够密实，造成隧道衬砌与围岩不能紧密贴合，一般称为“背后空洞”。

Due to voids or the uncompacted backfill between the tunnel lining and the surrounding rock, the tunnel lining and the surrounding rock cannot closely fit, which is generally called “cavity behind lining”.

衬砌背后空洞既与隧道施工工艺、工法有关，又与隧道周围地质水文条件、隧道防排水方式相关。隧道施工过程中，由于施工工艺与工法等原因，背后大多存在空洞或回填不密实，特别在拱顶与拱腰等部位极易产生该类施工问题。衬砌背后回填物中可能存在松散土体，在长期的运营过程中，地下水会将它们冲走而形成空洞。此外，隧道围岩中包含易溶成分，在地下水溶解与冲蚀作用下也可能产生空洞。

The cavity behind the lining is not only related to the tunnel construction technology and construction method, but also related to the geological and hydrological conditions around the tunnel and the waterproof and drainage mode of the tunnel. In tunnel construction, due to the construction process and construction method, there are cavities or uncompacted backfill behind the lining, especially at the arch crown and arch waist. There may be loose soil in the backfill behind the lining, which will be washed away by groundwater during long-term operation and form cavities. If there are soluble components in the tunnel surrounding rock, cavities will be developed under the dissolution and erosion of groundwater.

衬砌背后空洞会影响衬砌结构与围岩之间的相互作用以及结构的承载状态，即可能会造成应力集中，形成偏压效应，导致衬砌受力不均衡或局部承载，引发或加剧其他类型的衬砌病害。

The cavities behind the lining will affect the interaction between lining structure and surrounding rock and the load bearing status of struture. They may bring about stress concentration and form unsymmetrical loads, which leads to the unbalanced or local load bearing of lining and cause or aggravate other types of lining diseases.

(3)不均匀沉降

(3) Differential settlement

隧道穿越平原丘陵、崇山峻岭,区段地质条件千差万别。隧道赋存区域岩层可能存在大量的节理、溶洞、裂隙与断层等不良地质构造。隧道施工期间的扰动往往加剧了地层之间的相互运动或地层内部变形,不同区域地层变形的不一致则可能造成隧道发生不均匀变形和承受不利荷载;隧道运营过程中,地下水冲刷、溶洞、围岩物理力学性质不均匀、各向异性等因素都可能造成隧道周围地层发生不均匀变形或运动,引发衬砌结构不均匀沉降,使其发生变形与裂损。

The tunnel passes through plains, hills and mountains where the geological conditions are various. There may be a large number of joints, karst caves, large fissures, faults and other unfavorable geological structures in the rocks around the tunnel. The disturbance during the tunnel construction often intensifies the mutual movement between the strata or the internal deformation of the strata, and the inconsistency of stratum deformation in different areas may cause uneven deformation and unfavorable load of the tunnel. During operation, groundwater scouring, karst caves, inhomogeneous and anisotropic mechanical properties of surrounding rock may cause uneven deformation or movement of the stratum around the tunnel, which will lead to uneven settlement of the lining structure and result in its deformation and cracking.

(4)内空侵限

(4) Intruding into structure gauge

隧道内设备或衬砌结构侵入隧道建筑限界时,将对隧道的运营产生严重的安全隐患,内空侵限的主要原因有:

When the equipment or lining structure in the tunnel intrudes into the tunnel structure gauge, it brings hidden danger to tunnel operation. The main reasons are as follows:

① 围岩后期沉降过大。围岩后期沉降引起衬砌结构变形过大,从而使衬砌结构侵入建筑限界内。这一般多发生于膨胀性围岩或软质岩等大变形地段。

① Excessive post-construction settlement of surrounding rock. The post-construction settlement of surrounding rock causes excessive deformation of lining structure and makes the lining structure intrude into the structure gauge, which usually occurs in large deformation sections such as expansive surrounding rock or soft rock.

② 施工原因。施工过程中,施工放样误差、浇筑二次衬砌混凝土时跑模等情况可能引起隧道断面内空不足。为了避免因施工原因而引起的内空侵限问题,施工中必须加强测量放样工作,开挖与喷射混凝土施工后应复核断面内空尺寸,并须验算模板台车的整体刚度,防止模板变形等问题的发生。

② Construction reasons. During the construction, the errors of construction layout and the formwork shifting during the secondary lining concrete pouring may make the internal space of tunnel insufficient. In order to avoid the problems, surveying and setting out must be tighten up during construction. After excavation and shotcrete construction, the section internal space should be rechecked, and the overall stiffness of the formwork trolley must be calculated to prevent the deformation of formwork and other problems.

3.1.3 衬砌劣化

3.1.3 Lining deterioration

地铁运营环境下，按照规范进行耐久性设计的隧道混凝土衬砌通常能满足设计年限要求。但由于隧道渗漏水和裂损病害的影响，衬砌性能的劣化也是地铁隧道不可忽视的重要病害形式之一。

Under the environment of metro operation, the tunnel concrete lining based on durability design can usually meet the requirements of service life. However, due to tunnel leakage and crack damage, the deterioration of lining performance is also one of the common disease of subway tunnel that can not be ignored.

长期的渗漏水容易导致衬砌混凝土风化剥落，水中的侵蚀性介质还会加剧混凝土的劣化。衬砌开裂后，内壁空气中的二氧化碳和外壁地下水中的腐蚀离子侵入速度大大加快，混凝土的碳化速度和劣化速度显著增加。同时，混凝土保护层的失效会导致钢筋直接接触外部潮湿空气和地下水，发生锈蚀膨胀，进一步加剧衬砌开裂，以致发生局部衬砌脱落。

Long term water leakage is easy to lead to the weathering and peeling of lining concrete, and the corrosive medium in the water will also aggravate the deterioration of concrete. Lining cracking accelerates the invasion of carbon dioxide in the inner air and corrosive ions in the outer groundwater and increases the carbonation and deterioration of concrete. At the same time, the failure of the concrete protective layer makes the reinforcement close to the external moist air and groundwater directly, which will lead to corrosion and expansion, aggravate the lining cracking, and cause local lining to fall off.

衬砌劣化使衬砌结构强度减小，使用寿命缩短，甚至会导致钢轨及扣件腐蚀，危及行车安全。

The lining deterioration will reduce the strength of lining structure, shorten the service life, and even lead to the corrosion of rails and fasteners, which endangers the driving safety.

3.1.4 道床病害

3.1.4 Diseases of track bed

轨道交通区间隧道的结构形式一般为两种，即柔性结构和刚性结构。前者是采用盾构法施工的预制拼装衬砌，后者是采用明挖和暗挖法施工的现浇混凝土衬砌。

Rail transit interval tunnels can be divided into flexible structure and rigid structure. The former is precast and assembled lining constructed by shield method, and the latter is cast-in-situ concrete lining constructed by open excavation and underground excavation method.

柔性结构隧道整体道床病害特征表现在水沟两侧与道床出现渗漏水、翻浆、冒泥。由于隧道不均匀沉降、管片拼装误差等产生的管片错位，致使管片外侧土体泥浆返渗到管片内，引起水沟内翻浆冒泥。

The diseases of monolithic track bed in flexible structure include water leakage, frost boiling and mud pumping on both sides of the ditch and on the track bed. The different settlement of the tunnel and the assembling error of the segments lead to the segments dislocation, let the mud outside the segments seep back into the tunnel, cause mud pumping in the ditch.

刚性结构区间隧道整体道床的病害较柔性结构隧道复杂,除受到外部地质条件的影响,还与内部的结构形式和施工质量有关。特别是暗挖隧道结构形式,整体道床的病害尤为复杂和明显。主要表现为

The diseases of monolithic track bed in rigid structure interval is more complex than these of flexible structure tunnel, which is not only affected by the external geological conditions, but also related to the internal structure and construction quality. Especially for the underground tunnel, the diseases of the monolithic track bed are particularly complex and obvious. It mainly includes:

① 整体道床病害的起始特征为道床两侧水沟渗水、漏水。

① The diseases of the monolithic track bed are developed from the seepage and leakage of the ditches on both sides of the track bed.

② 道床与两侧水沟出现裂缝,隧道内出现裂缝、冒水、冒泥浆。

② Cracks are found on the track bed and the ditches on both sides, and cracks, water and mud are found in the tunnel.

③ 整体道床出现横向裂缝,变形缝严重漏水、冒泥,并与隧道主体结构产生严重剥离。

③ The monolithic track bed has transverse cracks, and the deformation joints with serious water leakage and mud pumping are seriously stripped from the tunnel.

3.2　隧道检查
3.2　Tunnel inspection

3.2.1　隧道结构设施的检查内容
3.2.1　Inspection contents of tunnel structural facilities

1. 隧道结构设施检查分类
1. Classification of tunnel structural facilities inspection

隧道结构设施检查分为年度检查、月度检查及不定期检查。

The inspection of tunnel structural facilities is divided into annual inspection, monthly inspection and irregular inspection.

(1)隧道年度检查

(1) Annual tunnel inspection

每年秋季对隧道设备定期进行全面、全方位检查的工作称为年检(即秋检)。年检对本年度设备进行全面鉴定、评估,并为编制次年设备维修计划提供依据。

The annual inspection (autumn inspection) is the regular and comprehensive inspection of tunnel equipment every autumn. The annual inspection is to comprehensively appraise and evaluate the equipment this year and provide the basis for the equipment maintenance plan next year.

(2)隧道月度检查

(2) Monthly tunnel inspection

隧道月度检查工作每月进行一次,作为次月生产计划工作内容确定的依据。

The monthly inspection of the tunnel shall be conducted once a month to provide the basis for making the production plan for the next month.

(3)隧道不定期检查

(3) Irregular tunnel inspection

根据隧道在运营年限中的沉降变形资料及相关重点病害区段的变化状态,开展不定期检查及时获取隧道质量状态信息。

According to the settlement and deformation of tunnel in service and the change of serious disease sections, irregular inspection is carried out to obtain the information of tunnel qualitative status timely.

2. 隧道结构设施检查的主要内容

2. Inspection contents of tunnel structural facilities

① 隧道顶部滴漏、侧面渗水。

① Dripping at the top of tunnel and seepage at the side of tunnel.

② 隧道底部渗水。

② Seepage at the bottom of tunnel.

③ 管片、混凝土构件破损。

③ Damage of segments and concrete members.

④ 道床与管片间产生脱离。

④ Separation between track beds and segments.

⑤ 隧道内渗砂、漏泥。

⑤ Sand seepage and mud leakage in the tunnel.

⑥ 嵌缝条脱落。

⑥ Falling off of sealing strip.

⑦ 钢管片锈蚀,钢管片和结构连接处漏水。

⑦ Corrosion of steel segments, water leakage of joints between steel segments and structure connection.

⑧ 浮置板道床两侧防尘装置破损。

⑧ Damage of dust prevention devices on both sides of floating slab track beds.

⑨ 人防门是否符合规范要求。

⑨ Whether the civil defense door meets the standard requirements.

⑩ 其他附属物是否缺损。

⑩ Whether other accessories are damaged.

3. 检查工具

3. Tools for inspection

工具主要包括记录类、照明类以及量测类三部分。其中,记录类工具包括纸板夹、笔、记录单、数码相机等。照明类工具包括小手电、探照灯等。量测类工具包括废纸、计时器、钢尺、普通三角尺等。废纸可用于判断病害属于湿迹还是渗水类型,计时器可用于滴漏频率,钢尺与普通三角尺可用于测量病害特征尺寸。

The tools mainly include recording, lighting and measurement. Among them, recording tools include cardboard clips, pens, record sheets, digital cameras, etc. Lighting tools include small flashlights, searchlights, etc. Measurement tools includes waste paper, timer, steel ruler, set square, etc. Waste paper can be used to judge whether the disease belongs to moisture stains or seepage, timer can be used to measure dripping frequency, and steel ruler and set square can be used to measure the size of disease.

3.2.2　隧道检查的技术要求

3.2.2　Technical requirements for tunnel inspection

为确保病害检查成果的有效性,便于后期资料的汇总统计及分析,病害检查应保证一定的准确性,检查过程应规范化、标准化。病害检查流程如图 3-2 所示。

In order to ensure the effectiveness of disease inspection and facilitate the summary, statistics and analysis of later data, disease inspection shall be accurate, and the inspection process shall be standardized. The disease inspection process is shown in Figure 3-2.

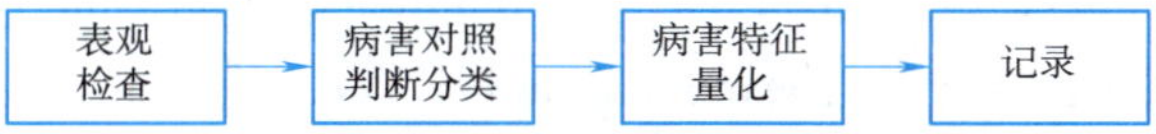

图 3-2　病害检查流程

Figure 3-2　Process of disease inspection

表观检查:visual inspection

病害对照判断分类: disease classification by comparison and judgment

病害特征量化:quantification of disease characteristics

记录:recording

表观检查依靠目测,初步确定病害类型,某些较难界定的病害通过一定检查方法加以分析判断。明确病害类型后,对病害特征进行量化,最后记录检查结果,并拍摄记录影像资料。

Visual inspection relies on naked eyes to preliminarily determine the disease, and some diseases that are difficult to define shall be analyzed and judged by certain inspection methods. After defining the disease, quantify the disease characteristics, finally record the inspection data, and shoot and record the images.

1. 渗漏水检查

1. Leakage inspection

管片渗漏水大多发生在管片接缝或注浆孔等部位,重点检查渗漏水从通道渗出后所形成的分布。

The leakage mostly occurs at the segment joints or grouting holes, and the water distribution after seeping from the channel shall be detected.

(1)检查内容

(1) Contents of inspection

渗漏水检查应区分出渗漏水病害类型，明确渗漏水位置（接缝、注浆孔、手孔或裂缝）、范围（结合展开图要素加以确定）及特征（具体量化指标），对于滴漏应通过秒表确定滴水频率。

The leakage inspection shall distinguish the classifications of leakage diseases, define the leakage location (joints, grouting holes, hand holes or cracks), scope (determined in combination with the unfolded drawing) and characteristics (specific quantitative indicators), and determine the drip frequency through the stopwatch for leakage.

(2)判别方法

(2) Discrimination methods

① 湿迹。

① Moisture stains.

对于湿迹现象，水分蒸发速度快于渗入量，用干手触摸有潮湿感，但无水分浸润感觉，在隧道内常规通风条件下，潮湿现象可能会消失。隧道腰部以上区域无法用手触摸，仅能依靠目测判断。

For moisture stains, the evaporation rate of water is faster than the infiltration amount. When touching by dry hands, it feels wet without moisture infiltration. Under the ventilation in the tunnel, the moisture may disappear. The area above the tunnel haunch which cannot be touched by hand shall be judged by visual inspection.

② 渗水。

② Water seepage.

渗水现象在加强人工通风的条件下也不会消失。用干手触摸，明显沾有水分；用废报纸贴于渗水处，废报纸将会被浸湿变色；对于腰部以上区域，可通过灯光照射，根据有无反光辅助判断是否为渗水。

Water seepage will not disappear under the artificial ventilation. The dry hand will be stained with water through touching. Waste newspaper posted on the water seepage will be wet and change colour. For the area above the haunch, whether there is water seepage can be judged according to whether there is reflection under the light.

某些情况下，病害可能介于湿迹与渗水之间，较难区别。此时，应多种检查方法并用，只要一种检查结果为渗水，则应按不利原则考虑归为渗水病害。

In some cases, the disease may be moisture stains or water seepage, which is difficult to distinguish. Thus, multiple inspection methods shall be adopted. As long as one of the results is water seepage, it shall be classified as water seepage according to the adverse principle.

③ 滴漏。

③ Dripping.

滴水现象与其他渗漏水病害较容易区分，但由于滴漏速度有快慢，当检查速度较快时，容易漏检。在检查过程中，可注意道床表面是否有水迹或少量积水，如存在，极有可能是隧道顶部滴漏的结果。

Dripping is easy to distinguish from other leakage diseases. However, due to the speed of dripping, it is not be detected under the quick examination. During the inspection, if there is water or small ponding on the surface of track bed, it may be caused by dripping from the top of tunnel.

④ 漏泥沙。

④ Mud leakage.

漏泥现象较易判断，漏泥时通常渗水量相对较大，且夹带新鲜泥沙，导致渗出物浑浊。

Mud leakage is easy to judge. When mud leakage occurs, the water seeps out with fresh sediment, resulting in turbidity of the exudation.

(3)病害标志

(3) Disease symbol

病害标志说明见表 3-1。

The description of disease symbol see Table 3-1.

表 3-1　渗漏水病害标志

病害		标志符号	解释	记录要求
渗漏水	湿迹		虚线填充的闭合曲线	曲线边界依据实际湿迹分布确定
	渗水		斜线填充的闭合曲线	曲线边界由实际渗水分布确定
	滴漏		由竖线、椭圆以及数字三部分组成，数字表示滴水频率（滴水数/min）	①当小于 1 滴/min 时，椭圆内应标注 <1。②当大于 60 滴/min 时，可认为滴漏已形成线流，此时应按照渗流标注符号"∞"
	漏泥		点及小三角填充的闭合曲线	曲线边界依据实际漏泥边界确定

注：①对于湿迹仅局限于裂缝，呈窄条状分布时，为提高检查效率，可不予以记录；

②如渗水现象明显，肉眼能观察到明显水流，则应备注栏予以补充说明。

Table 3-1 Symbol of water leakage diseases

Disease		Symbol	Interpretation	Recording requirements
Water leakage	Moisture stains		Closed curve filled with dotted lines	The curve boundary is based on the actual moisture stain
	Water seepage		Closed curve filled with slash	The curve boundary is determined by the actual seepage distribution
	Dripping		It is composed of vertical lines, ellipses and number. The number represent the frequecy of water dripping (water drops/min)	① When it is less than 1 drop/min, the ellipse should be marked with <1. ② When it is more than 60 drops/min, it can be considered that the drip has formed a linear flow. At this time, the sign "∞" should be marked according to the seepage
	Mud leakage		Closed curve filled with points and small triangles	The curve boundary is determined according to the actual leakage boundary

Note: ① When moisture stains are only limited to cracks and distributed in narrow strips, they can not be recorded to improve the inspection efficiency;

② If the water seepage is obvious and the water flow can be observed with naked eyes, the remarks shall be supplemented.

2. 管片损伤检查

2. Inspection of segment damage

(1)检查内容

(1) Inspection contents

管片损伤检查时,应明确隧道结构损伤的类型、位置和程度等信息。当管片裂缝发展到一定程度,与管片接缝贯通形成三维封闭体系时,会出现较罕见的混凝土成块碎裂现象。如在检查中发现,应准确记录碎裂的三维尺寸(面积与深度),并留存全面的影像资料。

During the segment damage inspection, the type, location and extent of tunnel structure damage shall be recorded. When the segment cracks develop to a certain extent and form a three-dimensional closed system with the segment joints, a relatively rare phenomenon of concrete fragmentation will occur. If it is found in the inspection, the three-dimensional size (area and depth) of the fragmentation shall be accurately recorded, and comprehensive image data shall be retained.

(2)判别方法

(2) Discrimination methods

管片损伤病害较为直观,管片裂缝与缺角主要通过目测进行检查。管片裂缝通常表现为颜色略深于管片内表面本色的细缝。管片缺角部位因表层混凝土缺失,缺角颜色同样会深于管片表面本色。

Segment damage diseases are more intuitive, cracks and broken corners are mainly inspected by visual inspection. Segment cracks usually appear as fine cracks whose color is slightly deeper than the true color of the segment inner surface. Due to missing the surface concrete, the color of broken corners is also deeper than the true color of segments.

(3)病害标志

(3) Disease symbol

病害标志说明见表 3-2。

The description of disease symbol see Table 3-2.

表 3-2 管片损伤病害标志

病害		定义	标志符号	解释
管片损伤	裂缝	表层混凝土裂开		①曲线或折线,以裂缝实际线形为依据,当裂缝宽度可量测时,应予以备注。 ②当裂缝较为严重,甚至出现混凝土碎裂的现象时,应特别予以备注,并留存详细的影像资料
	缺角	管片端部混凝土缺失		将实际缺角范围填实,管片缺角深度可量测时,同样予以备注
	缺损	管片纵缝两侧混凝土片状缺失		竖线代表发生缺损的纵缝,交叉线所代表区域与发生缺损区域一致

Table 3-2 Symbol of segment damage diseases

Disease		Definition	Symbol	Interpretation
Segment damage	Crack	Cracking of surface concrete		①The curves or broken lines shall be based on the actual line shape of cracks. When the crack width can be measured, it shall be noted. ②When the crack is relatively serious, or even the concrete fragments, special remarks shall be made and detailed image data shall be retained
	Broken corner	The concrete at the end of the segment is broken		Fill in the broken corner, and make remarks when the depth of broken corner can be measured
	Damage	The concrete flakes on both sides of the longitudinal joint of segments fall off		The vertical line represents the longitudinal joint with defect, and the cross lines represent the same area with damage

3. 管片错台检查

3. Inspection of segment dislocation

(1)检查内容

(1) Inspection contents

管片错台检查应明确错台位置及错台量。

The location and quantity of segment dislocation shall be recorded.

(2)判别方法

(2) Discrimination methods

管片错台初步判断可通过目测进行,对疑似处可通过手触确认,也可将探照灯平贴于管片朝疑似错台处照明，如存在错台现象，则光束在错台处会出现明显明暗对比。

Make a preliminary judgment on segment dislocation by visual inspection, confirm the suspected position by hand touch, or stick the searchlight on the segment to the suspected dislocation. If there is segment dislocation, the light beam will show obvious chiaroscuro at the dislocation.

错台量用钢尺进行量测。

The amount of dislocation can be measured by steel ruler.

(3)病害标志

(3) Disease symbol

病害标志说明见表 3-3。

The description of disease symbol see Table 3-3.

表 3-3 错台标志

病　害	定　义	标志符号	描　述
管片错台	管片间在环面或纵向接触面内发生相对错动的现象	6	直线与错台处接缝垂直并交叉，数字表示错台量

注：①错台量标志于相对朝隧道内的分块。对于环间错台情况，道床一侧可找出错台量最大处予以标注，无须连续标注。
②错台量通过钢尺垂直于管片进行测量。

Table 3-3 Symbol of segment dislocation

Disease	Definition	Symbol	Description
Segment Dislocation	Relative dislocation between segments in the circular or longitudinal contact surface	6	The straight line is perpendicular to and intersects with the joint at the dislocation, and the number represents the amount of dislocation

Note: ① The amount of segment dislocation is marked on the inner block. For the dislocation between rings, the dislocation with the largest amount on one side of track bed can be marked without continuous noting.
②The amount of dislocation is measured by a steel ruler perpendicular to the segment.

根据地铁盾构隧道纵向变形分析，当错台量超过 8 mm 时，将会影响到止水条防水性能。为提高检查效率，当错台量小于 8 mm 时，不予记录。

According to the longitudinal deformation analysis of the subway shield tunnel, when the displacement exceeds 8 mm, the waterproof performance of the waterstop will be affected. In order to improve the inspection efficiency, the dislocation of less than 8 mm will not be recorded.

对于单环相邻管片间出现错台情况，可在对应纵缝位置中部量测错台量。因检查条件的限制，通常只能检查到落底块(D)与标准块(B)间错台情况。

In case of dislocation between adjacent segments of a single ring, the dislocation can be measured at the center of the corresponding longitudinal joint. Due to the restriction of inspection conditions, only the dislocation between the floor block (D) and the standard block (B) can be detected.

4. 管片接缝张开检查

4. Inspection of segment joint splaying

(1)检查内容

(1) Contents of inspection

管片接缝张开检查应明确管片张开所在接缝,如张开处可目测出螺栓,应在备注栏予以明确说明。

During the inspection of segment joint splaying, the joint where the segments open shall be specified. If bolts can be seen at the opening, it should be clearly stated in the remark column.

(2)判别方法

(2) Discrimination methods

管片接缝张开初步判断通过目测进行,对于张开幅度较大处,灯光照射后能发现螺栓。具体接缝张开大小,需采用登高车实地量测。接缝张开一般发生在顶部纵缝位置。

The initial judgment of segment joint splaying is made by visual inspection. For the joints with large opening, bolts can be found in the light. The specific splaying amount of joints should be measured on the climb frame. Splaying of longitudinal joints generally occurs at the top of tunnel.

(3)病害标志

(3) Disease symbol

病害标志说明见表 3-4。

The description of disease symbol see Table 3-4.

表 3-4 接缝张开标志

病害	定义	标志符号	描述
管片接缝张开	顶部纵缝两侧管片未密贴,局部应力集中,出现倒 V 形空隙,即接缝张开	∧	受外界影响,导致隧道受力状态发生变化,严重时,顶部纵缝张开,能目测到环向螺栓

注:交点位置标于管片张开所在接缝处。

Table 3-4 Symbol of segment joint splaying

Disease	Definition	Symbol	Description
Segment joint splaying	The segments on both sides of the top longitudinal joint are not closely attached, which leads to local stress concentration, and an inverted V-shaped gap appears, that is, the segment joint splaying	∧	Due to the external influence, the stress state of tunnel changes. In serious cases, the longitudinal joints at the top are open, and the circumferential bolts can be observed visually

Note: The symbol is marked at the segments joint splaying.

5. 道床与管片脱开检查

5. Inspection for separation of track bed and segment

(1)检查内容

(1) Inspection contents

道床与管片脱开检查应明确脱开位置。对于整体式道床,由于两侧排水沟混凝土后于轨枕区域道床浇筑，管片脱开通常表现为两种形式：包括排水沟与管片脱开以及轨枕区域道床与管片脱开。在脱开现象较为明显的区域，道床混凝土可能会出现横向裂缝，对于此类情况，应在备注栏予以说明，必要时拍摄影像。

The separation position of track bed and segment shall be specified during the inspection. For the monolithic track bed, because the concrete of drainage ditches on both sides is poured later than the track bed in sleeper area, there are usually two forms of segment detachment, including the separation of drain and segment and the separation of track bed and segment. In the area where the separation is obvious, there may be transverse cracks on the concrete of track bed. For such cases, it should be detailed in the remark column, and images should be taken if necessary.

(2)判别方法

(2) Discrimination methods

道床与管片脱开主要通过目测进行检查，对于疑似处，可通过插硬卡片的方式确认两者是否脱开。

The separation of track bed and segment is mainly checked by visual inspection. For the uncertain part, the seperation can be judged by inserting hard card.

(3)病害标志

(3) Disease symbol

病害标志说明见表3-5。

The description of disease symbol see Table 3-5.

表3-5 道床与管片脱开标志

病害	定义	标志符号	描述
道床与管片脱开	道床与管片间存在间隙，纵向上明显存在		标志记录于道床与管片连接处

Table 3-5 Symbol for separation of track bed and segment

Disease	Definition	Symbol	Description
Separation of track bed and segment	There is a gap between track bed and segment, which is obvious in longitudinal direction		The symbol is marked at the connection between track bed and segment

将道床与管片脱开病害现象记录于管片平面展开图中，符号标记于脱开位置，并要求道床与管片脱开位置进行拍照存档。

The separation of track bed and segment shall be recorded in the segment plane unfolded drawing, and the symbol shall be marked at the separation position which is required to take photos for archiving.

6. 其他病害

6. Other diseases

此部分病害因较特殊，甚至从未出现过，无法对检查内容提出具体要求。一旦被发现，必须对病害的位置、范围以及特征进行详细的记录，并留存全面的照片及录像资料备查。

For the disease is special and even never appeared, we can not put forward specific requirements for inspection contents. Once it's detected, we must make detailed records of position, range and characteristic of the disease, and keep comprehensive photos and video data for future reference.

3.3　防水堵漏作业
3.3　Waterproofing and plugging operation

3.3.1　表贴式止水带施工作业
3.3.1　Construction of surface-mounted waterstop

表贴式止水带施工作业适用于矩形隧道变形缝渗漏水。

It's suitable for leakage of deformation joints in rectangular tunnels.

1. 所需材料和工器具
1. Materials and tools required

(1)所需材料(见表 3-6)

(1) Materials required (see Table 3-6)

表 3-6　表贴式止水带施工作业材料表

序号	名称
1	双快水泥
2	橡胶止水带
3	钢板
4	角铁
5	角铁
6	圆钢
7	嵌缝胶
8	化学锚栓

Table 3-6　Materials for construction of surface-mounted waterstop

No.	Name
1	Double fast cement
2	Rubber waterstop
3	Steel plate
4	Angle iron
5	Angle iron
6	Steel rod
7	Caulking glue
8	Chemical anchor

(2)所需工器具(见表3-7)

(2) Tools required(see Table 3-7)

表3-7 表贴式止水带施工作业工器具表

序号	名称
1	击钻
2	拖线盘
3	太阳灯
4	铝合金脚手架
5	钢丝钳
6	扳手
7	喷壶
8	榔头
9	凿子

Table 3-7 Tools for construction of surface-mounted waterstop

No.	Name
1	Churn drill
2	Towing reel
3	Sunlamp
4	Aluminum alloy scaffold
5	Wire-cutter
6	Spanner
7	Watering can
8	Hammer
9	Chisel

2. 操作程序

2. Operation procedure

① 找平处理堵漏后的基面。

① Level the surface after plugging.

② 根据止水带、角铁尺寸进行放样定位。

② Setting out and positioning according to the size of waterstop and angle iron.

③ 安装角铁架。

③ Install angle iron frame.

④ 将圆钢焊接至角铁架上。

④ Weld the steel rod to the angle iron frame.

⑤ 钻孔安装压板螺栓。

⑤ Drill holes and install press plate screw.

⑥ 安装止水带,并固定压板,见图3-3。

⑥ Install waterstop, and fix platen, see Figure 3-3.

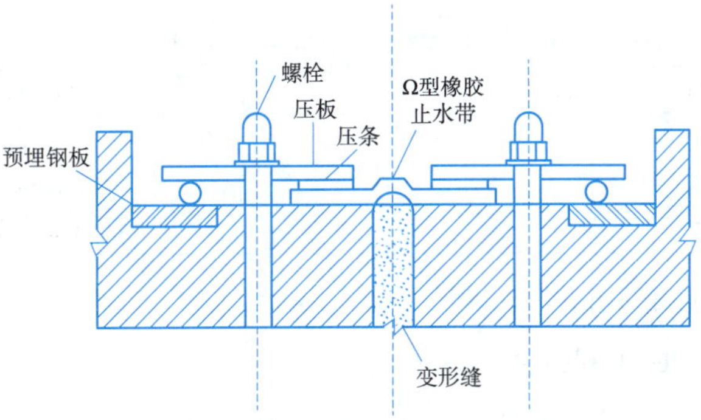

图 3-3　表贴式止水带示意图

Figure 3-3　Sketch map of surface-mounted waterstop

预埋钢板:embedded steel plate　压板:platen　压条:batten

Ω 型橡胶止水带:Ω rubber waterstop　变形缝:deformation joint

3. 质量控制

3. Quality control

① 基面找平到位,基层应坚固、密实,没有起砂、裂缝、蜂窝、麻面等现象。否则,应将基层表面用 1∶2 水泥砂浆整平,允许空隙不应大于 2 mm(用 2 m 直尺检查平整度)。

① The surface should be leveled, and the base should be strong, dense without sand, cracks, voids and pits. Otherwise, the base should be leveled with 1∶2 cement mortar, and the allowable gap should not be greater than 2 mm (check the flatness with 2 m ruler).

② 止水带接口应留在顶部。

② The waterstop joint should be set at the top.

3.3.2　引排水施工作业

3.3.2　Construction operation of water diversion and drainage

为了确保正常的运营安全,在时间、现场环境等客观因素的限制下,采用引排水施工。目前,引水施工主要采用埋管或设置引水槽的方法,该法适用于站线及矩形隧道顶板渗漏水。

In order to ensure the operation safety, construction of water diversion and drainage is adopted due to time, on-site environment and other objective factors. At present, diversion construction by burying pipe or setting trough, which is applicable to the roof leakage of station and rectangular tunnel.

1. 所需材料和工器具

1. Materials and tools required

(1) 所需材料(见表 3-8)

(1) Materials required (see Table 3-8)

表 3-8　引排水施工作业材料表

序号	名称
1	PVC 管
2	铅丝
3	不锈钢条

Table 3-8 Materials for construction operation of water diversion and drainage

No.	Definition
1	PVC pipe
2	Galvanized wire
3	Stainless steel strip

(2)所需工器具(见表3-9)

(2) Tools required (see Table 3-9)

表3-9 引排水施工作业工器具表

序号	名称
1	电锤
2	拖线盘
3	钢丝钳
4	扶梯

Table 3-9 Tools for construction operation of water diversion and drainage

No.	Name
1	Electric hammer
2	Towing reel
3	Wire-cutter
4	Staircase

2. 操作程序

2. Operation procedure

① 加工PVC管材(不锈钢引水槽)。

① Processing PVC pipe (stainless steel aqueduct).

② 确定安装位置。

② Determine the installation location.

③ 安装固定吊点。

③ Install the fixed lifting point.

④ 安装引水管(槽)。

④ Install the water pipe(aqueduct).

3. 质量控制

3. Quality control

① 引水管槽坡度不得小于5‰。

① Duct slope shall not be less than 5 ‰.

② 不得将引水管槽固定在其他管线上。

② The diversion pipe slot shall not be fixed to other pipelines.

4. 安全措施

4. Safety measures

① 施工人员必须穿戴工作服和手套等劳动防护用品。

① Construction workers must wear work clothes and gloves and other labor protection articles.

② 登高人员,必须穿戴安全带。

② Climbers must wear safety belts.

③ 施工完毕后,必须清理现场,做到工完料清。

③ After construction, the site must be cleaned up and the materials must be packed.

5. 作业验收

5. Operation acceptance

① 正确找出水源、漏水点。

① Find out the right location of water source and leakage.

② 施工作业符合相关的质量控制要求。

② Construction conforms to relevant quality control requirements.

③ 必须确保引水管(槽)安装牢固、排水通畅,且无漏水点在引水管(槽)外。

③ Ensure that pipe (trough) is firmly installed, diversion is unobstructed, and there is no leakage outside the pipe (trough).

3.3.3 堵漏施工作业

3.3.3 Leaking stoppage construction

堵漏施工的常用工艺包括:凿缝埋管灌浆堵漏法、钻孔灌浆堵漏法、管片接缝注浆堵漏法、环氧树脂注浆堵漏法和聚氨酯壁后注浆堵漏法。

The common construction for leaking stoppage includes: grouting after chiseling a seam and burying a pipe, grouting after drilling a hole, grouting segment joint, grouting with epoxy resin, grouting behind segments with polyurethane.

1. 凿缝埋管灌浆堵漏法

1. Grouting after chiseling a seam and burying a pipe

凿缝埋管灌浆堵漏法适用于矩形隧道变形缝渗漏水和钢筋混凝土结构不规则裂缝渗漏水。

The method is suitable for the seepage of deformed joints in rectangular tunnels and the seepage of irregular cracks in reinforced concrete structures.

(1)所需材料和工器具

(1) Materials and tools required

① 所需材料见表3-10。

① The materials requested are shown in Table 3-10.

表3-10 凿缝埋管灌浆堵漏法材料表

序号	名称	规格
1	双快水泥	快凝快干
2	聚氨酯	油溶性或水溶性

Table 3-10 Materials for grouting after chiseling a seam and burying a pipe

No.	Name	Specs.
1	Double fast cement	Fast setting, quick dry
2	Polyurethane	Oil soluble or water soluble

② 所需工器具见表 3-11。

② The tools required are shown in Table 3-11.

表 3-11 凿缝埋管灌浆堵漏法工器具表

序号	名称
1	冲击钻
2	电锤
3	电动注浆泵
4	手动注浆泵
5	拖线盘
6	太阳灯
7	铝合金脚手架
8	钢丝钳
9	割刀
10	榔头
11	凿子
12	扳手
13	喷壶
14	漆刷
15	水桶
16	注浆管

Table 3-11 Tools for grouting after chiseling a seam and burying a pipe

No.	Name
1	Churn drill
2	Electric hammer
3	Electric grouting pump
4	Manual grouting pump
5	Towing reel
6	Sunlamp
7	Aluminum alloy scaffold
8	Wire-cutter
9	Cutting knife
10	Hammer

continued

No.	Name
11	Plow bit
12	Spanner
13	Watering can
14	Paintbrush
15	Bucket
16	Grouting pipe

(2)操作程序

(2) Operation procedure

① 现场确定具体病害(裂缝)位置。

① Determine the location of diseases (cracks) on site.

② 病害位置开设 V 字槽(深度/宽度 = 1/2)。

② Open a V-shaped groove (depth/width = 1/2) at the location of disease.

③ 清洗孔位及 V 字槽。

③ Clean the hole and V-shaped groove.

④ 将注浆嘴预埋至孔内,并用双快水泥封缝。

④ Embed the grouting nozzle into the hole and seal the gap with double fast cement.

⑤ 对封堵的水泥进行浇水养护。

⑤ Cure the blocked cement with water.

⑥ 待水泥达到设计强度后,按比例配制浆液进行灌浆。

⑥ After the cement reaches the design strength, the grout shall be prepared in proportion for grouting.

⑦ 待浆液完全固化后去除注浆管,清理现场。

⑦ Pull out or cut off the grouting pipe and clean up the site after the slurry is completely solidified.

(3)质量控制(见图 3-4)

(3) Quality control (see Figure 3-4)

① 封堵孔位及 V 字槽时不得留有任何间隙。

① Do not leave any clearance when plugging the hole and V-shaped groove.

② 确保封堵水泥达到设计强度(一定的养护时间)后再注浆。

② Ensure that the plugging cement reaches the design strength (a certain curing time) before grouting.

③ 配制浆液时,搅拌时间不得少于 10 min。

③ Stir slurry for no less than 10 min when preparing it.

④ 灌浆时应观察周边情况,一旦出现漏浆、爆浆现象,应立即停止灌浆。

④ Observe the surroundings during grouting, and stop grouting immediately once slurry leakage or slurry explosion occurs.

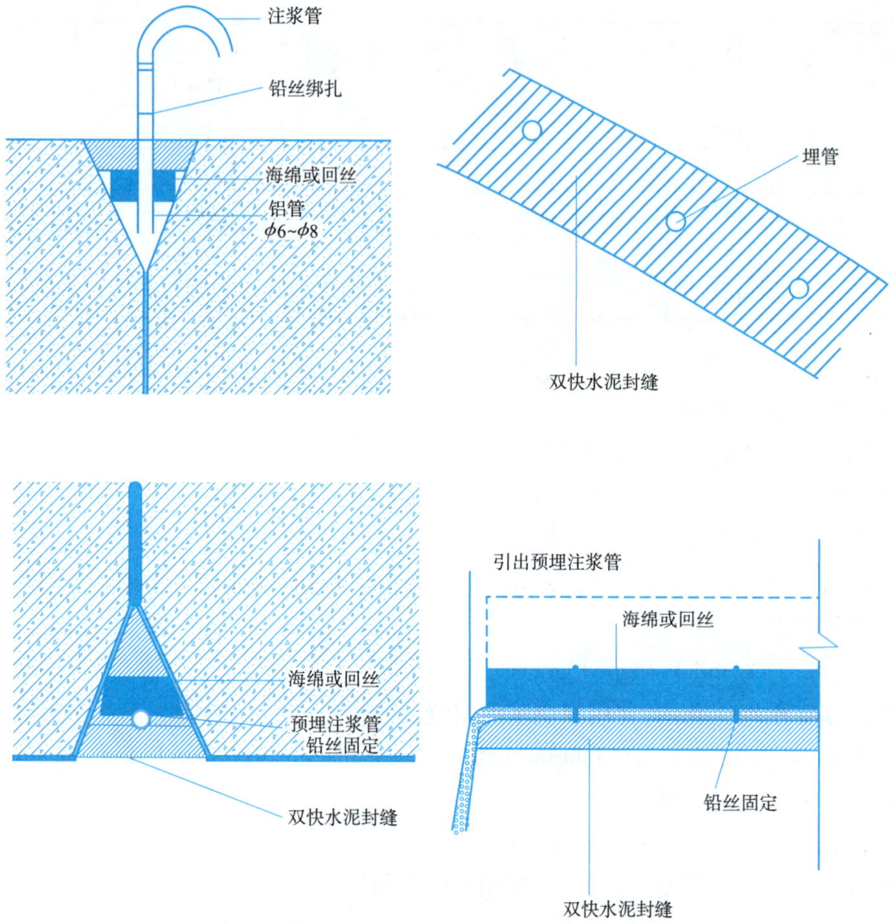

图 3-4 凿缝埋管注浆法

Figure 3-4 Grouting after chiseling a seam and burying a pipe

注浆管:grouting pipe　　铅丝绑扎:lead wire binding
海绵或回丝:sponge or rewind　　铝管:aluminium tube
预埋注浆管:embedded grouting pipe　　铅丝固定:lead wire fixation
埋管:buried pipe　　双快水泥封缝:double fast cement joint sealing
引出预埋注浆管:lead out the embedded grouting pipe

(4)安全措施

(4) Safety measures

① 施工人员必须穿戴护目镜、工作服和手套等劳动防护用品。

① Construction workers must wear goggles, work clothes and gloves and other labor protection articles.

② 登高人员,必须穿戴安全带。

② Climbers must wear safety belts.

③ 灌浆时必须对注浆孔进行遮掩。

③ The grouting hole must be concealed during grouting.

④ 施工现场不得堆放易燃易爆物品。

④ Inflammables and explosives shall not be stacked in construction site.

⑤ 施工完毕后，必须清理现场，做到工完料清。

⑤ After construction, the site must be cleaned up and the materials must be packed.

2. 钻孔灌浆堵漏法

2. Drilling grouting method for seepage plugging

钻孔灌浆堵漏法适用于矩形隧道变形缝渗漏水和钢筋混凝土结构不规则裂缝渗漏水。

The method is suitable for the seepage of deformed joints in rectangular tunnels and the seepage of reinforced irregular cracks in concrete structures.

(1) 所需材料和工器具

(1) Materials and tools required

① 所需材料见表 3-12。

① The materials required are shown in Table 3-12.

表 3-12　钻孔灌浆堵漏法材料表

序号	名称
1	双快水泥
2	聚氨酯

Table 3-12　Materials for grouting after drilling a hole

No.	Name
1	Double fast cement
2	Polyurethane

② 所需工器具见表 3-13。

② The tools required are shown in Table 3-13.

表 3-13　钻孔灌浆堵漏法工器具表

序号	名称
1	冲击钻
2	电锤
3	电动注浆泵
4	手动注浆泵
5	拖线盘
6	太阳灯
7	铝合金脚手架
8	钢丝钳
9	割刀
10	榔头

续表

序号	名称
11	凿子
12	扳手
13	喷壶
14	漆刷
15	水桶
16	注浆管

Table 3-13　Tools drilling grouting method for seepage plugging

No.	Name
1	Churn drill
2	Electric hammer
3	Electric grouting pump
4	Manual grouting pump
5	Towing reel
6	Sunlamp
7	Aluminum alloy scaffold
8	Wire-cutter
9	Cutting knife
10	Hammer
11	Plow bit
12	Spanner
13	Watering can
14	Paintbrush
15	Bucket
16	Grouting pipe

(2)操作程序

(2) Operating procedure

① 现场确定病害(裂缝)位置。

① Determine the location of the disease (crack) on site.

② 针对病害(裂缝)类型,选择钻孔方式。

② According to the type of the disease (crack), select a drilling method.

③ 选用双快水泥或环氧胶泥封堵裂缝。

③ Use double fast cement or epoxy mortar to plug the crack.

④ 安装并紧固注浆嘴。

④ Install and fasten the grouting nozzle.

⑤ 待封堵材料达到强度后,按配合比配置浆液进行灌浆堵漏。

⑤ After the plugging material reaches the strength, grout shall be prepared in proportion for grouting and plugging.

⑥ 当灌浆材料完全固化后，除去注浆嘴，留下的注浆孔可以用双快水泥封闭。

⑥ After the grouting material is completely solidified, remove the grouting nozzle and seal the grouting hole with double fast cement.

(3)质量控制(见图3-5和图3-6)

(3) Quality control (see Figure 3-5 and Figure 3-6)

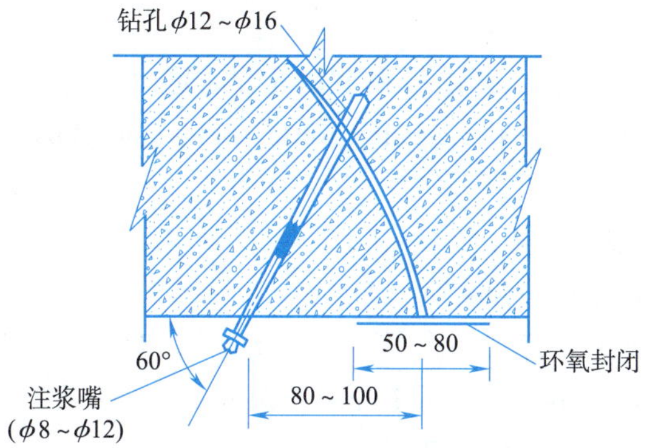

图3-5 钻斜孔注浆封缝细部构造图(单位:mm)

Figure 3-5 Structural details of crack sealing by drilling an inclined hole and grouting (Unit: mm)

钻孔:drilling hole 注浆嘴:grouting nozzle 环氧封闭:epoxy sealing

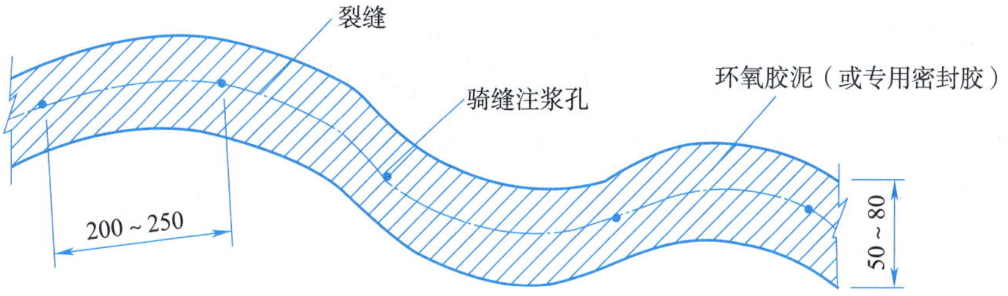

图3-6 骑缝注浆封缝布孔图(单位:mm)

Figure 3-6 Layout of holes for crack sealing by grouting along (Unit: mm)

骑缝注浆孔:hole for grouting along

环氧胶泥(或专用密封胶):epoxy mortar (or special sealant)

① 孔位应交错布置在裂缝周围，确保布设的斜孔穿过裂缝。

① The holes are staggered around the cracks to ensure that the holes cross the cracks obliquely.

② 裂缝延伸方向基本与衬砌表面垂直的裂缝可以布设骑缝孔。

② The crack extending direction is basically perpendicular to the lining surface.

③ 埋入注浆嘴深度应不小于注浆嘴总长的2/3，灌浆孔孔距控制在200～250 mm范围内。

③ The embedded depth of grouting nozzle should not be less than 2/3 of the total length of grouting nozzle, and the spacing of grouting holes should be within 200 - 250 mm.

④ 配制浆液时，配料搅拌时间不得少于 10 min。

④ During slurry preparation, the stirring time shall not be less than 10 min.

⑤ 灌浆时应观察周边情况，一旦出现漏浆、爆浆现象，应立即停止灌浆。

⑤ Observe the surroundings during grouting, and stop grouting immediately once slurry leakage or slurry explosion occurs.

(4)安全措施

(4) Safety measures

① 施工人员必须穿戴护目镜、工作服和手套等劳动防护用品。

① Construction workers must wear goggles, work clothes and gloves and other labor protection articles.

② 登高人员，必须穿戴安全带。

② Climbers must wear safety belts.

③ 灌浆时必须对注浆孔进行遮掩。

③ The grouting hole must be concealed during grouting.

④ 施工现场不得堆放易燃易爆物品。

④ Inflammables and explosives shall not be stacked in construction site.

⑤ 施工完毕后，必须清理现场，做到工完料清。

⑤ After construction, the site must be cleaned up and the materials must be packed.

3. 管片接缝注浆堵漏法

3. Grouting and plugging method for segment joints

管片接缝注浆堵漏法适用于圆形隧道管片拼接缝处渗水。

The method is applicable to the seepage at the segment joints of circular tunnel.

(1)所需材料和工器具

(1) Materials and tools required

① 所需材料(见表 3-14)。

① Materials requested (see Table 3-14).

表 3-14　管片接缝注浆堵漏法材料表

序号	名称
1	弹性环氧
2	环氧树脂
3	环氧胶泥
4	注浆管
5	注浆嘴
6	铁丝
7	尼龙棒
8	胶带

Table 3-14 Materials for grouting and plugging method for segment joints

No.	Name
1	Elastic epoxy
2	Epoxy resin
3	Epoxy mortar
4	Grouting pipe
5	Grouting nozzle
6	Iron wire
7	Nylon stick
8	Adhesive tape

② 所需工器具(见表 3-15)。

② Tools requested (see Table 3-15).

表 3-15 管片接缝注浆堵漏法工器具表

序号	名称
1	电锤
2	电动式注浆泵
3	手动式注浆泵
4	拖线盘
5	太阳灯
6	平板车
7	钢丝钳
8	活动扳手
9	榔头
10	喷壶
11	SM 胶枪
12	切割机
13	油灰刀
14	毛刷
15	美工刀
16	烘干枪

Table 3-15 Tools for grouting and plugging method for segment joints

No.	Name
1	Electric hammer
2	Electric grouting pump
3	Manual grouting pump
4	Towing reel

continued

No.	Name
5	Sunlamp
6	Flatbed trailer
7	Wire cutter
8	Monkey wrench
9	Hammer
10	Watering can
11	SM glue gun
12	Cutting machine
13	Scraper
14	Brush
15	Utility knife
16	Drying gun

(2)操作程序

(2) Operation procedure

① 根据实际情况,确定本施工工艺是否适用于现场病害整治。

① According to the actual situation, determine whether the disease is applicable to the operation procedure.

② 根据治理范围,制作隔断节点。

② Make partition nodes according to the scope of treatment.

③ 用水试压节点附近的注水口,检验节点隔断效果。

③ Test the nozzles near nodes with pressure water to check the isolation effect of nodes.

④ 在病害环缝内安装注浆嘴。

④ Install grouting nozzle in the circumferential joints.

⑤ 对病害环缝进行嵌缝处理。

⑤ Caulk the circumferential joints.

⑥ 将弹性环氧进行配制,对灌浆孔由下而上进行灌浆。

⑥ Prepare elastic epoxy and inject it into the holes from bottom to top.

⑦ 铲去粘贴于管片上的胶带和多余环氧胶泥。

⑦ Remove the adhesive tape stuck on the segment and excessive epoxy mortar.

(3)质量控制

(3) Quality control

① 环缝内的嵌缝水泥须彻底凿除。

① Chisel the cement in the circumferential joint thoroughly.

② 用毛刷清理环缝内的粉尘,否则会影响后续嵌缝的密封效果。

② Use a brush to clean the dust in the joint, or it will affect the subsequent sealing.

③ 节点应设置在封顶块、邻接块、标准块、拱底块的拼缝处；每处作为一个节点组，每组制作节点 2 个，注水孔 1 个。注水孔布置在两个节点的中间位置，最外侧节点离环缝中心距不得大于 200 mm。每环须制作 12 个节点组。

③ The nodes should be set at the joints of the top block, adjacent block, standard block and bottom block. Each joint is treated as a node group, which includes 2 nodes and 1 water injection hole. The water injection hole is set in the middle of two nodes, and the outermost node shall not be more than 200 mm from the circumferential joint. Each ring shall be made of 12 node groups.

④ 节点内先用环氧胶泥填充满，再塞入尼龙棒，提高节点的隔断效果。

④ The nodes shall be filled with epoxy mortar first, and then stuffed with nylon sticks to improve the partition effect of nodes.

⑤ 待环氧胶泥固化后，将注水孔与手动泵连接，用清水进行试压。如果压力表显示有压力，压不进水，并且节点处无水溢出，则说明该节点已起到隔断效果，可进行下一道工序；如有水溢出，则须重做节点。

⑤ After curing of epoxy mortar, connect the water injection hole with the manual pump and test the pressure with clear water. If the pressure gauge shows that there is pressure, and water cannot be injected and no water overflows at the node, it means that the node has been isolated, and the next process can be carried out. If water overflows, the node must be redone.

⑥ 每块管片各设 3 个注浆嘴，均匀分布（如遇渗水量较大，可适当增加注浆嘴数量）。注浆孔深度为 150 mm，直径为 14 mm；封顶块相邻两侧注浆孔深度要求为 250 mm，埋设塑料软管，伸入深度为 200 mm，使顶部环缝内更密实的填充满浆液，起到堵漏效果。

⑥ Each segment is equipped with 3 grouting nozzles evenly(if the amount of seepage is large, the number of grouting nozzles can be increased). The depth of grouting hole is 150 mm, the diameter is 14 mm. The depth of grouting holes on both adjacent sides of top block is 250 mm and the depth of grouting holes is 200 mm, which makes the top circumferential joint full of grout and improves the plugging effect.

⑦ 在环缝两侧各 30 mm 处沿环缝方向粘贴胶带。

⑦ Attach adhesive tape along the circumferential direction at 30 mm each side of the joint.

⑧ 胶带粘贴后，在环缝表面涂上环氧树脂。前后工序不能颠倒，否则胶带将无法粘贴于管片上。

⑧ After pasting adhesive tape, apply epoxy resin to the surface of the circumferential joint. The procedures can not be reversed, or the tape can not be pasted on the segment.

⑨ 将环氧胶泥嵌入环缝内，要求嵌缝饱满、表面平滑，并溢出环缝檐口宽 30 mm，厚 2 mm。

⑨ Embed epoxy mortar in the circumferential joint. The caulking shall be full and the surface shall be smooth. The cornice of the circular joint shall be 30 mm wide and 2 mm thick.

⑩ 待环氧胶泥固化后，采用电动注浆泵，以 0.4 MPa 的压力同时从隧道最低处注浆嘴向两侧进行灌浆。

⑩ After the epoxy mortar is solidified, an electric grouting pump is used to simultaneously inject elastic epoxy into grouting nozzles from the lowest to both sides at a pressure of 0.4 MPa.

⑪ 灌浆灌到相邻上一注浆嘴出浆,封闭低处注浆嘴,移至上一注浆嘴继续灌浆。依此类推,直至最后一个注浆管(顶部塑料软管)压力达到0.4 MPa并保持10 min不变,完成灌浆。

⑪ Grouting shall not be stopped until the grout is discharged from the adjacent upper grouting nozzle. Plug the lower grouting nozzle and inject the upper grouting nozzle. By analogy, the grouting is completed until the pressure of the last grouting pipe (top plastic hose) reaches 0.4 MPa and remains constant for 10 min.

(4)安全措施

(4) Safety measures

① 施工人员必须穿戴护目镜、工作服和手套等劳动防护用品。

① Construction workers must wear goggles、work clothes and gloves and other labor protection articles.

② 登高作业须穿戴安全带。

② Climbers must wear safety belts.

③ 灌浆时必须对注浆孔进行遮掩。

③ The grouting hole must be concealed during grouting.

④ 施工现场不得堆放易燃易爆物品,并配备防火设备。

④ The construction site shall not pile up inflammables and explosives.

⑤ 施工完毕后,必须清理现场,做到工完料清。

⑤ After construction, the site must be cleaned up and the materials must be packed.

4. 聚氨酯壁后注浆堵漏法

4. Grouting behind segments method with polyurethane

聚氨酯遇水后会发泡,膨胀快,膨胀率大(大于2 000%),强度好,有弹性,对渗水量大的地下工程堵漏效果良好,能加固地基。固结体有良好的抗渗性,在水中永久保持原形,并具有耐低温性,与水具有良好的混溶性,诱导时间(10~1 200 s)可以通过配比进行调节。聚氨酯壁后注浆堵漏法适用于圆形隧道壁后防水堵漏。

After encountering water, the polyurethane will foam and expand quickly with a large expansion rate (greater than 2 000%), good strength and elasticity. It has good plugging effect on underground engineering with large seepage volume and can strengthen the foundation. The consolidated body, which can keep its original shape forever in water, has good impermeability and low temperature resistance. Due to good miscibility with water, the induction time (10-1 200 s) can be adjusted by mixing ratio. The method is applicable to the waterproof plugging behind segments in circular tunnel.

(1)所需材料和工器具

(1) Materials and tools required

① 所需材料(见表3-16)。

① Materials requested (see Table 3-16).

表 3-16　聚氨酯壁后注浆堵漏法材料表

序号	名称
1	球阀
2	生料带
3	聚氨酯

Table 3-16　Materials for grouting behind segments method with polyurethane

No.	Name
1	Ball valve
2	PTFE TAPE
3	Polyurethane

② 所需工器具(见表 3-17)。

② Tools required (see Table 3-17).

表 3-17　聚氨酯壁后注浆堵漏法工器具表

序号	名称
1	变频器
2	齿轮泵
3	电锤
4	五坑钻头
5	注浆管
6	回流管
7	进浆管

Table 3-17　Tools for grouting behind segments method with polyurethane

No.	Name
1	Frequency transformer
2	Gear pump
3	Electric hammer
4	SDS-MAX
5	Grouting pipe
6	Return pipe
7	Grout inlet pipe

(2)操作程序

(2) Operation procedure

① 预置球阀。

① Preset ball valve.

a. 准备好球阀、生料带、两寸孔口管,孔口管为球阀与管片连接的媒介。

a. Prepare ball valves, PTFE TAPE and orifice pipes which is the medium of connecting ball valves and segments.

b. 施工前应对球阀及孔口管进行质量检查。

b. Before construction, inspect the quality of ball valves and orifice pipes.

c. 分别于孔口管两头以顺时针方向充分缠上生料带,并把细螺纹一头接入球阀。

c. Wrap PTFE TAPE on the both ends of orifice pipe in a clockwise direction, and insert the fine thread end to the ball valve.

② 注浆孔清理。

② Clean grouting holes.

a. 打开管片预留注浆孔闷头。

a. Open the bulkhead of the grouting hole reserved in the segment.

b. 清理注浆孔内部杂物。

b. Clean the debris in the grouting hole.

c. 检查注浆孔螺纹。

c. Inspect the grouting hole thread.

③ 安装球阀。

③ Install the ball valve.

a. 将已预置球阀以孔口管粗螺纹一端接入注浆孔。

a. Connect the preset ball valve to the grouting hole with the coarse thread end of orifice pipe.

b. 用管子钳分别紧固球阀与孔口管以及孔口管与管片注浆孔螺纹间的连接。

b. Fasten the connection between the ball valve and the orifice pipe and the connection between the orifice pipe and the segment grouting hole thread with pipe wrenches.

c. 关闭球阀。

c. Close the ball valve.

④ 钻注浆孔。

④ Drill grouting hole.

a. 打开管片注浆孔上球阀。

a. Open the ball valve on the segment grouting hole.

b. 用冲击钻通过球阀沿注浆孔打穿管片。

b. Drill the segment along the grouting hole through the ball valve with an impact drill.

c. 抽出钻头,并关闭球阀。

c. Pull out the drill bit and close the ball valve.

⑤ 接注浆管及注浆。

⑤ Connect the grouting pipe to the ball valve and grout.

a. 组装好变频器、齿轮泵、注浆管、吸浆管及回流管。

a. Assemble frequency transformer, gear pump, grouting pipe, slurry suction pipe and return pipe.

b. 将注浆管接入球阀及紧固。

b. Insert the grouting pipe to the ball valve and fasten them.

c. 打开电源,启动变频器控制齿轮泵。当浆液进入齿轮泵时关闭回流管阀门,并且同时打开注浆管与球阀的阀门，使得浆液通过注浆管及球阀注入管片壁后。注浆结束后，同时关闭球阀及注浆管的阀门，打开回流管阀门，再打开注浆管阀门进行卸压。

c. Turn on the power and start the transformer to control the gear pump. When the slurry enters the gear pump, close the valve of return pipe, open the valve of the grouting pipe and ball valve at the same time, and grout through the grouting pipe and ball valve. After grouting, close the ball valve and the valve of grouting pipe, open the valve of return pipe, and then open the valve of grouting pipe for pressure release.

d. 卸除注浆管。

d. Remove the grouting pipe.

⑥ 施工完毕后现场清理。

⑥ Site cleaning after construction.

a. 待聚氨酯固化后清除管片、球阀上残留物。

a. Remove residues from segments and ball valves after polyurethane curing.

b. 清洗齿轮泵、注浆管、吸浆管和回流管，以免残留浆液固化堵塞管道。

b. Clean gear pump, grouting pipe, slurry suction pipe and return pipe to avoid residual slurry solidification to clog pipes.

(3)质量控制

(3) Quality control

① 齿轮泵压力应进行控制。

① Control the pressure of gear pump.

② 每孔注浆量应进行控制。

② Control the grouting amount of per hole.

③ 注浆顺序：隧道纵向上，每次隔两环注浆一环；横向上，根据注浆孔分布情况，从下向上依次注浆。

③ Grouting sequence: longitudinally, each time grout one ring every two rings; transversely, according to the distribution of grouting holes, grout from bottom to top in turn.

④ 经过多次注浆后，须达到一定止水效果。

④ After multiple rounds of grouting, water stop must be achieved.

(4)安全措施

(4) Safety measures

① 建立安全生产责任制，责任落实到人。

① Establish responsibility system for production safety and assign responsibility to each person.

② 岗前须进行安全教育，掌握本施工安全生产的基本知识和技能。

② Safety education must be carried out before work, and make workers grasp the knowledge and the skill of safety production in construction.

③ 施工人员必须穿戴好防护用具、穿工作服、戴防护眼镜和口罩。

③ Construction workers must wear protective equipment, work clothes, protective glasses and masks.

④ 建立安全防护制度,并在施工中严格执行。

④ Establish a safety protection system and strictly implement it in construction.

⑤ 为防止漏浆,所有注浆作业须在接触网停电、验电及做接地保护后进行。

⑤ In order to prevent slurry leakage, all grouting operations shall be carried out after power failure of catenary, electricity inspection and grounding protection.

⑥ 无法安装孔口管的注浆孔须采用特殊工法封孔。

⑥ The grouting hole which can not install the orifice pipe shall be sealed by special method.

⑦ 安装的球阀必须满足限界要求。

⑦ The installed ball valve must meet the requirement of gauge.

⑧ 注浆前后球阀均应处于关闭状态,每次注浆撤场前须专人进行状态确认。

⑧ The ball valve before and after grouting shall be closed, and the status shall be confirmed by a special person before grouting operation withdraws from the site.

⑨ 施工现场严禁烟火,禁止吸烟,且须配备灭火器具。

⑨ Fireworks and smoking are prohibited on the construction site, and fire extinguishers must be equipped.

⑩ 施工完成后,须工完料清,经安全负责人现场确认后方可消点。

⑩ After construction, the site must be cleaned up and the materials must be packed. The person in charge must confirm safety on site before eliminating operation.

5. 堵漏作业验收

5. Acceptance of plugging operation

① 正确找出水源、漏水点。

① Find out the right location of water source and leakage.

② 采用正确的堵漏施工作业工法。

② Adopt the proper plugging operation.

③ 施工作业符合相关的质量控制要求。

③ Construction conforms to relevant quality control requirements.

④ 浆液配比正确,调配均匀。

④ The slurry is correctly proportioned and evenly mixed.

⑤ 注浆顺序由下而上,正确控制注浆压力,观察周边情况,一旦出现漏浆、爆浆现象,应立即停止灌浆。

⑤ Grout from bottom to top, and control the grouting pressure correctly. Observe the surroundings during grouting, and stop grouting immediately once slurry leakage or slurry explosion occurs.

⑥ 水泥封堵不起鼓,水泥砂浆刮抹平整光滑。

⑥ The plugging cement shall not bulge, and the cement mortar shall be flat and smooth.

⑦ 环氧胶泥嵌缝应嵌密、压实、抹平,表面平整一致。

⑦ The epoxy mortar caulking shall be compacted and leveled, and the surface shall be flat.

3.4 加固作业
3.4 Reinforcement operation

3.4.1 整体道床轨道支撑块加固作业
3.4.1 Reinforcement of track support board on monolithic track bed

整体道床轨道支撑块加固作业适用于整体道床轨道支撑块开裂、破损。

The reinforcement of track support board on monolithic track bed is suitable for cracking and breakage of track support board on monolithic ballast bed.

1. 所需材料和工器具
1. Materials and tools required

(1)所需材料(见表 3-18)

(1) Materials required (see Table 3-18)

表 3-18 整体道床轨道支撑块加固作业材料表

序号	名称
1	双快水泥
2	环氧树脂
3	铅丝
4	注浆管

Table 3-18 Materials for reinforcement of track support board of monolithic track bed

No.	Name
1	Double fast cement
2	Epoxy resin
3	Galvanized wire
4	Grouting pipe

(2)所需工器具(见表 3-19)

(2) Tools required (see Table 3-19)

表 3-19 整体道床轨道支撑块加固作业工器具表

序号	名称
1	电锤
2	手动式注泵
3	拖线盘
4	太阳灯
5	钢丝钳
6	喷壶

Table 3-19 Tools for reinforcement operation of track support board of monolithic track bed

No.	Name
1	Electric hammer
2	Manual grouting pump
3	Towing reel
4	Sunlamp
5	Steel wire cutter
6	Watering can

2. 操作程序

2. Operation procedure

① 清理支撑块及周边道床基面。

① Clean the support board and the track bed surface.

② 布设孔位及钻孔。

② Set and drill holes.

③ 清孔,清洗孔内粉尘。

③ Clear up holes and rinse dust out of holes.

④ 封缝及埋设注浆管。

④ Seal cracks and embed grouting pipes.

⑤ 进行注浆。

⑤ Carry out grouting.

3. 质量控制

3. Quality control

① 清洗干净支撑块及周边道床表面。

① Clean the support board and the track bed surface.

② 注浆材料需按配合比进行调和。

② Grouting materials shall be prepared according to the mix proportion

③ 封缝时应封堵密实,注浆时不得出现跑浆。

③ The cracks shall be sealed tightly and no grout runs out during grouting.

④ 注浆时应低压缓注,压力需控制在 0. 2 ~0. 4 MPa。

④ Inject grout slowly under the low pressure which is kept within 0. 2-0. 4 MPa.

⑤ 注浆结束,注浆管结扎牢固。

⑤ After grouting, the grouting pipe shall be firmly fastened.

4. 安全措施

4. Safety measures

① 施工人员必须穿戴护目镜、工作服和手套等劳动防护用品。

① Construction workers must wear goggles, work clothes and gloves and other labor protection articles.

② 灌浆时必须对注浆孔进行遮掩。

② The grouting hole must be concealed during grouting.

③ 施工现场不得堆放易燃易爆物品。

③ Inflammables and explosives shall not be stacked in construction site.

④ 施工完毕后,必须对现场进行清理,做到工完料清。

④ After construction, the site must be cleaned up and the materials must be packed.

3.4.2 整体道床结构注浆补强加固作业

3.4.2 Grouting reinforcement of monolithic track bed structure

整体道床结构注浆补强加固作业适用于整体道床结构开裂、整体道床与排水沟结合部位开裂、整体道床与隧道管片拱底块脱离或存在空隙、轨枕与整体道床间脱开和其他混凝土结构开裂。

The grouting reinforcement of monolithic track bed structure is applicable to the cracking of monolithic track bed, the cracking of joint between monolithic track bed and drainage ditch, the separation or gap between monolithic track bed and the tunnel arch bottom block, the separation between sleeper and monolithic track bed, and the cracking of other concrete structures.

1. 所需材料和工器具

1. Materials and tools required

(1)所需材料(见表 3-20)

(1) Materials required (see Table 3-20)

表 3-20 整体道床结构注浆补强加固作业材料表

序号	名称
1	双快水泥
2	环氧树脂
3	注浆管
4	铝管
5	铅丝

Table 3-20 Materials for grouting reinforcement of monolithic track bed structure

No.	Name
1	Double fast cement
2	Epoxy resin
3	Grouting pipe
4	Aluminum tube
5	Galvanized wire

(2)所需工器具(见表 3-21)

(2) Tools required (see Table 3-21)

表 3-21 整体道床结构注浆补强加固作业工器具表

序号	名称
1	电锤
2	手动式注浆泵
3	拖线盘
4	太阳灯
5	平板车
6	钢丝钳
7	割刀
8	喷壶

Table 3-21 Tools for grouting reinforcement of monolithic track bed structure

No.	Name
1	Electric hammer
2	Manual grouting pump
3	Towing reel
4	Sunlamp
5	Flatbed trailer
6	Steel wire cutter
7	Cutting knife
8	Watering can

2. 操作程序

2. Operation procedure

① 现场确定具体病害(裂缝)位置。

① Determine the location of diseases (cracks) on site.

② 针对所确定病害进行钻孔。

② Drill holes for the disease.

③ 清除钻孔及 V 字槽内杂物。

③ Remove the debris in the hole and V-shaped groove.

④ 将铝管预埋至孔内,并用双快水泥封堵。

④ Embed the aluminum pipe into the hole and block it with double quick cement.

⑤ 封堵的水泥进行养护。

⑤ Cure the cement.

⑥ 待水泥达到强度后,连接塑料注浆管至注浆泵。

⑥ After the cement reaches the strength, connect the plastic grouting pipe to the grouting pump.

⑦ 环氧树脂按 1∶3 比例配制,充分搅拌后进行灌浆加固,如图 3-7 和图 3-8 所示。

⑦ The epoxy resin is prepared in proportion of 1∶3 and used for grouting reinforcement after full stirring, as shown in Figure 3-7 and Figure 3-8.

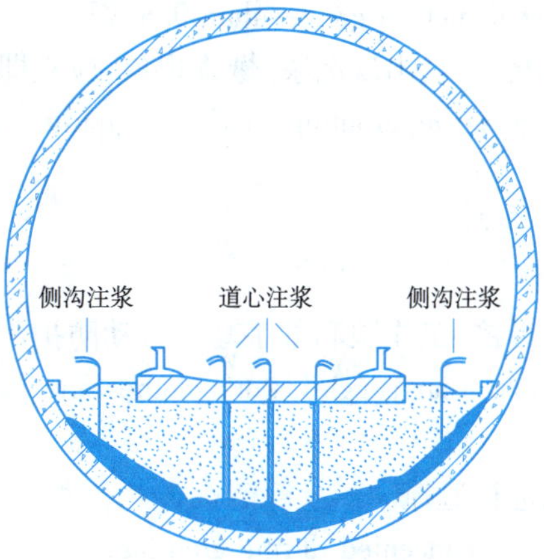

图 3-7　混凝土整体道床加固剖面图

Figure 3-7　Sectional drawing of concrete monolithic track bed reinforcement

道心注浆:grouting at the center of road　　侧沟注浆:grouting at the side ditch

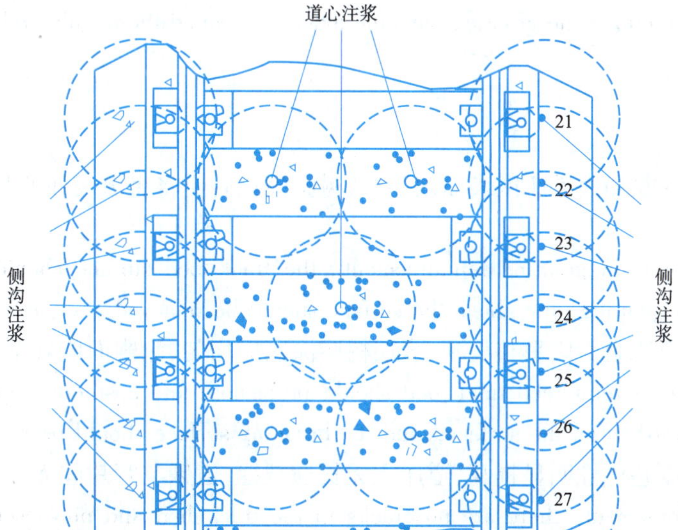

图 3-8　混凝土整体道床加固平面图

Figure 3-8　Plan of concrete monolithic track bed reinforcement

3. 质量控制

3. Quality control

① 封堵孔位时不得留有任何间隙。

① No gap shall be left when plugging the hole.

② 确保对封堵水泥的养护时间。

② Ensure enough curing time of plugging cement.

③ 环氧树脂按比例配制后,应对浆液进行充分搅拌,不得低于 10 分钟。

③ After preparing epoxy resin in proportion, stir it fully for at least 10 minutes.

④ 灌浆压力不得大于0. 4 MPa。

④ The grouting pressure shall not be greater than 0. 4 MPa.

⑤ 灌浆时应观察周边情况,一旦出现漏浆、爆浆现象,应立即停止灌浆。

⑤ Observe the surroundings during grouting, and stop grouting immediately once slurry leakage or slurry explosion occurs.

4. 安全措施

4. Safety measures

① 施工人员必须穿戴护目镜、工作服和戴手套等劳动防护用品。

① Construction workers must wear goggles, work clothes and gloves and other labor protection articles.

② 灌浆时必须对注浆孔进行遮掩。

② The grouting hole must be concealed during grouting.

③ 施工现场不得堆放易燃易爆物品。

③ Inflammables and explosives shall not be stacked in construction site.

④ 施工完毕后,必须清洗干净注浆机,做到工完料清。

④ After construction, the grouting machine must be cleaned thoroughly and the materials must be packed.

5. 验收标准

5. Acceptance criteria

① 环氧树脂注浆加固道床区表面须平整,树脂固化后应将突出表面的封堵水泥和注浆管清除。

① After epoxy resin grouting reinforcement, the track bed surface should be flat, and the sealing cement and grouting pipe above the surface should be removed after resin curing.

② 加固范围道床表面应平整美观,表层树脂涂刷应均匀,涂刷面应规整。

② The surface of reinforced track bed should be smooth and aesthetic appearance, the resin should be evenly brushed on the surface, and the brushing surface should be regular.

③ 加固后道床整体性明显提高,道床上无贯通裂缝,道床与管片间无松脱。

③ After reinforcement, there are no cracks in the track bed and no loosening between track bed and segment, so that the integrity of track bed is obviously improved.

④ 加固范围较大缺损须用水泥砂浆修补,表面须与原道床在同一平面内。

④ Large defects should be repaired with cement mortar and the surface should be in the same plane with the original track bed.

⑤ 道床与管片间缝隙须充满环氧。

⑤ The gap between track bed and segment shall be filled with epoxy.

⑥ 施工范围内无加固材料污损的道床、钢轨,且没有遗留施工垃圾。

⑥ There are no track beds and steel rails contaminated by reinforcement materials within the construction scope, and there is no construction waste left.

3.4.3　转辙机基坑结构补强加固作业
3.4.3　Reinforcement of track switcher foundation pit structure

整体道床转辙机基坑结构补强加固作业适用于道岔区转辙机基坑结构开裂、破损。

It is applicable to crack and damage of track switcher foundation pit structure in turnout area.

1. 所需材料和工器具
1. Materials and tools required

(1)所需材料(见表 3-22)

(1) Materials required (see Table 3-22)

表 3-22　转辙机基坑结构补强加固作业材料表

序号	名称
1	双快水泥
2	水泥基渗透结晶型涂料
3	铅丝

Table 3-22　Materials for reinforcement of foundation pit structure of transfer machine

No.	Name
1	Double fast cement
2	Cementitious capillary crystalline coating
3	Galvanized wire

(2)所需工器具(见表 3-23)

(2) Tools required (see Table 3-23)

表 3-23　转辙机基坑结构补强加固作业工器具表

序号	名称
1	电锤
2	拖线盘
3	太阳灯
4	喷壶

Table 3-23　Tools for reinforcement of foundation pit structure of transfer machine

No.	Name
1	Electric hammer
2	Towing reel
3	Sunlamp
4	Watering can

2. 操作程序

2. Operating procedure

① 清除基坑坑底及周边疏松混凝土。

① Remove the loose concrete at the bottom and around the foundation pit.

② 清理基坑。

② Clean the foundation pit.

③ 用快封水泥进行回填、砌筑。

③ Use quick plug cement for backfilling and masonry.

④ 养护。

④ Curing.

⑤ 在基坑坑底及周边涂刷水泥基渗透结晶型涂料。

⑤ Apply cementitious capillary crystalline coating at the bottom and around the foundation pit.

3. 质量控制

3. Quality control

① 清除疏松混凝土时,如基坑两侧排水沟有积水情况,需做好围堰。

① When removing the loose concrete, if there is ponding in the drainage ditches on both sides of the foundation pit, the cofferdam shall be constructed.

② 清理时,应注意将基坑坑底浮层清除干净。

② During cleaning, remove the residues at the bottom of the foundation pit.

③ 回填、砌筑时,应保持原基坑形状及尺寸不变。

③ The shape and size of the original foundation pit shall be kept unchanged during backfilling and masonry.

④ 养护时间要充分,以免表面产生细缝。

④ Make sure enough curing time and avoid fine cracks on the surface.

⑤ 需涂刷水泥基渗透结晶型涂料二遍。

⑤ Apply two coats of cementitious capillary crystalline coating.

4. 安全措施

4. Safety measures

① 施工人员必须穿工作服和戴手套等劳动防护用品。

① Construction workers must wear work clothes and gloves and other labor protection articles.

② 施工现场不得堆放易燃易爆物品。

② Inflammables and explosives shall not be stacked in construction site.

③ 施工完毕后,必须对现场进行清理,做到工完料清。

③ After construction, the site must be cleaned up and the materials must be packed.

3.4.4 排水沟作业

3.4.4 Drainage ditch operation

排水沟作业适用排水沟结构开裂、破损。

It is suitable for crack and damage of drainage ditch structure.

1. 所需材料和工器具

1. Materials and tools required

(1)所需材料(见表 3-24)

(1) Materials required (see Table 3-24)

表 3-24　排水沟作业材料表

序号	名称
1	普通水泥
2	双快水泥
3	黄沙

Table 3-24　Materials for drainage ditch operation

No.	Name
1	Portland cement
2	Double fast Cement
3	Sand

(2)所需工器具(见表 3-25)

(2) Tools required (see Table 3-25)

表 3-25　排水沟作业工器具表

序号	名称
1	凿破机
2	石材切割机
3	拖线盘
4	榔头
5	凿子
6	喷壶
7	泥工工具

Table 3-25　Tools for drainage ditch operation

No.	Name
1	Chipper
2	Marble Cutter
3	Towing reel
4	Hammer
5	Chisel
6	Watering can
7	Masonry tools

2. 操作程序

2. Operation procedure.

① 确定修补位置。

① Determine the position for repair.

② 开凿部分损坏水沟。

② Chisel the damaged parts of ditches.

③ 拌制混凝土。

③ Mix concrete.

④ 沟内找坡。

④ Make slope in the ditch.

⑤ 混凝土养护。

⑤ Curing concrete.

3. 质量控制

3. Quality control

(1)开凿处的基面清理干净。

(1) Clean the excavation surface.

(2)混凝土充分搅拌。

(2) Mix concrete fully.

(3)沟内的坡度,不得小于5‰。

(3) The gradient in the ditch shall not be less than 5‰.

(4)新修补的混凝土不能有开裂现象。

(4) The newly repaired concrete shall be free from cracking.

4. 安全措施

4. Safety measures

(1)开凿排水沟时,应注意其他管线走向,不得影响其他管线正常使用。

(1) When digging drainage ditches, the direction of other pipelines does not affect the normal use of other pipelines.

(2)施工人员必须穿工作服和戴手套等劳动防护用品。

(2) Construction workers must wear work clothes and gloves and other labor protection articles.

(3)施工完毕后,必须清理现场,做到工完料清。

(3) After construction, the site must be cleaned up and the materials must be packed.

5. 验收标准

5. Acceptance criteria

(1)排水沟作业范围边界须规整。

(1) The boundary of drainage ditch shall be neat.

(2)作业范围表面应与道床齐平,且与原道床黏结牢固。

(2) The surface of repaired drainage ditch shall be flush with the track bed and firmly bonded with the original track bed.

(3)原破损、松散混凝土应凿除彻底。

(3) The original damaged and loose concrete shall be chiseled thoroughly.

(4)排水沟内表面光滑流畅,具有适当排水坡度,一般不得小于 5‰。

(4) The internal surface of drainage ditch shall be smooth with proper drainage slope which shall not be less than 5‰ generally.

(5)新施工排水沟混凝土表面无开裂现象。

(5) There is no crack on the concrete surface of the newly constructed drainage ditch.

(6)施工范围内无水泥污损的道床、钢轨和地坪,且无施工垃圾遗留。

(6) The track bed, steel rail and floor within the construction scope are not stained by cement and there shall be no construction waste left.

3.4.5 双液微扰动注浆加固作业

3.4.5 Reinforcement of dual-liquid microcisturbance grouting

双液微扰动注浆加固作业适用由于邻近隧道建筑活动的加卸载引起隧道不均匀沉降;由于隧道在渗漏条件下经受列车长期振动而发生振陷;当隧道穿越不均匀而又极软弱地层时,在盾构施工扰动下发生较大施工期沉降和工后沉降;隧道渗漏造成地基水土流失引起的不均匀沉降;隧道进出洞及旁通道处冻结法施工引起的融沉和区域不均匀沉降等。

The reinforcement of daul-liquid microcisturbance grouting is suitable for the uneven settlement of tunnel caused by the loading and unloading of the adjacent construction activities; the vibration subsidence caused by the long-term vibration of train under leakage circumstance; the large settlement during construction and post-construction under the disturbance of shield construction when the tunnel passes through uneven and extremely weak stratum; the uneven settlement caused by soil erosion due to tunnel leakage; the thaw settlement and regional uneven settlement at tunnel entrance and exit and side passage caused by freezing method construction.

微扰动注浆是在治理范围内沿隧道纵向以合理间距布设注浆孔,对每个注浆孔少量、多次地自隧道底部向下分层叠加注浆。每次注浆引起的隧道上抬量 ΔV 总大于或等于隧道自然沉降和超孔隙水压力部分消散而产生的固结沉降量之和 ΔS(见图 3-9)。在初始阶段,适当减少各次注浆的间隔时间 ΔT,增大每次注浆有效抬升量。当隧道总抬升量 $\sum(\Delta V-\Delta S)$ 达到预期值时,暂停注浆一段时间,待隧道下卧土层因注浆引起的超孔隙水压消散殆尽后,确认隧道地基最终抬升量是否满足要求。

Perturbation grouting is to arrange grouting holes at a reasonable distance along the longitudinal direction of tunnel within the treatment scope, and grout little slurry multiple times from the tunnel bottom downward in layers. The tunnel uplift ΔV caused by each grouting is always greater than or equal to the sum ΔS of the tunnel natural settlement and the consolidation settlement caused by the partial dissipation of excess pore water pressure (see Figure 3-9). In the initial stage, the interval time ΔT between grouting shall be appropriately reduced, and the effective lifting amount of each grouting shall be increased. When the total lifting amount $\sum(\Delta V-\Delta S)$ of the tunnel reaches the expected value, the grouting will be suspended for a period of time. After the excess pore water pressure of substratum caused by grouting completely dissipates, confirm whether the final lifting amount of tunnel foundation meets the requirements.

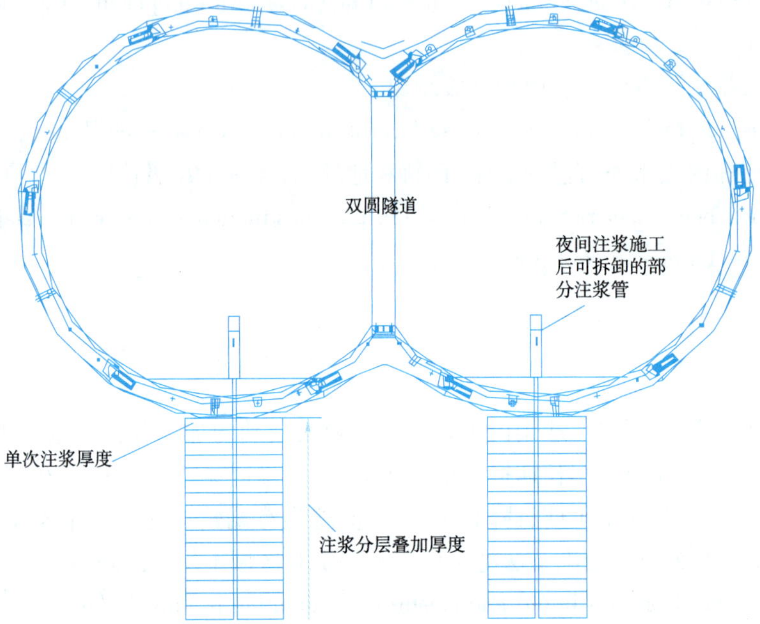

图 3-9 微扰动注浆治理断面图

Figure 3-9 Section of perturbation grouting treatment

双圆隧道:double circular tunnel

夜间注浆施工后可拆卸的部分注浆管:removable grouting pipe after construction at night

单次注浆厚度:thickness of single grouting

注浆分层叠加厚度:superimposed thickness of grouting layers

1. 所需材料和工器具

1. Materials and tools required

(1)所需材料(见表 3-26)

(1) Materials required (see Table 3-26)

表 3-26 双液微扰动注浆加固作业材料表

序号	名称
1	水泥
2	水玻璃

Table 3-26 Materials for reinforcement of dual-liquid microcisturbance grouting

No.	Name
1	Concrete
2	Water glass

(2)所需工器具(见表 3-27)

(2) Tools required (see Table 3-27)

表 3-27 双液微扰动注浆加固作业工器具表

序号	名称
1	注浆泵
2	混合器
3	流量计
4	注浆前端装置
5	注浆管
6	下管器
7	拔管器

Table 3-27 Tools for reinforcement of dual-liquid microcisturbance grouting

No.	Name
1	Grouting pump
2	Mixer
3	Flow counter
4	Grouting front end device
5	Grouting pipe
6	Pipe laying device
7	Pipe extracting device

2. 操作程序

2. Operating procedure

微扰动注浆加固作业操作程序如下:

The operation procedure for preturbation grouting reinforcement is as follows:

(1)放样

(1) Setting out

钻孔需要考虑管片类型、管片布筋等不同情况,尽量避开钢筋。如受条件限制可能会破坏箍筋,但一定要确保主筋不受损害。放样是微扰动注浆加固作业的第一步操作,放样的精度直接影响到注浆孔能不能避开钢筋。

Different conditions such as segment type and segment reinforcement shall be considered for drilling to avoid reinforcement as much as possible. Sometimes the stirrup may be damaged, but the main reinforcement must not be damaged. Setting out is the first step of perturbation grouting reinforcement, and the accuracy of setting out directly affects whether the grouting hole can avoid reinforcement.

(2)一次钻孔

(2) Primary drilling

由于运营隧道夜间施工时间有限,第一次钻孔不能将管片钻穿,待全部打孔工作完成后,开始注浆时，对当晚注浆的位置进行二次开孔，以防止泥浆和砂涌入隧道。第一次钻孔直接影响到钻孔位置的精确度，因此，钻孔设备的选择和定位十分关键。

Due to the limited construction time at night, the segment cannot be drilled through by the first drilling. Before grouting, the second drilling shall be conducted at the grouting position at that night to prevent mud and sand from flowing into the tunnel. The first drilling directly affects the accuracy of drilling position, so the selection and positioning of drilling equipment is very critical.

（3）安装孔口管

(3) Install orifice tube

孔口管安装时，其管壁和隧道管片之间的空隙必须充分填满黏结剂，如图 3-10 所示。

During the installation of orifice pipe, the gap between tube wall and tunnel segment must be fully filled with adhesive, as shown in Figure 3-10.

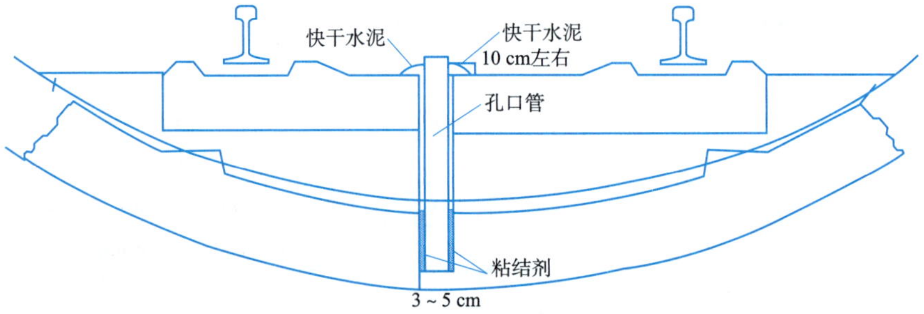

图 3-10 孔口管安装的示意图

Figure 3-10 Schematic diagram of orifice pipe installation

快干水泥：fast drying cement　黏结剂：adhesive　孔口管：orifice tube

（4）安装球阀

(4) Install ball valve

安装球阀时其撕口应进行适当处理，保证球阀关闭后的密水性。

When installing the ball valve, its orifice shall be properly treated to ensure the water tightness after the ball valve is closed.

（5）二次钻孔

(5) Secondary drilling

二次钻孔一般采用冲击钻，直接将管片剩余厚度打穿。值得注意的是，二次开孔只对当天作业点实施，在上下行隧道对称地打开球阀，打穿管壁，直至计划深度，完成二次钻孔。

Use the impact drill to pierce the remaining thickness of segment directly. It is worth nothing that the secondary drilling is only implemented for the day's work spot. Open ball valves symmetrically in the up and down tunnels, penetrate segments to the planned depth, and complete the secondary drilling.

（6）浆液的拌制和运输

(6) Mix and transport slurry

浆液的拌制和运输应满足连续施工要求。浆液的配比应综合考虑流动性、凝固时间、固结体强度等因素，避免堵管的发生。

The mixing and transportation of slurry shall meet the requirements for continuous construction. When preparing slurry, factors such as fluidity, setting time and strength of consolidation body shall be comprehensively considered to avoid pipe plugging.

(7)安装防喷装置

(7) Install blowout preventer

防喷装置是在每次注浆前安装在球阀上,防止注浆时压力较大导致浆液喷出。

Install the blowout preventer on the ball valve before each grouting to prevent grout from ejecting due to high grouting pressure.

(8)压管

(8) Press tube

注浆管由注浆头及管身组成。压管前要准备好注浆管,并在其底部连接喷浆头。为防止插入过程中堵塞注浆头,先用胶布将注浆头固定。管身长 1 m,按照注浆深度的不同可接长。

The grouting pipe is composed of grouting head and pipe. Before pressing pipe, prepare a grouting pipe and install the shotcrete head to its bottom. In order to prevent the grouting head from being blocked during insertion, the grouting head shall be fixed with adhesive tape. The pipe length is 1 m, which can be extended according to the different grouting depth.

(9)注浆

(9) Grouting

当参数设定好后,按照注浆要求,通过多项控制操作,完成注浆加固作业,保证运营隧道的安全。

After setting parameters, complete the grouting reinforcement through multiple control operations according to the grouting requirements to ensure the safety of operating tunnel.

(10)拔管

(10) Extract pipe

用专门的拔管设备拔出注浆管。

Use a special equipment to extract the grouting pipe.

(11)关闭球阀

(11) Close the ball valve

注浆结束后,关闭球阀,拆除防喷装置。

After grouting, close the ball valve and remove the blowout preventer.

(12)封孔

(12) Seal hole

完成注浆施工后,应进行封孔,避免水土从注浆孔内流出,如图 3-11 所示。

After grouting construction, seal the hole to prevent water and soil from flowing out, as shown in Figure 3-11.

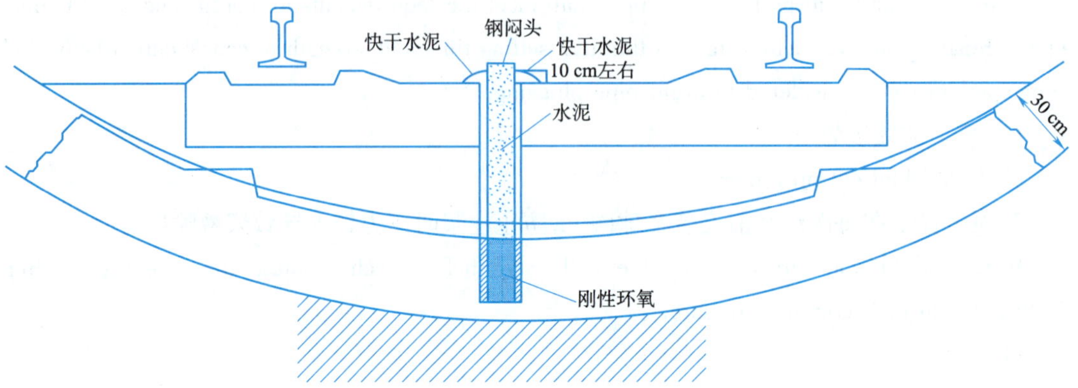

图 3-11 封孔示意图

Figure 3-11 Schematic diagram of hole sealing

钢闷头:steel bulkhead 刚性环氧:rigid epoxy

3. 安全措施

3. Safety measures

① 施工人员必须严格穿工作衣、戴防护手套、防护镜等劳动防护用品。

① Construction workers must wear work clothes, protective gloves, protective glasses and other labor protection articles.

② 施工现场不得堆放易燃易爆物品。

② Inflammables and explosives shall not be stacked in construction site.

③ 施工完毕后,必须对清理现场,做到工完料清。

③ After construction, the site must be cleaned up and the materials must be packed.

3.4.6 衬砌裂缝注浆补强作业

3.4.6 Reinforcement of lining crack grouting

衬砌裂缝渗漏水一般采用堵水注浆处理。待衬砌结构基本稳定和混凝土达到设计强度后,进行裂缝注浆。

The leakage of lining crack is generally treated by water-sealing grouting. Crack grouting shall be carried out after the lining structure becomes stable and the concrete reaches the design strength.

1. 所需材料

1. Materials required

防水混凝土结构出现宽度小于 2 mm 的裂缝可视为无害裂缝,如产生渗漏水可采用水泥基结晶渗透型材料涂抹施工;宽度大于 2 mm 的混凝土裂缝产生渗漏水应采用化学注浆处理,注浆材料宜采用环氧树脂、聚氨酯、丙烯酸盐等浆液;除堵漏外,为达到良好的注浆补强效果,注浆材料宜采用超细水泥、改性水泥浆液或特殊化学浆液。

Cracks with a width less than 2 mm in waterproof concrete structure can be regarded as harmless cracks. If leakage occurs, cement-based crystal permeable materials can be used for coating construction. The leakage of concrete cracks with a width greater than 2 mm shall be treated by chemical grouting such as epoxy resin, polyurethane, acrylate, etc. In addition to plugging, ultra-fine cement paste, modified cement paste or special chemical paste should be used as grouting materials to achieve good grouting reinforcement effect.

2. 质量控制

2. Quality control

① 浅裂缝应骑槽粘埋注浆嘴，必要时，沿缝开凿 V 字槽并用水泥砂浆封缝。

① For a shallow crack, stuck a grouting nozzle along the groove. If necessary, cut a V-shaped groove along the crack and seal gaps with cement mortar.

② 深裂缝应骑缝钻孔至裂缝深处，孔内埋设注浆管，间距应根据裂缝宽度而定，但每条裂缝至少有一个进浆孔和一个排气孔。

② For deep cracks, drill holes to the depth of crack and embed grouting pipes in the holes. The spacing should be determined according to the width of cracks, but there is at least one inlet hole and one exhaust hole for grouting in each crack.

③ 注浆嘴及注浆管应设于裂缝的交叉处、较宽处及贯穿处等部位，对封缝的密封效果应进行检查。

③ Locate grouting nozzle and grouting pipe at the intersection, wide and through parts of cracks and check the sealing effect.

④ 采用低压低速注浆，化学注浆压力宜为 0.2 ~ 0.4 MPa, 水泥浆灌浆压力宜为 0.4 ~ 0.8 MPa.

④ Grout under low pressure and low speed. The grouting pressure of chemical materials should be 0.2 -0.4 MPa, and the grouting pressure of cement paste should be 0.4 -0.8 MPa.

⑤ 注浆后，直到缝内浆液初凝而不外流时，方可拆下注浆嘴并进行封口抹平。

⑤ After grouting, remove the grouting nozzles and seal the holes neatly when the grout in the crack initially set and does not flow out.

3. 验收标准

3. Acceptance criteria

① 补强后的裂缝表面须清洁美观，无浆液溢流污损。

① After reinforcement, the crack surface must be neat and good-looking without slurry overflow and dirt.

② 补强范围表面应平整，无凸凹不平的水泥封堵面。

② The surface within the reinforcement range shall be flat without uneven cement.

③ 待浆液完全凝固后，彻底清理注浆管和注浆嘴。

③ After the grout has completely solidified, thoroughly clean the grouting pipe and nozzle.

④ 尽可能骑缝安埋注浆嘴，无明显次生损坏结构现象。

④ Set grouting nozzles along the crack as much as possible without obvious secondary damage to the structure.

⑤ 补强后裂缝无明显渗漏水，尤其影响接触网、钢轨和转辙机等设备的渗漏水。

⑤ After reinforcement, there is no obvious water leakage, especially the water leakage which affects equipment such as catenary, rail and switch machine.

⑥ 施工范围无补强材料污损道床、钢轨或地坪现象,且没有遗留施工垃圾。

⑥ The track bed, steel rail and floor within the construction scope are not stained by cement and there shall be no construction waste left.

3.5 隧道维护验收及质量评定
3.5 Acceptance and quality assessment of tunnel maintenance

3.5.1 隧道维护
3.5.1 Tunnel maintenance

车站建筑及隧道结构设施维护分为综合维修和保养。综合维修占设施总数的20%或以上,保养占设施总数的80%。

The structural facilities maintenance strategies of station building and tunnel structure strike a balance between comprehensive maintenance and preventative maintenance. Approximately 80% of all maintenance activities are performed under a preventative maintenance approach, while comprehensive maintenance activities accounts for 20%.

1. 隧道保养
1. Tunnel preventative maintenance

保养的定义:根据生产调度的报修及上月巡检的病害资料,以及隧道设施病害的特点,有计划地对综合维修计划外的隧道设施进行维修。掌握隧道设施技术状态,及时、主动地消除病害,以防止病害扩大,按期做好季节性工作,确保使用安全。

Preventative maintenance: according to the repair report of production scheduling, the disease data of last month's patrol inspection, and the characteristics of tunnel infrastructure diseases, the tunnel infrastructure beyond the comprehensive repair plan are maintained in a planned way. Grasp the status of tunnel infrastructure, eliminate diseases timely and actively to resist early decay or damage, do seasonal work on schedule, and ensure the safety of use.

保养的主要工作内容包括:

The main contents of preventative maintenance include:

① 地铁工程结构、变形缝等滴漏及滴漏以上处理。

① The leakage water treatment of subway engineering structure and deformation joints.

② 管辖内隧道设施的露筋破损修理。

② The repair of exposed reinforcement and damage of tunnel infrastructure within the jurisdiction.

③ 掌握隧道设施的质量状态,及时处理和上报影响结构安全和运营安全的病害。

③ Grasp the quality status of tunnel infrastructure, deal with and report diseases affecting structural safety and operation safety timely.

④ 应急处理和观测。

④ Emergency treatment and observation.

⑤ 隧道人防门、防淹门、旁通道隔断门、侧向平台零星病害修复。

⑤ Repair sporadic diseases from civil defense door, flood door, side channel partition door and side platform.

⑥ 使用和管理隧道内管片编号的油漆。

⑥ Use and manage the paint for segment numbering in tunnels.

⑦ 每季节清洗隧道一遍。

⑦ Clean the tunnel once every season.

⑧ 处理各类临时报修。

⑧ Handle all kinds of temporary repair requests.

2. 隧道综合维修

2. Tunnel comprehensive maintenance

综合维修的定义：有计划、按周期地对已发生和可能发生的破损、病害进行维修，保持隧道设备经常处于良好状态，延长使用寿命。

Comprehensive maintenance: repair the existing and potential damages and diseases periodically to keep tunnel infrastructure in good condition and improve its life.

根据隧道设备状态，以五年为一个周期，安排综合维修计划。隧道人防门的综合维修周期不受五年一个周期的限制，但不能大于五年一个周期。

According to the state of tunnel infrastructure, a comprehensive maintenance plan is arranged with a period of five years. The comprehensive maintenance cycle of tunnel civil defense door is not limited by a cycle of five years, but cannot be greater than a cycle of five years.

综合维修主要工作内容如下：

Main contents of comprehensive maintenance are as follows:

(1)盾构法隧道综合维修内容(见表 3-28)

(1) Comprehensive maintenance contents of shield tunnel (see Table 3-28)

表 3-28　盾构法隧道综合维修内容

综合维修项目	内　容
混凝土管片	混凝土管片开裂、掉块、露筋的治理 渗泥沙的治理 环纵缝、注浆孔、螺栓孔渗漏水的治理 注浆闷头缺尖的修补 螺栓脱落、缺失现象修补 双圆隧道钢保护壳除锈补漆 嵌缝条脱落的治理
钢管片	钢管片除锈补漆 渗漏水、渗泥沙治理 内格腔混凝土掉块修补 注浆闷头缺失的修补

续表

综合维修项目	内　容
端头井	渗漏水、渗泥沙治理 混凝土开裂、掉块、露筋的治理
旁通道、泵站及集水井	渗漏水、渗泥沙治理 混凝土开裂、掉块、露筋的治理 集水井暗管的疏通
中间风井	渗漏水、渗泥沙治理 混凝土开裂、掉块、露筋的治理
整体道床	道床与管片、管片与排水沟间产生脱离现象整治，整体道床的开裂、轨枕与道床间裂隙现象整治 注浆闷头缺失的修补 注浆孔渗漏水、渗泥沙治理
侧向平台	松动支架紧固 破损复合板材更换 防火涂层修补 金属部件除锈补漆
中间隔墙(双圆、大盾构)	防火隔断板松动、破损的治理 中隔墙开裂、破损的修补 大盾构中隔墙限位角钢的除绣处理 大盾构中隔墙防火密封胶的修补
人防门	门体、门框的除锈上漆 密封条的更换 传动机构涂油 链条等紧固件松动的治理
防淹门(不含电气部分)	门体、门槽及其零部件的除锈上漆 密封条的更换 添加或更换润滑油脂 对变形、腐蚀、损坏的部位及零部件进行整修、更换
旁通道隔断门	锁头、门铰链轴承等机械转动部位添加润滑油 五金件的更换 紧固各类松动构件 除锈补漆
其他	隧道内碳素纤维等补强材料的脱落抽丝现象整治 其他附属物缺损的维护 若发现管片螺栓崩裂、环缝纵缝张开和错台错缝超过技术标准规定，应及时报上级部门，委托设计部门做出综合治理方案，委托有资质单位实施维修工作

Table 3-28　Comprehensive maintenance contents of shield tunnel

Comprehensive maintenance item	Content
Concrete segment	Treatment of concrete segment cracking, falling block and exposed reinforcement Treatment of sediment seepage Treatment of water leakage from longitudinal ring joints, grouting holes and bolt holes Repair of losing angle of grouting bulkhead Repair of bolt falling off and missing Rust removal and paint repair of steel protective shell of double round tunnel Treatment of caulking strip falling off

continued

Comprehensive maintenance item	Content
Steel segment	Rust removal and paint repair of steel segment Treatment of water and sediment seepage Repair of concrete block falling in internal lattice Repair of missing grouting bulkhead
End well	Treatment of water and sediment seepage Treatment of concrete cracking, falling block and exposed reinforcement
Connecting passage, pump station and collecting wells	Treatment of water and sediment seepage Treatment of concrete cracking, falling block and exposed reinforcement Dredging of pipes in collecting wells
Air shaft	Treatment of water and sediment seepage Treatment of concrete cracking, falling block and exposed reinforcement
Monolithic track bed	Treatment of separation between track bed and segment, segment and drainage ditch, cracking of monolithic track bed, and gap between sleeper and track bed Repair of missing grouting bulkhead Treatment of water and sediment seapage from grouting holes
Lateral platform	Fastening of loose support Replacement of damaged composite plate Repair of fireproof coating Rust removal and paint repair of metal parts
Mid-partition wall (double round and large shield)	Treatment of loose and damaged fire partition board Repair of cracked and damaged middle partition wall Derusting treatment of limiting angle steel of middle partition wall of large shield Repair of fire sealant for middle partition wall of large shield
Civil defense door	Derusting and painting of door and frame Replacement of sealing strip Oiling of transmission mechanism Treatment of loose fasteners such as chains
Flood door (excluding electrical part)	Derusting and painting of door, slot and other parts Replacement of sealing strip Add or replacement of lubricating oil Repair and replacement of deformed, corroded and damaged parts and components
Partition door of connecting passage	Adding lubricating oil to mechanical rotating parts such as lock head and door hinge bearing Replacement of hardware Fastening various loose components Rust removal and paint repair
Other	Treatment of peeling and wire drawing of carbon fiber and other reinforcement materials in tunnel Maintenance of defects of other attachments If some segment bolts are cracked, the longitudinal joints of the circumferential joints are opened, and the staggered joints exceed the provisions of the technical standards, it shall be reported to the superior department in time, and the design department shall be entrusted to make a comprehensive treatment plan, and the qualified unit shall be entrusted to carry out the maintenance work

(2)明挖法隧道综合维修内容(见表3-29)

(2) Comprehensive maintenance content of open cut tunnel (see Table 3-29)

表3-29　明挖法隧道综合维修内容

综合维修名称	内　容
顶板	渗漏水、渗泥沙的治理 混凝土开裂、掉块、露筋的治理 引水管、槽松动的治理 变形缝渗漏水，止水带破损、脱落的治理
侧墙	渗漏水、渗泥沙的治理 混凝土开裂、破损、露筋的治理 引水管松动的治理 变形缝渗漏水、止水带破损的治理 侧墙倾斜的治理
整体道床	道床与排水沟间产生脱离现象整治、整体道床的开裂、轨枕与道床间裂隙现象整治 转辙机坑洼处渗漏水的治理
泵房、集水井	渗漏水、渗泥沙的治理 混凝土开裂、破损、露筋的治理 集水井暗管的疏通
其他	隧道内纤维类等补强材料的脱落抽丝现象 拆除遗留的施工模板 车站站线风道板开裂、松动的治理 紧固其他附属物的脱落松动 其他附属物缺损的维护

Table 3-29　Comprehensive maintenance contents of open cut tunnel

Comprehensive maintenance item	Content
Roof	Treatment of water and sediment seepage Treatment of concrete cracking, falling block and exposed reinforcement Treatment of looseness of diversion pipe and trough Treatment of water leakage at deformation joints, damage and falling off of waterstops
Side wall	Treatment of water and sediment seepage Treatment of concrete cracking, damage and exposed reinforcement Treatment of looseness of diversion pipe Treatment of water leakage at deformation joints, damage and falling off of waterstops Treatment of side wall inclination
Monolithic track bed	Treatment of separation between track bed and drainage ditch, cracking of monolithic track bed and gap between sleeper and track bed Treatment of leakage water in the pit of transfer and withdrawal machine
Pump station and collecting wells	Treatment of water and sediment seepage Treatment of concrete cracking, damage and exposed reinforcement Dredging of concealed pipes in collecting wells
Other	Falling off and wire drawing of reinforcing materials such as fiber in the tunnel Remove the remaining construction formwork Treatment of crack and looseness of air duct board above the station tracks Fastening falling off and loosening of other accessories Maintenance of defects of other attachments

3.5.2　隧道维护验收

3.5.2　Acceptance of tunnel maintenance

1. 综合维修验收标准

1. Acceptance standard of comprehensive maintenance

隧道综合维修作业质量的验收，要严格执行工区自验，生产维护部门、公司联合验收制，分级把关，控制质量。每天应在作业中及收工前进行质量自检、互检和回检，发现不符合标准的项目应及时返修达标。每次检查的情况都应填记在日计划完成表或施工日志上。

The quality acceptance of tunnel comprehensive maintenance operation should strictly carry out self-inspection of work area, joint acceptance of maintenance department and company, grading check and quality control. Self-inspection, mutual inspection and in-return inspection shall be carried out in the operation and before the end of operation every day. If some items that do not meet the standard should be repaired in time. Each inspection should be recorded in the maintenance log.

综合维修验收主要内容：

Main contents of comprehensive maintenance acceptance are as follows:

① 隧道病害综合维修应以消除渗漏水和漏泥沙、管片开裂、整体道床开裂及旁通道病害为主，综合维修过程中对结构的改变应尽量恢复。

① The comprehensive maintenance of tunnel diseases should mainly eliminate water and sediment seepage, segment cracking, monolithic track bed cracking and connecting passage diseases, and the structural changes in the process of comprehensive maintenance should be restored as far as possible.

② 综合维修后隧道区间应消除管片开裂破损、漏水、漏泥沙、嵌缝条脱落、道床开裂、螺栓脱落缺失、注浆孔螺帽缺失、各种附属设施的松动脱落等病害。

② After comprehensive maintenance, the diseases, such as segment cracking and damage, water leakage, sediment leakage, caulking strip falling off, track bed cracking, bolt missing, grouting hole nut missing, loosening and falling off of various auxiliary facilities, shall be eliminated in tunnel interval.

③ 隧道整体状态达到 2 级防水标准，即不允许漏水，结构表面可有少量湿渍；湿渍总面积不大于总防水面积的 2/1 000，单个湿渍面积不大于 0.2 m^2，任意 100 m^2 防水面积不超过 3 处；平均渗漏水量不大于 0.05 L/(m^2 · d)，任意 100 m^2 防水面积的渗漏水量不大于 0.15 L/(m^2 · d)。

③ The overall state of the tunnel reaches the waterproof grade 2, that is, no water penetration is acceptable, but there can be a small amount of wet stains on the structure surface; the total area of wet stains shall not exceed 2/1 000 of the total waterproof area, the area of single wet stain shall not exceed 0.2 m^2, and the waterproof area of any 100 m^2 shall not exceed 3 wet stains; the average water leakage is not more than 0.05 L / (m^2 · d), and the water leakage of any 100 m^2 waterproof area is not more than 0.15 L / (m^2 · d) .

④ 相邻管片环向错台 ≤15 mm，径向错台 <10 mm。

④ Circumferential dislocation of adjacent segments shall be less than 15 mm, radial dislocation shall be less than 10 mm.

⑤ 混凝土管片、钢管片注浆口螺栓要严格按设计要求拧紧，不得缺失。

⑤ The grouting hole bolts of the concrete segment and steel segment shall be tightened strictly according to the design requirements and shall not be missing.

⑥ 验收后需填写相关质量验收表和状态评定表，建立相应台账。

⑥ After acceptance, the relevant quality acceptance form and status assessment form shall be filled in, and the corresponding ledger shall be established.

2. 保养验收标准

2. Acceptance standard of preventative maintenance

① 隧道保养质量的验收频次为各保养施工独立验收。

① The acceptance frequency of tunnel maintenance quality is the independent acceptance of each preventative maintenance operation.

② 隧道保养质量验收由工区、生产维护部门、公司三方共同完成。隧道保养质量验收须通过工区自验，生产维护部门质量评定，公司质量验收。

② The acceptance of tunnel maintenance quality is jointly conducted by work area, maintenance department and company. It must pass the self inspection from work area, the quality assessment from maintenance department, and the quality acceptance from company.

③ 隧道保养应以不损坏原有结构为基础，在此基础上使渗漏水、漏泥沙、混凝土开裂等影响结构安全的病害得以治理，达到保护结构的目的。

③ The preventative maintenance of tunnel diseases should be based on the original structure without damage, on which leakage, mud leakage, concrete cracking and other diseases affecting the safety of the structure can be treated to achieve the purpose of protecting the structure.

④ 隧道结构保养质量评定是根据该设备各部分存在的问题，按照《隧道结构保养质量评分标准》的规定，根据扣分的情况来评定保养的优劣。验收标准详见《隧道结构单项作业验收标准》。

④ According to the provisions of the "Tunnel Structure Maintenance Quality Scoring Standards", the maintenance quality of tunnel structure is assessed based on the problems existing in various parts of the equipment and the score deduction. See "Acceptance Standard for Single Operation of Tunnel Structure" for acceptance standard.

3.5.3 隧道质量等级评定

3.5.3 Quality assessment of tunnel

综合维修的隧道区间需进行状态质量评定，年检是对全线设施的质量状态进行评定，并以此作为对一年来维修工作质量评价和考核的依据，以及为编制次年的维修计划提供依据。隧道结构质量分为"优秀"、"合格"和"不合格"三个等级评定，详见表3-30。

The tunnel under comprehensive maintenance shall be subject to status quality assessment. The annual inspection is to assess the quality status of the facilities along the whole line, which is the basis for the quality evaluation and assessment of the maintenance work in the past year, as well as the basis for the preparation of the maintenance plan for the next year. The tunnel structure quality is classified into"excellent""qualified" and "unqualified", see Table 3-30.

表 3-30 隧道结构状态评定表

评定等级	评定标准	病害类型	数量
优秀	无漏泥沙或线漏	漏泥沙或线漏	
	单个湿迹面积不大于 0.2 m^2	单个湿迹面积大于 0.2 m^2	
	任意 100 m^2 防水面积上的湿渍不超过 3 处	任意 100 m^2 防水面积上的湿渍	
	任意 100 m^2 渗水量不大于 0.15 L/(m^2·d)	任意 100 m^2 渗水量大于处 0.15 L/(m^2·d)	
	平均渗水量不大于 0.05 L/(m^2·d)	平均渗水量大于 0.05 L/(m^2·d)	
	隧道顶部无滴漏	隧道顶部滴漏	
	隧道内表面潮湿面积不大于 2/1 000 的总内表面积	隧道内表面潮湿面积大于 2/1 000 的总内表面积	
合格	无漏泥沙或线漏	漏泥沙或线漏	
	单个湿渍面积不大于 0.3 m^2	单个湿渍面积大于 0.3 m^2	
	单个漏水点的漏水量不大于 2.5 L/d	单个漏水点的漏水量大于 2.5 L/d	
	任意 100 m^2 防水面积上的湿渍不超过 7 处	任意 100 m^2 防水面积上的湿渍	
不合格	任意 100 m^2 防水面积的平均漏水量大于 2.5 L/(m^2·d)	任意 100 m^2 防水面积的平均漏水量大于 2.5 L/(m^2·d)	
	隧道内发生涌沙、线流或漏泥沙，侧墙出现连续渗流	隧道内出现涌沙、线流或漏泥沙，侧墙出现连续渗流	
	道床与管片产生脱离现象	道床与管片产生脱离现象	
	混凝土结构发生贯穿性裂缝或严重破损	混凝土结构发生贯穿性裂缝或严重破损	
	管片发生严重错台错缝或环纵缝张开超过 1 cm	管片发生严重错台错缝或环纵缝张开超过 1 cm	

注：每个评定等级只要有一项未达到要求即下降一个等级直至到不合格为止。

Table 3-30 Evaluation standards of tunnel structure state

Grade	Evaluation standard	Disease type	Number of diseases
Excellent	No mud and sand leakage or line-like leakage	Mud and sand leakage or line leakage	
	The area of a single wet stain shall not be greater than 0.2 m^2	The area of a single wet stain is greater than 0.2 m^2	
	No more than 3 wet stains on any 100 m^2 waterproof area	Wet stains on any 100 m^2 waterproof area	
	The seepage volume of any 100 m^2 is not more than 0.15 L/(m^2·d)	The seepage volume of any 100 m^2 is greater than 0.15 L/(m^2·d)	
	The average water seepage is not more than 0.05 L/(m^2·d)	The average water seepage is greater than 0.05 L/(m^2·d)	
	No dripping at the top of the tunnel	Dripping at the top of the tunnel	
	The wet area of tunnel inner surface is not more than 2/1 000 of the total inner surface area	The wet area of tunnel inner surface is greater than 2/1 000 of the total inner surface area	

continued

Grade	Evaluation standard	Disease type	Number of diseases
Qualified	No mud and sand leakage or line leakage	Mud and sand leakage or line leakage	
	Single wet stain area is not more than 0.3 m^2	Single wet stain area is greater than 0.3 m^2	
	The water leakage of a single water leakage point is not more than 2.5 L/d	The water leakage of a single water leakage point is greater than 2.5 L/d	
	No more than 7 wet stains on any 100 m^2 waterproof area	Wet stains on any 100 m^2 waterproof area	
Unqualified	The average water leakage is greater than 2.5L/(m^2·d) on any 100 m^2 waterproof area	The average water leakage is greater than 2.5 L/(m^2·d) on any 100 m^2 waterproof area	
	Sand gushing, linear flow or mud leakage occurs in the tunnel, and continuous seepage occurs on the side wall	Sand gushing, linear flow or mud leakage occurs in the tunnel, and continuous seepage occurs on the side wall	
	Track beds are separated from segments	Track beds are separated from segments	
	Penetrating cracks or serious damage occur in concrete structures	Penetrating cracks or serious damage occur in concrete structures	
	Segments are seriously staggered; The opening of circumferential or longitudinal joint exceeds 1 cm	Segments are seriously staggered; The opening of circumferential or longitudinal joint exceeds 1 cm	

Note: As long as the evaluation grade of any item fails to meet the requirements, it will descend one grade until it is unqualified.

隧道结构维修质量可按表3-31评定。

The maintenance quality of tunnel structure can be evaluated according to Table 3-31.

表3-31 隧道结构维修质量评定表

维修项目	扣分标准	扣分/处
裂缝堵漏	封堵表面不平整	3分
	封堵处有湿渍、渗漏点	10分
变形缝堵漏，安装止水带	出现渗漏水	21分
	止水带安装不密贴	3分
道床加固	道床与排水沟脱离、渗水	8分
防水砂浆抹面	抹面表层不平整	2分
	抹面表层有湿渍	5分
引水板引水施工	抹面表层空鼓、不密实	3分
	引水板安装出现倒落水	35分
	引水板安装有松动，出现移动	10分

注：满分为100分标准，扣除缺点分后，80~99分为优良；60~79分为合格；60分以下为不合格。

Table 3-31 Evaluation standards of tunnel structure maintenance quality

Maintenance item	Deduction criteria	Deduction/position
Crack plugging	The plugging surface is uneven	3
	There are wet stains and leakage points at the plugging place	10
Sealing of deformation joint, installation of waterstop	Water leakage occurs	21
	The waterstop is not installed tightly	3
Track bed reinforcement	The track bed is separated from the drainage ditch and water seepage occurs	8
Waterproof mortar plastering	The plastering surface is uneven	2
	There is wet stain on the plastering surface	5
Diversion construction of diversion plate	The plastering surface is hollow and not dense	3
	The installation of water diversion plate has fallen	35
	The water diversion plate is loose and moves	10

Note: The full score is 100 points. After deducting the defect score, 80-99 points are excellent; 60-79 is qualified; a score below 60 is a unqualified.

课 后 练 习
Exercises

1. 隧道常见病害有哪些?
1. What do common tunnel diseases include?
2. 简述隧道渗漏水的成因和危害。
2. Briefly describe the causes and hazards of water leakage in tunnels.
3. 衬砌裂损病害分哪几类?
3. What types of lining cracks can be classified?
4. 隧道结构设施检查的主要内容包括哪些?
4. What are the main contents of tunnel structural facilities inspection?
5. 钻孔灌浆堵漏法需要哪些材料和工具?
5. What materials and tools are required for the drilling grouting plugging method?
6. 简述整体道床结构注浆补强加固作业的验收标准。
6. Briefly describe the acceptance criteria for grouting reinforcement of monolithic track bed.
7. 车站建筑及隧道结构设施维护分为哪两类?
7. What two types can maintenance of station buildings and tunnel structures be classified?
8. 隧道保养的主要工作内容包括哪些?
8. What are the main work contents of tunnel preventative maintenance?
9. 盾构法隧道综合维修内容有哪些?
9. What are the contents of shield tunnel comprehensive maintenance?

参考文献

[1] 上海申通地铁集团有限公司轨道交通培训中心. 城市轨道交通桥隧技术[M]. 北京:中国铁道出版社,2012.

[2] 蒋伟,王金山. 城市轨道交通桥隧工[M]. 北京:中国铁道出版社,2015.

[3] 仇朝东,卜邦梅. 桥隧工:城轨:三级[M]. 北京:中国劳动社会保障出版社,2016.

[4] 李术希. 城市轨道交通隧道施工与维护[M]. 2 版. 北京:中国劳动社会保障出版社,2018.